American by Choice

An Immigrant's Journey

Walter M. Kroner

Professor Emeritus, Rensselaer Polytechnic Institute (RPI)

7·30·2010

Dear Guy and Anne,

Your encouragement not only
led to creating this book but
this _second printing_ is hopefully
of a quality you expect.

Walter Kroner

SHIRES
PRESS

4869 Main Street
P.O. Box 2200
Manchester Center, VT 05255
www.northshire.com/printondemand.php

American by Choice
An Immigrant's Journey
©2009 Walter M. Kroner, Professor Emeritus, Rensselaer

ISBN Number: 978-1-60571-048-8
Library of Congress Number: 2009910944
Library of Congress Cataloging-in-Publication Data

Kroner, Walter M.
American by Choice: An Immigrant's Journey/ Walter M. Kroner
1. Kroner, Walter M. - Childhood to Adulthood
2. World War, 1934-1945 – Personal Narratives, German
3. World War, 1939-1945 – Children-Germany-Biography
4. World War 1939-1945 – Hitler Youth, Germany
5. Germany History 1945-1954 Biography
6. Emigration/Immigration-United States/Germany 1952-1955: Biography
7. United States of America 1954-2008 – Personal Narratives

Building Community, One Book at a Time
This book was printed at the Northshire Bookstore, a family-owned, independent bookstore
in Manchester Ctr., Vermont, since 1976. We are committed to excellence in bookselling.
The Northshire Bookstore's mission is to serve as a resource for information,
ideas, and entertainment while honoring the needs of customers, staff, and community.

Printed in the United States of America
using an Espresso Book Machine from On Demand Books

Permissions

Photographs scanned from, *Stadt Neu-Ulm 1869-1994, Texte und Bilder zur Geschichte, Stadtarchiv Neu-Ulm 1994*:

Abb. 15, page 299, Aufnahmefeier der Zehnjährigen ins Jungvolk im April 1942 vor dem Neu-Ulmer HJ-Heim, Aufnahme Karl Sigel, Photoarchiv August Welte, Neu-Ulm. Permission from Lora Brehm, Stadtarchiv Neu-Ulm, Germany.

Abb. 26, page 329, 21 August 1940. Neu-Ulmer Jungvolk vor örtilcher Prominenz in der Augsburger Straße. Kreisleiter Roedel und SA-Sturmbannführer Kahler mit »deutschen« Gruß. Privatarchiv August Welte. Permission from Lora Brehm, Stadtarchiv Neu-Ulm, Germany.

Abb. 27, 27 Juli 1942. Neu-Ulms Jugend ertüchtigt sich. Heimatmuseum der Stadt Neu-Ulm. Permission from Lora Brehm, Stadtarchiv Neu-Ulm, Germany.

Abb. 1, page 366, Zu über 70 Prozent ist Neu-Ulm nach den zahlreichen Bombenangriffen im Zweiten Weltkrieg – die schwersten 1944 und 1945 – zerstört. Photo by Heinz Leiwig: Deutschland Stunde Null. Motorbuch-Verlag, Stuttgart, 2. Aufl. 1988. Permission from Heinz Leiwig and from the Paul Pietsch Verlage.

Photograph scanned from, *Ulm in Trümmern Bilder einer vergessenen Zeit*, by Eberhard Neubronner, Endres Verlag, 2nd Auflage 1992.

Abb. page 36, "707 Ulmerinnen und Ulmer fielen dem 17 Dezember zum Opfer: Beisetzung der Toten am 30 Dezember 1944. Permission from Eberhard Neubronner.

To my wife and soul mate Jean Anne Stark;
her love, critique, and support
are the fulfillment of my dreams.

To my grand-daughter Olivia Jane Hoagland;
may she never have to guess
about her Opa.

Introduction

Originally, I intended to write a series of stories about being a German child soldier during the Second World War, surviving its aftermath, and my experiences, hopes and dreams as an immigrant in the United States. Over the years I have shared these stories with family, friends, colleagues, architectural clients, and students. Again and again I was encouraged to capture the tales of my life on paper. What finally convinced me to write this book, however, was the birth of my first grandchild, Olivia Jane Hoagland. I want her and her descendents to know this part of their history, and how they came to live in this great country that I love so deeply.

At first I thought I would write an autobiography, but my achievements are similar to other survivors of WW II, as well as many other immigrants to the United States. I can not lay claim to being famous or to having had a significant impact on important events, so an autobiography didn't seem appropriate. I also considered the possibility of creating a journal of my life's journey of seventy-plus years, but the documents needed to create such a diary do not all exist and the task was beyond the bounds of possibility.

That is how I came to write this memoir. This book, based on contemporaneous journals, interviews, news articles, and my own diaries and memories, chronicles my life history and that of my immediate family. With the exception of a few names that I have changed out of respect for the individuals' privacy, all of the names, places, and events in this book are accurate.

Reflecting on my past, I realize little has changed since the beginning of my childhood. The same formative forces and events that shaped my life continue to impact the lives of millions around the world. Child soldiers are still forced to fight wars they don't understand. We in the United States are surprised and horrified when innocent men, women, and children are killed as soldiers wage war around them, although this has been the case since the dawn of time. Immigrants unfamiliar with the language and culture of their new homes are still abused and exploited, here and abroad. Some leaders rape the resources of their countries, diminishing the quality of life of their own people. Political and religious extremism continues throughout the world, depriving people of their right to think and decide freely how they choose to live. The soldiers in our military - who are the real heroes of our democracy - are often ignored, while those who seek self aggrandizement and personal wealth are made famous by the media.

As a result of conditions like these around the world, tens of thousands continue to dream of a better life in the United States of America, just as I did. Only when one has lived and survived such perils and succeeded in achieving the American dream, can one understand the profundity of an immigrant's love for all the good things about America, and the immigrant's compassion for what we have yet to change. The stories of the American immigrant and the magnetism of America need to be better understood and appreciated. This to me was an equally compelling reason for writing this book.

I have attempted to write an honest portrayal of my life. Any omissions, errors, or lapses in memory are mine. It has taken many years to complete and many people have helped to make it a reality. First and foremost, I would like to express my heartfelt gratitude to all of the people named in this book who have helped me survive through perilous times, on both sides of the Atlantic Ocean. To my colleagues, students, clients, and friends that kept encouraging me to put to paper the stories of my life, thank you for being persistent. I am especially grateful to my children Robert, Kevin, Reneé and her husband Tim, for making me see that the experiences and lessons learned from my journey are as meaningful today as they were in the past. I am also grateful to Professor Guy Garrett's review of the manuscript and his gentle commentary and perspective. He encouraged me to finish what I had started.

This book has been touched by the creative spirit and suggestions of the love of my life, Jean. She lovingly rejected the first two drafts, and then helped me create the final manuscript. She has enriched the stories through graphics, time-lines, photographs, and images in an attempt to create a visual context that would take the reader beyond the words. Without her critique, design contributions, readings, and corrections, this book would have remained mere words on a page.

Considering that English is my second language, I admired the attempts Jean and Naomi Miller made to read and correct the various drafts. However, my English grammar was beyond voluntary editing. Therefore, I am forever indebted to Ms. Louise Jones for her editorial services and acute eye that transformed my writing into a readable book.

I owe a debt of deep gratitude to my son Kevin Kroner who performed the final editing of this book. His devotion to detail and his ability to correct my misuse of the English language leaves me uncharacteristically speechless.

I am grateful for the research my sister Marianne performed to help me discover our family secret and for her bibliographic research in Germany. I am equally thankful to my brother Karlheinz for filling in the informational gaps related to the last few days of his time in the Hitler Youth at the end of the war.

Mr. August Welte, Chairman of the Bürgerverein Neu-Ulm, provided detailed chronicles of the bombing attacks on Neu-Ulm and Ulm, as well as the information of the capture of the two cities by American troops.

Finally, I want to express my heartfelt appreciation to my fellow Americans whom I have met along my journey. For me, you embody the spirit of this amazing land, these United States of America.

Contents

Book One

WORLD EVENTS 1901-1946

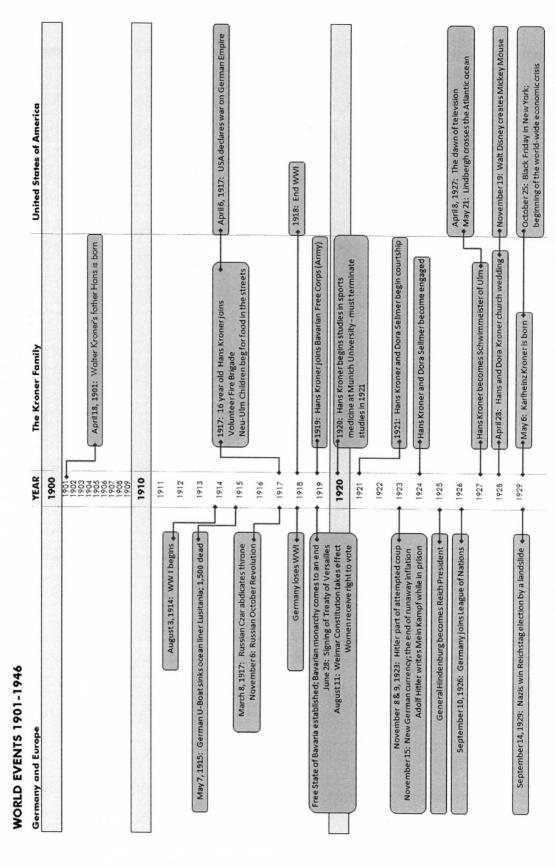

Germany and Europe

The Kroner Family

United States of America

YEAR

1900

April 18, 1901: Walter Kroner's father Hans is born

1910

1911

August 3, 1914: WW I begins

1912

1913

May 7, 1915: German U-Boat sinks ocean liner Lusitania; 1,500 dead

1914

1917: 16 year old Hans Kroner joins Volunteer Fire Brigade
Neu-Ulm Children beg for food in the streets

1915

March 8, 1917: Russian Czar abdicates throne
November 6: Russian October Revolution

1916

1917

April 6, 1917: USA declares war on German Empire

Germany loses WWI

1918

1918: End WWI

Free State of Bavaria established; Bavarian monarchy comes to an end
June 28: Signing of Treaty of Versailles
August 11: Weimar Constitution takes effect
Women receive right to vote

1919: Hans Kroner joins Bavarian Free Corps (Army)

1920: Hans Kroner begins studies in sports medicine at Munich University – must terminate studies in 1921

1920

1921

1921: Hans Kroner and Dora Sellmer begin courtship

1922

November 8 & 9, 1923: Hitler part of attempted coup
November 15: New German currency; the end of runaway inflation
Adolf Hitler writes Mein Kampf while in prison

1923

Hans Kroner and Dora Sellmer become engaged

1924

General Hindenburg becomes Reich President

1925

September 10, 1926: Germany joins League of Nations

1926

Hans Kroner becomes Schwimmeister of Ulm

1927

April 8, 1927: The dawn of television
May 21: Lindbergh crosses the Atlantic ocean

April 28: Hans and Dora Kroner church wedding

1928

November 19: Walt Disney creates Mickey Mouse

September 14, 1929: Nazis win Reichstag election by a landslide

1929

May 6: Karlheinz Kroner is born

October 25: Black Friday in New York; beginning of the world-wide economic crisis

2

Timeline

Germany and Europe	The Kroner Family	YEAR	United States of America
	1930: Worldwide Depression begins	**1930**	1930: Worldwide Depression begins
		1931	
May 1932: Ban against Sturm Abteilung is lifted		1932	
January 30, 1933: Hitler becomes Reich Chancellor; February 2: Burning of the Reichstag; October 14: Germany leaves League of Nations		1933	March 5, 1933: President Roosevelt takes office
June 30, 1934: Röhm Putsch; Night of the Long Knives	June 28: Walter Kroner is born in Neu-Ulm	1934	
September 15, 1935: Jews lose civil rights in Germany		1935	
July 17, 1936: Beginning of Spanish Civil War; August 1, 1936: Opening of Olympic Games in Berlin		1936	August 4, 1936: Jesse Owens wins four gold medals at Berlin Olympics
May 7, 1937: Zeppelin Hindenburg crashes		1937	
November 9-10, 1938: Kristallnacht; Dec. 3: Germans march on Austria		1938	June 23, 1938: Joe Louis crushes Max Schmeling (world boxing match)
March 15, 1939: Germany invades Czechoslovakia; May 1: Worlds Fair in New York; August 24: Germany & Russia sign non-aggression pact; September 1: Germany invades Poland – WWII begins; Spanish Civil War ends	June 10, 1939: Marianne Kroner is born; Karlheinz in Hitler youth	1939	
	1940: Walter starts elementary school in Neu-Ulm	**1940**	
June 22, 1941: Germany attacks Soviet Union; December 11: Germany declares war on United States of America		1941	December 7, 1941: Japan bombs Pearl Harbor
January 20, 1942: Germany adopts the "final solution" – the Holocaust; July 7: Anne Frank goes into hiding		1942	November 8, 1942: American Armada in North Africa under Eisenhower
January & February 1943: Germans defeated at Stalingrad	1943: Hans and Karlheinz Kroner help local farmers with harvest	1943	
July 20, 1944: Assassination attempt on Adolf Hitler; October 14: Hitler assassinates Rommel	March 16, 1944: Bombing of Ulm & Neu-Ulm; April 20: Walter joins Hitler Youth; September 10: Major bombing raid–Ulm & Neu-Ulm; December 17: 75% of Ulm & Neu-Ulm destroyed	1944	June 6, 1944: Normandy Landing by Allied Forces
April 30, 1945: Hitler commits suicide; May 7: WWII ends; Germany signs unconditional surrender	February 1945: Karlheinz Drafted into the Volksturm; March 1 & 4: Bombing raids on Ulm & Neu-Ulm; March 6: Kroner family escapes to Kirchhaslach; April: Walter sent to fight in the war as a child soldier; April 24: 10th US Armored Division takes Ulm	1945	April 12, 1945: President Roosevelt dies; August 6: USA drops atomic bomb on Hiroshima; September 2: Japan surrenders
March 6, 1946: Advent of the Iron Curtain; October 2: Nüremburg Trial sentences handed out	1946: Hoover feeding program begins in German schools	1946	

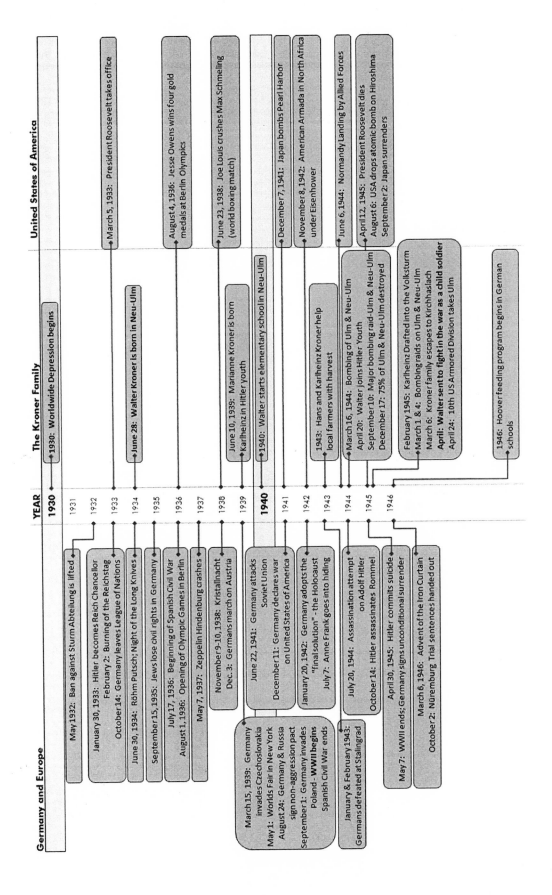

Fall 2009

I was ten years old when I was drafted into the German Hitler Youth movement. At the age of eleven, I was forced to fight in WW II, barely surviving bombs and fighter planes until the American liberation forces arrived. Despite the horrors of bombing raids, the killings, and the destruction of my home town - Neu-Ulm - I did not develop a hatred for the "enemy," which included Americans. After the American occupation of Neu-Ulm, I developed an affinity for the GIs that reinforced my desire to someday go to America.

That dream had all but evaporated by the age of eighteen, but it was replaced with two tempting offers. The first was a job with my employer in a large hat-making factory as an industrial electrician journeyman. Once I received my masters qualification, the position of master electrician and lifelong employment would be mine. If that was not to my liking, I was offered the position of personal chauffeur and mechanic for the factory owner for as long as I wanted. On a cool April evening in 1953, I sat in my hideaway by the Danube River, peering into the rushing water. I had to make a decision between economic security in Germany and a potentially greater opportunity that held much uncertainty in America. I always had a great deal of difficulty with others trying to stop me from dreaming about a different kind life. I decided to run from a world that constantly told me, "Remember your place in society," and "Stick with your own kind." I dreamed of a life where I could discover who I was and what I could become. The decision I made would change me forever. Just as there was no clarity in the foaming rapids of the river, there was no clear path for me to follow into my future. I was ready to jump into the river of life to discover my potential by following the natural course of things. People say that unless you are well prepared, you cannot succeed. I discovered that is untrue. I was completely unprepared for what lay ahead of me. However, if I had not believed in myself and trusted the river of life, I would still be sitting in my hideaway by the Danube. I would be wondering what kind of life I had let flow by me, instead of sitting at my desk looking out across the Hudson River, telling you the story of my life.

Thirty years after that cool April night, I received a phone call from Dr. Ursel Köstlin telling me that my father was in the hospital in Memmingen, Germany, and there was very little hope he would survive an aneurism. She said, "This may be your last chance to see him." I was afraid he would not live long enough to reveal the secrets I knew he held. I immediately made arrangements for a flight from Boston, Massachusetts to München, Germany. After leaving the airport, I pushed the BMW to its limits on the Autobahn while I rehearsed the questions I wanted to ask my father; questions he had refused to answer for forty-five years. I had always been rebuffed by him with, "We will never talk about that!" or, "You wouldn't understand if I told you."

I wanted to know why he joined the Sturmabteilung (SA) which was a part of the Nazi system. In addition, I wanted to know more about my paternal great-grandfather. Could it be that my brother and I, who were drafted into the Hitler Youth movement, were part Jewish? No one in my family would ever discuss my paternal grandfather's roots. He had taken his secret to the grave in 1950. I was bound and determined to keep my father from doing the same. There was so much to ask and to learn. "He must not die," was all I could think of as I tried to find the hospital in Memmingen where Ursel was Chief of Pediatrics. I was so very close to achieving the professional goals I had set for myself and wanted to share this with my father. He, of all the people in my life, needed to know that what I had learned from him had helped me to navigate the river of life. At the time, I could not foresee the rapids still ahead.

Karlheinz (left), Dora, Walter (right) and Marianne in front, on the banks of the Danube, circa 1941

View of Ulm from Neu-Ulm with the Münster (Cathedral) in the background.

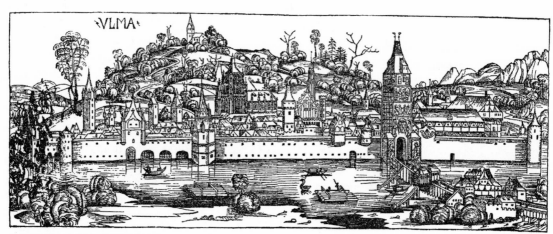

Holzfchnitt aus Schedel's Weltchronik   Ulm um 1493

Ulm circa 1493, woodcut from Schedel's Weltchronik

The Swabians

Dora Kroner would take her regular Sunday stroll along the Danube River with her three children, except when it snowed or rained. Along the bank of the river, on the Neu-Ulm side, were large deposits of washed river stones. The feeder river Iller, running from the Alps into the Danube west of the two cities, brought these once rough and sharp stones to the Danube. The stones were smooth and round and many were perfectly flat - ideal for skipping across the water. On each side of the river bank was a park-like landscape forming the promenade along the river's edge. Dora and her children would walk from their apartment in Neu-Ulm two blocks north, past the hospital, before they reached the river's east-west promenade. Looking across the Danube they could see the historic panorama of Ulm's fortification and half-timbered houses with their red-tiled roofs. Within this setting of old medieval houses sat the Rathaus (City Hall), built during the Renaissance in 1357. The jewel of Ulm is its Gothic Cathedral, the Münster. The cathedral was paid for entirely by the citizens of Ulm and given to the Church as a gift. Its spire has a height of 161 meters and is the tallest cathedral tower in the world. This segment of the Danube became the playground for Dora's children, away from their co-op apartment complex and the family's garden.

Ulm has a history of eleven-hundred years, whereas Neu-Ulm is only about two centuries old. In 1181, Ulm became an Imperial City with its own traders and craftsmen. Ulm was positioned at the crossroads of important trade routes extending to Italy. The City became Protestant in 1530. Around 1700, Ulm was alternately invaded several times by French and Bavarian soldiers. In the wars following the French Revolution, the city was occupied by French and Austrian forces; the former destroyed the City fortifications. In 1810, Ulm was incorporated into the Kingdom of Württemberg and lost its neighborhoods on the south banks of the Danube, which came to be known as Neu-Ulm (New Ulm).

The symbol of Ulm is the Ulmer Spatz (The Sparrow of Ulm) with a straw in its beak. The story of the Ulmer Spatz has been handed down from medieval times to every child growing up in Ulm and Neu-Ulm. During the construction of the Cathedral the workers were trying to move long tree trunks through the gates of the walled city, but the trunks lay cross-ways on the cart. The width of the gate was too narrow compared to the length of the logs. Just as they were about to demolish and enlarge the city gate the city fathers saw a sparrow with a straw in its beak trying to enter through a small hole in the fortification. The bird, having the same problem as the workers, turned the straw lengthwise and pushed it through the small hole. The workers learned from the Spatz, stopped the demolition of the gates, and took the logs from their carts and individually moved them lengthwise through the city gates. Being grateful for the lesson taught by the sparrow, the citizens made it their icon. A replica of the Sparrow sits on the roof above the nave of the Cathedral.

Der Ulmer Spatz ist weithin bekannt
Im Unterland, im Oberland
Und sonst an tausend Plätzen ...
Sein Denkmal gar, aus Meisterhand
Blickt hoch vom Domfirst in das Land
Denn dorthin tat man's setzen.

7

Ulm (left) and Neu Ulm, separated by the Donau (the Danube).
The star marks the location of the Kroner apartment.

Ulm is located in the state of Baden-Württemberg,
while Neu-Ulm is located in the state of Bavaria.

Flowing between Ulm and Neu-Ulm is the river Danube, which first becomes navigable at Ulm. The Danube became an important trading route with the eastern countries such as Austria, Hungary, Serbia and Romania. The river terminates at the Black Sea in Russia. The citizens of Ulm are true Swabians whereas the citizens of Neu-Ulm are politically Bavarian. Nonetheless, Neu-Ulm citizens, whether in cases of politics, religion, or national crises have always felt a kinship to Ulm and therefore consider themselves mostly Swabian. Historically, culturally, and politically Swabians are a unique group of people. They are frugal, clever, entrepreneurial and hard-working, as well as the butt of many jokes. They are sometimes made out to be simpletons by non-Swabians. Swabians will say: "Wir können alles, ausser Hochdeutsch." (We are capable of doing anything, except speaking High German.)

Swabians like to point to their famous sons and daughters including: astronomer Johannes Kepler, inventors Gottlieb Daimler, Karl Benz, Rudolf Diesel, and Robert Bosch whose inventions continue to impact transportation systems. The citizens of Ulm are very proud of physicist and Nobel Laureate Albert Einstein, who was born in Ulm. Swabians are equally proud of a group of individuals who opposed Adolf Hitler and gave their lives in support of the opposition, including the famous desert fox, General Erwin Rommel. Rommel was born in Heidenheim, Swabia and his last residence was in Herrlingen near Ulm. Ulm is also the home of siblings Hans and Sophie Scholl, who were members of a secret student organization called the White Rose that stood in opposition to the Nazi Regime. The Scholl siblings distributed leaflets to many universities throughout Germany and were caught in the act of placing leaflets at the University of München. They were tried and executed by the Nazis on February 22, 1943. Another Swabian was Staff Officer Claus von Stauffenberg who was born in Jettingen, near Ulm. He was responsible for placing the bomb that was supposed to assassinate Adolf Hitler on July 11, 1944.

Albrecht Ludwig Berblinger, a famous citizen of Ulm, was a tailor, inventor, and flight-pioneer, who lived from 1770 to 1829. Berblinger had a passion for mechanics, especially a hangglider based on his observations of flying owls. He became the joke of the city even though King Friedrich von Württemberg gave support for the idea. To prove the possibility that humans could fly, he demonstrated to the King's brother and several princes his prototype on May 31, 1811. He intended to take off from a wooden platform constructed on top of the city's fortification and fly across the Danube, landing on the Neu-Ulm side. However, the demonstration failed in part because of the wind and thermals and Berblinger fell into the river. One hundred and seventy-five years later on a hill outside of Ulm, an exact copy of the hangglider was flown successfully, proving its flight worthiness.

The Tailor von Ulm

Perseverance seems to be in the blood of Swabians who are known to work hard and play hard. Those of us from Ulm and Neu-Ulm are proud of our fellow Swabians, their discoveries, and inventions. Most Swabians strive to own, if not build, their own home. Their homes, or "Häusle" as they call them, are usually two-family, two-story, masonry houses surrounded by little fenced-in gardens. The second floor was typically planned for taking in the wife's parents, or as a means to subsidize the income by renting it. There is always the requisite cellar with its various types of storage rooms, work shop, pantry, laundry and ironing room, and a place to store at least a year's supply of fuel for the winter.

Born in 1901, Hans Kroner was the son of a railroad switch master and one of eleven children who were born and grew up in Neu-Ulm. As a young child, Hans was raised by his older sisters and his mother, a stubborn matriarch. At the age of sixteen, Hans was the youngest volunteer fireman in Neu-Ulm. In the devastating wake of the First World War, children were roaming the streets of Neu-Ulm, begging for food from anyone, but particularly from the Bavarian soldiers stationed at the local barracks. As a way out of this misery, Hans, and his twenty year old brother Jakob, joined the military in 1918. Hans joined the Bavarian Army and Jakob signed up for the German Navy. Their motivation was simple: "At least the military feeds its soldiers." Their adventures were short-lived due to the signing of the Treaty of Versailles. Hans then joined several sports and gymnastic clubs, clubs for singing, mountain climbing, skiing, and swimming. His greatest passion, however, was the water. Through the Deutsche Lebens Rettungs Gesellschaft or DLRG (National Life Guard Association) Germany issued its very first lifeguard certificate to Hans Kroner in 1922.

Hans became a national sports figure in track and field, as well as swimming. As a result of his accomplishments, he was selected to study sports medicine at the University of München. Due to the political and economic upheaval of the time, Hans' academic career came abruptly to an end one year later. The only job he could find was in a factory that made brooms and brushes. Hans would never forget that one week's wages in 1923, paid in cash, was so much paper money that it had to be brought home in a wheel barrow. Its value, however, was just enough to buy a small loaf of bread.

Hans won the German Sport Bronze Medal at the age of twenty. Much later, at the age of 41, he won the German Sport Gold Medal. To win a medal he had to accomplish specified goals within a twelve months period. The requirements for the gold medal were: Swim 300 meters in nine minutes; high-jump 1.35 meters; walk 400 meters in 68 seconds; throw an iron ball weighing 7.25 kilograms for a distance of 8 meters; and do a 10,000 meter walk in 50 minutes.

He had many medals, all of them on colored ribbons. The medals were in the form of pointed crosses denoting honorable service for heroic rescues. There is one medal in the shape of a Helvetica cross held by a circular band. On the surface of the white cross are red flames denoting a connection with fire rescue. In the center of the cross was a piece of red tape Hans had cut out and placed over the circular center. Behind the tape was a place for an insignia that had been removed. It must have been a swastika. None of these medals were for killing, but instead they were for saving lives.

Dora Sellmer, who grew up in Ulm during that same period of hunger, starvation, and unemployment. She was one of five children, including one sister and three brothers. Her

Hans and Dora, 1921

father was a carpenter at the Magirus factory, a manufacturer of fire-engine trucks. By the age of sixteen, Dora became a certified seamstress. In contrast to Hans' family, Dora's family was a cohesive, sustaining, family unit supporting each other. Dora's strength and conviction came from her parents and siblings, whereas Hans' came from his personal experiences outside of the family context and his membership in numerous sport and social clubs. Dora and her siblings learned to be content by doing without while Hans learned that you had to plan and compete for what you wanted.

It must be true that opposites attract because Hans Kroner was by any measure a nationally recognized athlete, and Dora Sellmer did not have an athletic bone in her body. In fact, Dora would practically stop breathing if she went into a pool of water that reached her ankles. She never learned to enjoy the water, much less how to swim. The couple met at a soccer match when Hans hit Dora in the head with a soccer ball. Dora and a girlfriend kept returning to watch Hans play soccer. Hans evidently had his eye on her, and some time after 1921 they started dating.

During their courtship Dora worked for Herr and Frau Unkauf, a wealthy industrialist family living on Olgastrasse in Ulm. The Unkauf's were involved in several ventures including a cheese factory. The Unkauf's had one daughter, Ursel, who studied to become a medical doctor. In those days, wealthy people had their own in-house seamstresses who took care of things like clothing, bed linens, embroidery, and the like. At the end of each workday, Hans would go to the Olgastrasse address and meet Dora to walk her home.

Before they became engaged, Hans and Dora pooled their money so they could pay cash for furniture and household items for their future home. This was a Swabian tradition. The rest of their money was invested for their dream, a "häusle" of their own. They lived frugally in order to deposit as much money as possible into a savings and loan bank with a contract to build on a pre-determined site in Neu-Ulm. On November 1, 1923, Hans and Dora paid 65 billion marks for their bedroom armoire. By November 15, 1923, when the inflation ended and a new currency was instituted, Hans and Dora's life savings was destroyed. They had forever lost their dream of raising a family in their own home. Dora used to say, "Men can change the world with just the stroke of a pen."

11

Hans and Dora became engaged on Pentecost in 1924. This news was not well received by Dora's parents because Hans had yet to make something of himself. "He's just a broom-maker," they said. Since Dora's father and brother Karl worked at Magirus, Hans soon obtained work as a milling-machine operator. Over the next three years, studying at night, Hans obtained all of his national and state certifications to become a Schwimmeister and a state certified masseur and physical therapist. In 1927 the City of Ulm offered Hans the City's Schwimmeister position with the responsibility for all swimming and bathing facilities in the city. This meant he was totally responsible for health and safety procedures, teaching programs related to swimming, as well as the treatment and therapeutic programs offered by the Stadtbad (City Bath). However, a prerequisite for that position was that the Schwimmeister had to be married.

Hans Kroner, Schwimmeister at the Donaubad.

Dora Sellmer's father had just passed away in April 1927 and a year of mourning was the minimum waiting period before there could be a wedding. In Germany, marriage involves two events: A civil ceremony presided over by the mayor of the city, and a church wedding. In October 1927, the civil ceremony took place. As far as Dora was concerned, however, the real wedding day was April 28, 1928 when they were married in her favorite place of worship, the Münster, the Cathedral of Ulm. Hans and Dora Kroner, my parents, moved into an apartment on Maximilian Strasse in Neu-Ulm.

Stadtbad Ulm (City Bath)

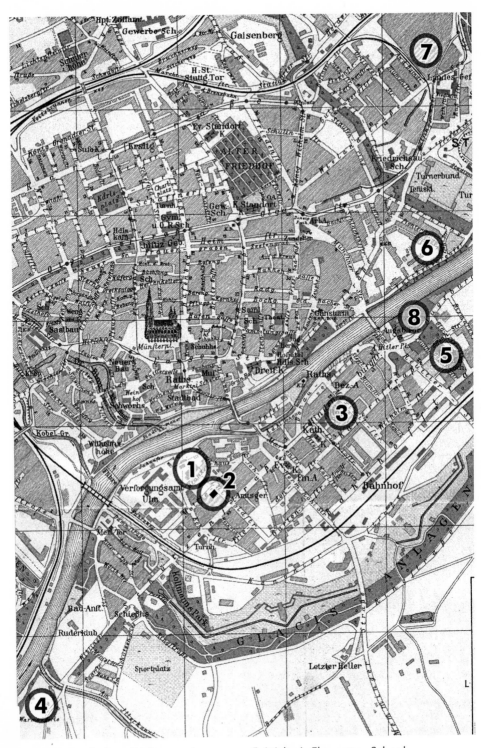

1 Hospital where Walter was born   5 Walter's Elementary School
2 Kroner Apartment   6 Walter's Bakery
3 Walter's Realschule (Middle School)   7 Mayser's Hutfabrick
4 Kroner Garden on the Donau   8 Augsburger Gate

Ulm, from the "Amtlicher Plan der Stadt Ulm," 1937

The Garden

"Over there beyond the park, see that tan-colored stucco house with the brown shutters? That was supposed to be our häusle," mother used to tell us on the way to our garden. Swabians like to end certain words with the suffixes –le, -el and –li. Haus (house) became Häusle. There was always a tone of sadness in her voice and a distant look in her eyes, when she described "our häusle." For almost fifty years, as she walked or bicycled to the garden, she was reminded of a dream lost; a hope never realized; and a labor of love without a tangible result.

The Kroners lived at Moltkestrasse 25 (3rd floor). After WWII the street was renamed Silcherstrasse.

Hans and Dora grew up in co-op housing projects. In 1931 they were able to join the newly formed coop housing group in Neu-Ulm located at Moltkestrasse 25. In the twenties and thirties, co-op housing consisted of blocks of four-story masonry buildings capped by mansard roofs and punctuated by large windows, each with operable shutters for shading, privacy, and protection from bombing raids. These city blocks were about one-hundred meters long, twenty meters deep, and contained somewhere between forty and fifty apartments. On the public side was a sidewalk and at the backside was a Hof (courtyard). The Hof functioned as a communal play ground, work area, and open storage area. Eight apartments shared a main entrance and staircase. These apartments also shared a multi-purpose annex that had a large boiling vessel for doing laundry, and hook-ups for water-driven washing machines. The annex could also be used for making repairs to household items or building small furniture.

Each apartment had access to a strip of land across the street from the co-op complex that was four meters wide and twenty-five meters in length - just large enough for several small gardens. My parents used a portion of this land for a vegetable and herb garden.

While saving money never lost its significance to Dora, investing in the future or working for dreams was too risky to be trusted to bankers, investors, industrialists and politicians. She kept her money in a box in the house. Dora was committed to saving the family's money. She thought spending too much of it was at best risky, and at worst foolish. If Dora said it once she said it a thousand times while her children were growing up:

> "Die Menschen machen Pläne aus,
> Gott Vater schaut zum Himmel raus und sagt,
> 'Wird nichts daraus.'"

It means, "People plan, God looks from heaven and says, 'Nothing may become of it.'"

In 1861, Dr. Daniel Gottlieb Moritz Schreber stated that people living in dense cities needed to spend more time outdoors, exposed to sunlight and fresh air. "At minimum, Germans should have small little gardens where they teach their children the basics of gardening," he proclaimed. Germany followed his advice and cities made possible the leasing of land at the outskirts of towns. Citizens could create small gardens and lawns with a small structure to get out of the rain, store tools, etc. During World War I and World War II, these gardens grew in importance as sources of otherwise hard-to-get fruits and vegetables. Today, these gardens - called Schrebergartens - are found at the edge of every German city, along railroad tracks, and in river valleys.

So, in addition to the garden across the street from the co-op apartment, my family had a second garden – our personal Schrebergarten. Hans leased the land from the city of Ulm in 1934 and created a beautifully landscaped garden within a few blocks of the Danube River. If Hans and Dora couldn't have their häusle, Hans would do the next best thing - he would create a garden with a miniature häusle where the Kroner-Sellmer clan could gather on weekends. The Kroner's garden became the place where the clan could play, bond, bring friends, or simply change into bathing suits to go swimming in the Danube. For the Kroner-Sellmer clan, it was to become the emotional and spiritual hearth for the extended family. Its harvest helped them survive during the difficult period toward the end of and following WW II.

The railroad passenger car that served as a cabin in Hans and Dora Kroner's Schrebergarten.

The Schrebergarten lease with the city of Ulm required the removal of any structures if the city needed the land. Hans' stroke of genius was to place an old railroad passenger car on the property. He was given the railroad car free of charge. Hans' bungalow of steel could easily be moved, if necessary, compared to the wooden structures that everyone else built. Hans converted the passenger car into a mobile home without altering its exterior. It had a bedroom, sleeping accommodations for five people, a small kitchen with a wood-fired cooking stove, a hand-operated well pump, a soapstone sink, and a living/dining room. There was an outhouse connected to the mobile home via a breezeway. A concrete box set into the earth, and accessible from the shaded deck, functioned as a cooler.

The garden was a 30-minute, leisurely walk from the co-op apartment along Schützenstasse, in the direction of Wiblingen, west of Neu-Ulm. After crossing the Illerkanal Bridge, one took a sharp right turn at the casket maker's barn onto a paved path. Across the street from the barn was a small market that sold such essentials as beer and soda. The market also raised beavers, which were always fun to watch. The path carved its way through tall grass and led to the area set aside for Schrebergartens. This area, to the north of the paved path, was a strip of land about 220 meters wide and roughly 500 meters long. It was divided up into garden parcels. To the north of this Schrebergarten region was a forest area adjacent to the grassy banks of the Danube.

Hans' half-acre garden was enclosed by a hedge tall enough to hide the fencing, and to provide the all important visual privacy. When passing through the metal gate, the garden partially revealed itself. Behind the hedge was a moat-like grassy area, which would completely flood during the spring. The garden itself would only flood from spring snow melt in extreme

cases. The arbor ahead of the entry gate framed a wild-flower area. Just past the arbor on the left was the garden's only gooseberry bush, whose fruit facing the path always mysteriously "disappeared." For some reason no one seemed to be able to walk past this bush without picking its green prickly fruit. On the same side as the gooseberry bush were at least fifty red currant bushes. At the end, the path turned to the right and opened up to a vista edged by gladiola flowers and bean stalks. The view ended at the railroad car's green metal skin that was punctured by classical passenger car windows. The walk led past a hand-operated well pump and the metal drums that were used to store water for the garden. A grassy gathering area lay at the end of the walk. There were terraced areas with permanent benches, a bowling play area, play-swings of all types, a large sand box, and an unforgettable lilac bush with its beautiful and aromatic fragrance. Along the other edges of the garden were outbuildings for tools and furniture storage, and a small work shed. Initially, there was a large grass area for playing soccer, pitching tents, badminton games, and stacking hay. Eventually, however, Hans subdivided this space so that his sister Anna and our neighbors, the Brauns, could put up their own little cabin and gardens.

During the summer, the Kroner family lived and slept in the garden and returned to the co-op apartment only as items were needed. In the summer Hans would go to work at the nearby Donaubad - an outdoor swimming and recreational complex directly on the Danube - where he managed a staff of about twenty to thirty people. Hans was also the Chief Lifeguard for the Donaubad. The complex was open seven days a week from early morning to sunset. The

Donaubad was a public playground with ping-pong tables, netball courts, and "swimming pools" in the river. The pools were metal cages floating in the river. They were designed to allow the current to flow through them, keeping the swimmers inside the cages safe. One could also choose to dive into the river from the floating pools, or from an arrangement of one-meter and three-meter diving boards. Along the river bank were exit floats with ladders, anchored to the bank, as a means of getting onto dry land. Others would walk west along the Danube, past the boundary of the Donaubad, cross the Illerkanal Bridge, with its dangerous whirlpools below, and after thirty minutes reach the confluence of the river Iller and the Danube. It is the Iller that moves all of the stones from the glaciers and rivers of the German Alps to the Danube's river bed. One could swim, float, or race down the river for a distance of over two kilometers, or 3.5 miles.

Across from the Donaubad was an area that was off-limits for swimmers. A large dredging boat was anchored with iron chains to the river bottom. Its rotating shovels extracted river stones for the construction industry. The danger was that if a swimmer got too close to the dredger, they could get pulled under the boat and potentially get trapped by the shovels. Since the dredger was directly across from the Donaubad, saving swimmers from drowning in this dangerous area was one of Hans' responsibilities. More than once he had to rescue swimmers from the chains of the anchor before they were pulled under.

Summer evenings and nights in the garden were quiet, serene, and beautiful. We could hear the birds and the wildlife in the wooded area between the Schrebergartens and the Danube. Sometimes my father would make a small fire in a pit and we would sit around listening to classical music on the radio. I remember thinking this must be what life is like in those villas and mansions surrounded by private gardens and landscapes. Quiet, in fact silence, was the result of the physical distance from other people, not people refusing to speak. Calm did not depend on having quiet or silent neighbors. I began to understand why having your own "häusle" was very much a desirable dream.

Our family performed a ritual every Sunday evening before the clan left to go home. Hans would gather whatever was ready to be harvested - vegetables, flowers, or fruit - and place the bounty in baskets for siblings and in-laws. If anyone wanted lingenberries, raspberries, blueberries, or strawberries, they had to pick them themselves. Only the boysenberry bush was off-limits to everyone except Hans' family.

While the garden was a most enjoyable and rejuvenating place, it was also a lot of work for Hans and his sons. There were many chores. Each day, flowers and vegetable beds had to be watered. This chore required using four 55-gallon drums of water that had to be filled with the hand pump. Slag had to be hauled from the City Bath Boiler House to the garden and placed between the pavers on all walking paths. In the summer, berries had to be harvested and processed to store for winter. Everyone hated having to pick berries, but everyone enjoyed Dora's marmalade, jams, canned fruit, fruit drinks, and jelly items that were stored in the cellar of the apartment house. After World War II, when there was no food and not much of anything else, Hans raised chickens and rabbits in the garden. Hans did the butchering and, in the case of the rabbits, converted the pelts into items of clothing and slippers. The garden was slowly transformed over time from a place of fun and pleasure to a tool for survival - both in terms of food and shelter - particularly during WW II. Only after the war and the prolonged period of minimal food and resources that followed were over, did the garden once again become a tranquil compound for the Kroner-Sellmer clan.

Dora and Frau Unkauf

Besides the extended family, the only other person appearing regularly in the garden was a tall, blond, beautiful and statuesque woman that everyone referred to as Frau Unkauf - Dora's former employer. Everyone called her by her last name and she would always address my mother as "Frau Kroner" and my father as "Herr Kroner." This was the custom in German society unless the parties involved agreed formally to call each other by their first names. Such an agreement never took place between Frau Emma Unkauf and my parents primarily because they belonged to a very different socio-economic group.

Dora used to tell her children: "You must always remember who you are and where you belong." The emphasis was on belonging. She was referring to socio-economic class. She used to say this as if to suggest that the Kroners and Sellmers belonged to one socio-economic group and Frau Unkauf to another, and that somehow the two should always be mindful of their position in society. This was my first introduction to class division. Hans and Frau Unkauf regularly went together on a four week skiing vacation since Dora had no interest in skiing. They stayed at the Ski and Mountain Club's cabin near Sonthofen in the Gunzenrieder's Valley. This was their base camp from which they went cross-country skiing, climbed mountains on their skis using ski-pelts, and then skied downhill to the next series of mountains.

After working in the garden, Hans would come home, enter the apartment, and give Dora a handpicked bouquet of flowers from the garden. There was no smile, no hello, no hugs or kisses just, "Here, these are for you." Then he would walk into the living room. Dora would arrange the flowers in a vase, set them near where Hans was sitting, and kiss him on the cheek. Both would have a sheepish grin on their face. It was their ritual, to be repeated as long as Hans had his garden. Dora rubbing her cheek against Hans' face was the most physical tenderness their children ever witnessed.

Marianne Karlheinz   Walter

The Sellmer Clan in the Garden circa summer 1941.

Uncle Christian   Aunt Marie Vater   Uncle Jakob Aunt Emmie Mutter

Karlheinz

Walter

The Kroner Clan: Anna & Jacob Kroner's Golden Wedding Anniversary, November 1938.

Walter in October 1935.

One-year old Walter in the Garden, 1935.

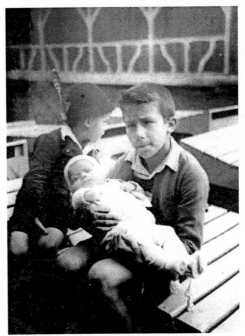

Walter, Karlheinz and Marianne, 1939.

Walter - Christmas 1937.

Walter on his first day of school in 1940.

Tranquility Base

In 1933, one year before I was born, Adolf Hitler became Reich Chancellor of Germany and disbanded all political parties except the National Socialistischen Deutsche Arbeiter Partei (NSDAP), also known as the Nazi Party. It was further decreed that any German citizen who held a political or civil service office must join the Nazi Party. Since Hans was a civil servant of the City of Ulm as Schwimmeister, he was required to become a Nazi. In doing so he had to prove that he had no bloodline connections to Jews, gypsies, or other "undesirables." To provide such proof he had to submit certificates related to births, weddings, and deaths as far back as his and his wife's grandparents.

Hans' membership in the Nazi Party started in the summer of 1933, four years after his first son Karlheinz was born. We always called him Heinz for short. It was considered desirable that the first-born be a male, in this way the continuity of the family name and lineage was assured.

It was Thursday, June 28, 1934 at 7:30 PM when Dora gave birth to their second child. Hans and Dora decided to wait until the baby was brought home to reveal the news to Heinz. When she placed the baby in the crib so Heinz could see it, he immediately asked, "What is it, a girl or a boy?"

"Say hello to your brother, Walter Manfred," was Dora's reply. "Send him back, I don't want him, I want a sister," he said and stormed out of the room.

Dora's favorite poet and lyricist was the 12th century minstrel Walther von der Vogelweide. In the modern form it was written as Walter. Dora, my mother, never provided an explanation where the middle name Manfred came from. In any case, she felt there was something poetic and romantic associated with the name.

Not until 1939 would my mother's and my brother's wish for a girl be fulfilled. Marianne Suse Kroner entered our life on June 10, 1939. I don't know whether my parents had planned to space their children five years apart, but it did impact my childhood as I never bonded closely with my brother or my sister when I was young. All three of us had our own set of friends in school and in the neighborhood, and seldom did we play together except in the garden. I spent the first ten years of my life under the influence of Mutter, which is what we called our mother. For some reason we never took much liking to words that other kids called their mother such as: Mutti, Muttile, Mutterle, Mama, etc. Similarly, we referred to our father simply as Vater.

The first ten years of my life were what I would describe as a tranquil period: a time when I developed a strong bond with Vater; struggled with the discipline and rules of Mutter; and, discovered the value of education through books and the efforts of my favorite teacher, Fräulein Herrmann. She took a personal interest in my learning, always answered my endless questions, and never punished me physically as some teachers would. We would walk together on the way home from school engaged in conversation. She walked proud and erect and her back was always straight even though she limped because one of her legs was shorter than the other. To compensate for the difference one of her shoes had a very thick shoe sole and heel.

It was a time when I discovered some of my favorite places around my hometown. One of these was my Vater's garden, and the other the River Danube. I felt a bond with its flowing water. There were beautiful, interesting, and fascinating things to see along its path; some man-made and some natural. There were forests, gardens, historic buildings, parks, and promenades. There were a few private villas where rich people lived. These villas actually had stairs leading out of the river up to the front doors of their mansions. But, it was the river that stimulated my dreams and fantasies. I built a paper boat and set it free on the river to float on a journey through Austria, Hungary, Romania, and on to the Black Sea. The river knew no borders, boundaries, dams, canals, and other objects that would deter my floating fantasies. Vater's library with its encyclopedia, books, and atlases provided me visual images of my boat's journey. There were many times when I walked west along the river to its confluence with the River Iller, where I would float on my back and stare at the sky. Sometimes, I would place a rhubarb leaf on my head as a shade and float downriver to the Donaubad. A little steering with my hands and careful slow breathing was all that was required to float free. For me, flowing free like my river became a metaphor for living my life.

I had a surrogate pet during this time, a German Shepherd named Arko who belonged to the restaurant Bräustüble at the end of the apartment block. I loved dogs more than any other animal, and after the owner of the Bräustüble let me take Arko around the neighborhood for walks, I was convinced that someday, somehow, I would have a German Shepherd of my own. I must have been around six or seven years old when a mixed-breed dog followed me home. My guess was that the dog was part shepherd. I brought him home and put him in the garden across the street from our apartment. I pleaded with Mutter to let me keep him. After much talk about responsibilities, the lack of outdoor space, money shortages, and the small size of our apartment, I realized she was right and that the luxury of dog ownership was an impossible dream. I had to return the dog to the park near the river where I had originally found him. It was within a week that I saw a railroad track-worker pick up a dead dog from the railroad track and throw it in the river. It looked like the dog that had followed me home. I was sure it was my short-lived pet and I crawled into a cluster of lilac bushes by the railroad bridge to cry. Witnessing this dog that I had loved, however briefly, being unceremoniously dumped into the river hurt deeply, and the image is imprinted on my brain and heart even today. There was something wrong with what I saw. My stomach hurt as I watched his motionless form of yellow-brownish hair and white underbelly floating helplessly in my river. It was at that moment that I realized a pet was no different from a human being; it needed love, a welcoming home, care, and a respectfully loving burial when that time came.

Arko became my personal playmate. He was the only life form that I was able to hold, hug, and stroke. Hugging, holding, kissing, and stroking were not something that happened amongst the members of my family, and certainly not given by Mutter. The closest I ever came to any form of hugging by another human being was by Frau Muschweck. She lived in the first floor apartment at Moltkestrasse 25. She was a short buxom lady - a little on the heavy side - but she radiated a warmth and genuine friendliness. I immediately warmed up to her. When she would see me she would say come here and draw me toward her with my face close to her bosom. Whenever I ran an errand for her I would always get a slice of bread with butter and jam as a thank you. Actually, she put more butter and jam on one slice than Mutter did on five slices. The only other person that expressed similar affection towards me was Uncle Jakob's wife, Tante Marie. However, I did not see her on a regular basis, so receiving her warmth and affection was limited to birthdays, Easter, and Christmas visits.

Vater and Mutter had worked out an arrangement where Mutter was totally in charge of the household including money, raising children, health, and religion. Skills useful for girls, such as cooking, sewing and homemaking were also Mutter's responsibility to teach her daughter.

Vater was responsible to provide economic stability for the family, a place to live, safety, and security. Basically, Mutter ruled at home and everything else was Vater's domain. Mutter was responsible for making sure her children were well behaved and completed their school assignments. However, when the report card had to be signed at the end of the school semester, it was Vater who had to sign the papers before they were returned to the School. This always struck me as a peculiar division of responsibilities.

By the time I had reached the age of ten, I had a very good understanding of my relationship with Mutter. We didn't get along. In fact, I disliked her and tried very hard to spend as little time around her as I could manage. There were divisions of chores: some for my brother, some for me, and some were shared on a rotating basis. Tasks ranged from washing and drying dishes, cleaning and shining every one's shoes every day, going to the cellar to bring up coal, potatoes, canned goods, or "Most" (fermented cider). These tasks were never a problem for me unless I had to go to the cellar at night. I was afraid to go when it was dark because I was sure someone was lurking in a dark corner of the cellar. In the winter, we had to get firewood from the attic, or take down the laundry that was hung out to dry on the second attic level.

For me, there were two major difficulties in my relationship with Mutter. The first was that she had many rules about behavior of which I often ran afoul. She had a definite idea about which activities were acceptable for her children, and which were not. That in itself never bothered me. The difficulty was when I asked, "Why?" or, "Why not?" The response was generally one of the following: "Because I said so; end of discussion." "It's not good for you." "You are too young to understand, just trust me."

It didn't matter how old I was, these responses never satisfied my curiosity, my wanting to know, or my desire to learn. Arguing about this lack of clarity was simply not allowed. She would say, "Children are supposed to be seen and not heard," or, "Speak when you're spoken to."

The second reason I had so much difficulty with Mutter was her method of supervising my homework assignments. In the first two years of homework, assignments had to be handed to the teacher on a slate tablet. One side of the tablet had permanent guide-lines while the other side was blank. We used griffels - slate pencil-like writing instruments - to write on the tablets. Actually it was more like scratching, and a wet sponge suspended from the tablet frame was used as an eraser. Whenever the quality of my work was unacceptable to my mother, she would take the wet sponge and make the work disappear so I had to do it over again. The school work that I enjoyed was handwriting, art, music, and reading. It was arithmetic that gave me trouble. The griffels were kept in a wooden box with a slide-out lid. Mutter would use the lid to hit me over the head every time I gave a wrong answer to an arithmetic question. There was never any tutoring or help. She knew when the answer was either right or wrong. I could memorize my multiplication tables - I was good at that- and I could add and subtract really fast in my head; but I had trouble when it came to long multiplication and division. I was sure that fractions were invented by the devil because they created a living hell for me, or at least for the back of my head.

In 1939, Mutter knew before I ever did that she essentially had five years to make something out of me before the Hitler Youth movement would take over. By 1939, Heinz was already in the Hitler Youth and Mutter legally could not interfere with his training program. She took her responsibility as a Mutter very seriously and she was bound and determined that her children would turn out to be decent human beings - what she called a "Mensch." A Mensch was a person that had good character, high morals, fortitude, and purpose.

Mutter was a good woman who could create wonders out of the limited food supply Vater brought home from his garden or from his patients who were farmers and millers. She could make her own dresses as well as clothing for her three children. She could convert any piece of fabric into a fashion statement. Her children were always dressed neat and clean and our shoes were always polished. As boys, my brother and I had to wear wool stockings held up by garters, something I hated with a passion. The relationship between Mutter and my brother Heinz was much more tender and loving than between her and I.

Vater was a big, muscular, athletic man and a public figure in Ulm and Neu-Ulm. He was a man of few words and even fewer outwardly visible emotions. "Never show your feelings, they make you vulnerable," he used to say. Another one of his and Mutter's sayings was, "Talking is silver, silence is gold."

I was proud to be seen with Vater, partially because everyone in town seemed to know him and respect him. At those times, most adult men wore hats and they would lift their hat as a form of greeting and point it towards the person they greeted. The person with the lower social standing would lift his hat first and point it to the person with the higher standing. The other person, in return, would reciprocate. What struck me as significant was the number of people who would extend to my father this sign of admiration and respect. At my young age, I had not yet learned of his accomplishments except to know that he had taught hundreds of people how to swim. Some even commented how he had saved many people from drowning. Vater would never boast, brag, or speak of his accomplishments. I just knew that this man seemed to be admired by everyone in Ulm and Neu-Ulm.

If I wanted to spend time with Vater I could always visit him at the Stadtbad, Donaubad, the fire station, or in his beloved garden. He wasn't the type of man who would come home from work and sit around listening to the radio or read the newspaper. He was a multi-tasking, multi-talented character, independent, capable, and the type of man one would want to be near in a time of crisis. He had very little to do with our formal education until after World War II. His commitment to providing for his family, his profession, and to community service organizations took him away from the family. His work responsibilities at the Stadtbad and Donaubad took him away six days a week. In addition, he had private clients that he saw in his physical therapy and massage practice. As Fire Marshall of the Neu-Ulm volunteer fire department, he manned the control desk mostly during the winter on Sundays. He was also an active founding member of the DLRG (Deutsche Lebensrettungs Gesellschaft). This group was committed to saving people from drowning, teaching swimming, and training other lifeguards. The remainder of his free time was spent in his garden, mountain climbing, or going on his traditional four-week skiing vacation with Frau Unkauf after Christmas.

Finding out who Vater really was, how he thought, and his attitudes toward different things was made possible by being next to him at the places he worked. In the beginning, Heinz and I would bring Vater his lunch at the Donaubad, the garden, or the fire station. When Vater was working at the Stadtbad in Ulm, he usually came home for lunch since there was additional staff to cover for him. At noon, on winter Sundays, the lunch delivery went to the fire house. When I reached the age of nine, I was allowed to make these lunch deliveries by myself using my bicycle.

Mutter would prepare the lunch and place it in three metal containers that stacked on top of each other and were held in place by a carrying strap. The bottom container usually had some type of desert like pudding, fruit, or something cold and sweet; the second container would
26

contain hot vegetables, potatoes, or spätzle (homemade pasta), and the upper metal container had the meat and gravy in it. The container had to be delivered exactly at noon. If Mutter was late preparing the lunch it had to be delivered by bicycle. Our family had the luxury of a motorcycle, but it was Vater's means of transportation. During the times where Vater could come home for lunch, it had to be ready to be served exactly at noon, and he was right on time, every time. Vater kept an exact schedule. He managed many people and he expected them to be timely and punctual. One of his many lessons to me was, "Be an example of what you would like others to be." A related saying of his was, "It is better to be one hour early than one minute late."

I often wondered whether it would be okay if his lunch showed up one hour early and got cold before he could eat it. I never had the courage to ask him because that would have been disrespectful. Even when he was working by himself in the garden, timing was still important because he was planning the day's work around a systematic way of completing a day's tasks. "You can't talk and do good work at the same time," was one of the first lessons I learned from him.

Vater did not chitchat while he worked. He did not want to be distracted by the radio, and he definitely did not like to be asked questions unless they were absolutely necessary to the work at hand. When he did talk it was short, specific, and clear. There was another reason why he didn't want to talk - he was busy thinking. He would often say, "Always analyze what you are doing and why, and then think about how you could improve on it." Another piece of advice was, "Be creatively lazy," meaning figure out how to do what you do more easily.

To me, it didn't matter what he was doing. I watched him like a hawk. When the time was right I would ask him why he did what he did. Later, I picked up on the rhythm of his work and anticipated what tools or supplies he might need and handed them to him at the right moment. He would never say thank you and he would never tell anyone at home what we did together, but I would know that I did well by him because of what he did after we finished working. At the end of the day, we rode his motorcycle to the local pub/restaurant. Vater would stop and go to his Stammtisch, a table reserved for regulars, and ask me to sit next to him. He would order a beer for himself in a stein the restaurant kept for him, and a small stein of beer and some bread, mustard, and sausages for me. "Go eat, and have some beer," he would say, pointing to the smaller stein. I knew then that he was pleased with what I did.

At the end of such a successful bonding experience with Vater, I would come home, clean up and lean on the kitchen window sill so I could look across the buildings of Neu-Ulm to the Münster of Ulm. With the Münster, the Swabians showed the world that whatever others could do, they could better. No matter where you were in the city of Ulm, you simply kept your eye on the Münster and you would find your way around town. In addition to the Cathedral being a feast for the eyes, its carillon provided music for the ears of everyone up and down the Danube valley and beyond to the hills surrounding Ulm. One did not need a clock; the bells of the Münster would let you know every half-hour what time it was. Home was a beautiful place and our home and lifestyle were secure. We didn't have a "häusle," but we had our garden, a wonderful place in the sun, and our swimming place, the "Blue" Danube, as the composer Richard Strauss referred to it.

It was a tranquil life that Vater and Mutter created. It was usually a peaceful, quiet home, except when the Kroner and Sellmer clan celebrated a birthday or New Year's Eve in our apartment. Cooking and baking were done in the kitchen on a wood-fired kitchen stove/oven that provided a constant source of warm water. We had a wood-fired hot water heater in the bathroom that was used mostly on weekends so Mutter could take a bath. She didn't want to go to the Stadtbad, where everyone else went to do their weekly bathing. The living room had a cast-iron stove. In the winter, the stove kept a hot water pot warm and the reflector shield provided a hanging surface to warm our pajamas before bedtime. The tasks of bringing fire wood from the attic and coal from the cellar always fell to Heinz and me. The bedrooms had no heatsource. Instead, we used hot water bed warmers. These copper containers were moved from bed to bed to pre-warm the space underneath the large down quilts.

When Mutter finally realized her dream of having a daughter in 1939, the nightmare of World War II was already underway. The war was raging far away from us, but it took my Uncle Ernst to Norway, Uncle Jakob to sea with the Navy, and Uncle Eugen to fight in France. At home, posters warned German citizens of "the enemy within our midst." We were told to keep our mouths shut because the enemy was listening. Huge posters with a mysterious figure in a black cape, black Mexican hat, with white sinister eyes were posted everywhere with the warning to be silent. Little did I know that the silence that I began to feel and experience in my own family was part of the fear that permeated all of Germany.

The early part of my tranquil life was interesting, secure, and predictable. It was life with Mutter the ruler and Vater the provider. However, just as the river carried its stones hidden from view, there were secrets in my family, or at least things that were never discussed. My parents never engaged in intellectual dialogue about anything, and there were few books in the apartment. Music from the radio, Mutter's singing, and table games were our form of entertainment. Every Thursday, Mutter and Vater would go to the Kino movie theather one block away, while our neighbors kept an ear out for us. We didn't have babysitters. Woe to us if the neighbors complained about too much noise. Once in a while we would go to the theater, but my memory of the plays and operas we saw has faded. Vater had more books in his garden than he had in his office at home. Books by Goethe, Schiller, and Karl May were plentiful, but I was too young to understand or appreciate them, with the exception of Karl May's adventure stories.

Reflecting on this comfortable period of my life reveals a rhythm of going to school, doing homework assignments, completing my chores, and playtime. After the daily chores were completed I could go down to the Hof, the apartment courtyard that was a protected playground area shared by all the co-op apartments. Our other play areas were the street, the old military hospital with its park one block away, and the Danube. Playing in the street was wonderful; there was plenty of space and little traffic. Neighbors would watch from their apartment windows and cheer us on. After sundown we would return to the apartment to practice our music lessons, do assigned readings, and once in a great while play table games.

In early spring, all of the mattresses, pillows, and carpets had to be taken into the Hof for cleaning and freshening. This meant transporting everything down three flights of stairs and then back up again. In the fall, firewood for an entire winter had to be split and carried to the attic, up four flights of stairs.

My dislike for Mutter was reinforced every time I received her physical punishments. The punishments were usually for lying or stealing. Fighting with other kids was absolutely forbidden.

Playing pranks on other people or calling them bad names was equally frowned upon. Having to go to bed without supper or not being allowed to play in the Hof didn't really produce the results Mutter desired. Up until I was ten years old, most of my punishments, were the result of my lying about eating things Mutter was saving for one reason or another. Mutter was intent on teaching us honesty, sharing, kindness, and above all, respect for others. For example, when I went to the baker, I usually received a pretzel as a gift, or a slice of sandwich meat from the butcher. Mutter expected me to bring it home and share it with my brother. I thought of the gift as an advantage and a reward for assisting Mutter with her shopping, so I always at it before arriving home. Mutter's verbal punishments, to me, were not really punishments; they were the price one had to pay for the pleasure gained. When the consequences escalated to physical punishment, it was usually a bamboo rugbeater that she used on me. I had to stand with my back to her and she would bring down the rugbeater on my back-side. Usually, I would cry loudly so she would stop, but the truth was that these lashings were not terribly painful because of the heavy lederhosen I wore. One day, I made the mistake of revealing this secret. Instead of crying, I laughed at her and told her it didn't hurt. After that I had to drop my pants for the punishments.

What made all of this "crime and punishment" worse was the fact that we lived in a very dense city. There were hundreds of eyes in the neighborhood watching what was going on, and the slightest transgression was reported to the appropriate parent. Neighbors, as well as aunts and uncles who lived within walking distance, would report my misdeeds to Mutter. The worst of these was my Tante Emmie, who lived next door. It was a waste of time trying to find out who the snitch was; it simply boiled down to taking whatever punishment Mutter seemed to think was appropriate. I never remember my brother being physically punished, but then I also don't remember my brother getting into difficulties like I did. I did not feel I was a bad person, I just didn't understand why curiosity was such a bad thing. My interactions with Mutter were mostly inquisitions, but since I knew right from wrong, and proper from improper, I became very good at deceiving, lying, making up stories, and acting innocent.

Let the River Flow

In the summer of 1940, I finally learned how to swim. My swimming lessons had been delayed because of a series of ear infections. I first learned the basic breast stroke while tied at the end of a looped pole. Vater guided me along the edge of a caged swimming pool that floated in the Danube. I always wore a safety device made out of two airpillow floats held together by two straps.

The time finally came for me to learn how to swim in the open Danube. The day of my first swim in the open river, Vater and I were sitting on his observation bench at the Donaubad. He reminded me not to be afraid of the water. He would be there, no matter what. Previously, he had me practice putting my head under water while keeping my eyes open.

"Are you ready?" came Vater's question. "Yes Vater," I told him. I felt sure, I felt secure, and I had the best Schwimmeister in all of Germany. I knew this man, my hero, would not let anything happen to me. I trusted him totally.

The Floating Cage, from "Wasserwacht Neu-Ulm"

I was holding on to the ladder on the side of the floating cage. Vatter instructed me to swim downriver to the last exit dock, about 20 meters from the caged pool. Beyond the last dock there was no way out of the river because of a ten meter high river wall; the next place to get out of the river was no less than one-thousand meters down stream. I held the ribbons that connected the two pillows against my chest and lay onto the water's surface.

The safety device worked for about three meters before the air escaped from the pillows. Suddenly I saw nothing but water in front of me. I was below the surface, but I kept on swimming. I saw the river's bottom of stones, and light coming from above bathing everything in a greenish hue. And of course, there were my air bubbles. I remember Vater's advice, "Don't fight the river. Fear will kill you." I was doing perfect breast strokes. Before I went under my head was aimed at the exit dock, so I just kept swimming in that the same direction.

It seemed like an eternity before I recognized the drums of the exit dock and a hand reached down to lift me out of the water. "Now you know how to swim!" said my father with a smile on his face, his cigar cantilevered from his lips. It was one of the few times that I remember him putting his arms on my shoulder, and we walked back to the caged pool.

My Vater stood with me on the same ladder as before and said, "Now jump in without the swimming pillows and do the same thing as before. But this time swim on top of the water." I said in a very low voice, so no one could hear me, "Vater I don't think I can do this." "You already did it. Your problem was that instead of looking up with your head out of the water, you were looking down into the water. Do you understand about keeping your head up?" he asked. "Yes Vater," I replied.

By then a group of children and adults had gathered around the big muscular man, Schwimm-Meister Kroner, with his massive chest and arms. He picked me up threw me in the river and said, "Do it again." There were no pillows to either side of me.

This time I kept my head above the water and looking up I could see Vater walking along the bank. He met me at the dock, and his booming voice said, "Now you are a free swimmer." "What is a free swimmer?" I asked. "It is one who is free to swim without aids in the river," he replied.

That summer could not have ended on a better occasion than to make my Vater proud of me and to be free of swimming restrictions. I still had a lot to learn, but it was the best feeling I had in a long time and I could tell Vater was pleased with me. That's all that mattered. I kept jumping into the river swimming to the same dock repeatedly.

On the way home Vater asked me, "Do you know how I know when a swimmer is in trouble even before the swimmer knows?" "No, tell me," I said. "When a swimmer's head is too low in the water it is the first sign that they are about to drown. The swimmer may be tired or there may be some other reason, but it's a clear sign. The next thing is that his head will go below the water and then they fight to keep their head above water; that fear will put them in danger; and then it's all over."

There was a long silence as we walked along. One more time Vater spoke, "Everyone gets tired and exhausted while swimming, but in the river you don't have to drown. In a lake if you go far from the shore you need to have the strength to swim back to the shore. In a river you can float free without much exertion and be saved." "I don't understand," I said.

"I will teach you how to float on your back in the river to safety. You lie on your back, you inhale/exhale very slowly so you will stay afloat, with your arms on your side, or stretched out like a "T." You move your hands only to steer yourself to the banks of the river. Remember, let the river's current carry you to safety on its banks."

The next day we practiced the new technique. I loved it. From that day forward I was never afraid of any river, no matter how fast or furious.

The Silence of Secrets

Lunch time at home was radio propaganda time. The noon meal was the main meal for the day, and Vater would arrive punctually at noon. The meal was on the table ready to be served by Mutter. Vater would turn on the radio, give a glance to his children seated around the table, and then he would listen to Herr Goebbels' propaganda or Hitler's latest screaming. There was no discussion between my parents - much less with us children - about what was talked about on the radio. In fact, there was never any kind of discussion on anything to do with the news, politics, the war, or current events. I knew that Mutter had some strong feelings about all this propaganda because her body language and the waving of her hand in a dismissive sort of way suggested her objection to whatever was said. Vater would turn to her and say "Frau!" with a serious stare as if to say to her, "Don't do that." You could sense that something was going on without knowing what. When I would ask what was going on I would be told, "This is too difficult to explain." or, "You are too young to understand." The one comment that always made me frustrated was, "We are not going to talk about that."

The first time I heard this was when I was five years old. I was in my parents' bedroom moving a chair up to the window sill to look out at a silent parade that was going down on the street. Red swastika banners were hanging from all the buildings and small red burning candles were on all of the window sills. Down below, the military, the SA, Hitler Youth boys and girls, and civilians were marching without music or talking. Just as I was about to move the sheer curtain aside to lean on the sill and watch, my mother said, "No! You don't do that." As always my response was, "Why not?"

She responded with, "You are too young to understand." I wasn't content with this answer and begged for an explanation. "We are not going to talk about that, now!" With that, she moved the chair behind the sheer curtain, so I could look at the parade through its veil. One of the uniforms I saw looked familiar to me. It was a brown shirt, black riding pants held up by a belt and belt buckle with an insignia. A leather strap was slung over the right shoulder fastened to the waist belt on the left side. Suspended from the belt was a long knife in a leather sheath. The boots where like riding boots and the hat was brown, but looked like an upside down pot with a visor. Where had I seen this uniform before?

By the time I made the connection, Mutter had left the room. I thought I had seen such a uniform in my parents' armoire, which was right there to my left with its full length mirror on one door. I could hear Mutter doing dishes in the kitchen. I locked the bedroom door and opened the door to the armoire. I moved the clothing that was suspended from a rod and, hidden to the right of a big overcoat, was that same type of uniform I had seen in the parade. Up on the shelf was the hat with an edelweiss insignia. That would be Vater's, I thought, since he was a mountain climber. A long dagger was suspended behind the uniform, fastened to the belt. My Vater belonged with those people, I realized, whoever they were.

The problem was that I could not let my parents know that I knew of the uniform because I wasn't supposed to snoop. I had never seen Vater wear it, but I needed to know what it was doing in the armoire. I could not leave this piece of knowledge alone and kept searching for more information. As I got older, I learned that these uniforms were worn by members of the SA mountain division. That is all I knew. I didn't even know what SA stood for.

One day, we were sitting at lunch without the radio playing and everybody seemed to be in a good mood. Since no one seemed to be anxious to talk, I asked, "What does SA mean?" Forks dropped to plates, Mutter stared into the center of her plate, and Vater looked at me quizzically and asked, "Where did you hear that?" "I heard it in a marching song that goes '… SA marschiert …"

With his sternest look and most intense tone in his voice, Vater replied, "We are not going to talk about this ever. Do you understand? Ever!" "Yes Vater," I replied, and that was the last of it. The uniform remained in the armoire for a while - I kept checking on it - until a year or two later, when it suddenly disappeared. There remained for me, however, a sense that there was a shameful, or some kind of skeleton still in the closet.

The second time I realized there was some kind of secret held by the adults in my family was in February of 1941. It was my grandmother Oma Kroner's birthday when the clan gathered for a celebration at my parents' home. As is usual after the noon meal, people would go for a Spaziergang - a long walk to help digest the food. It was a sunny, but cold February Sunday, and the adults decided to make a pilgrimage to Oma's birthplace, a farm in the village of Pfuhl east of Neu-Ulm. We would go see where my grandmother lived as a young woman before she married my Opa Kroner. On this Spaziergang, I asked my Opa Kroner a perfectly innocent question that created a level of discomfort for my adult relatives, the likes of which I had never seen. I remember the occasion, in part, because I have a photograph showing the group on our walk. There I was, almost seven years old, walking in front of the group, wearing an overcoat, woolen stockings, and a beret. I was using my Great-Uncle Michael's walking stick, pretending I was a grown-up.

There was Mutter, with a wool coat and felt hat with a green satin band, with her son Heinz hanging on her arm as always. Heinz was happiest when he was near to his Mutter. Heinz wore shorts with wool stockings, a jacket, and a beret. Opa Kroner, in his usual dark suit and Homburg hat, was bringing up the rear. Uncle Michael's wife Marie had an overcoat with a fascinating fox fur wrapped around her shoulder. The fox's mouth clamped itself to the tail to keep the fur snug around her shoulders. Then there were Vater's sisters, Walburga and Emmie, also with overcoats and felt hats. Emmie's children, my cousins, Herbert and Helga were there looking as well dressed and proper as always. Helga's pigtails were so long they were formed into a loop. Looking over the back of her stroller was my sister Marianne, not yet two-years old. The kids were smiling and the adults paused long enough for Vater to take the picture.

Three generations of Kroners set out to visit Pfuhl, about 2.5 miles from Neu-Ulm. Oma Kroner was not with us on this particular walk, but I remembered the farmhouse from previous visits. Someone else was living there now. The adults explained how our grandmother had lived there, and showed us which window was her room at the time when my grandfather Jakob came to court her. As we stood there in front of my grandmother's former home I asked my grandfather, "Opa, where did you grow up?" Since everyone was always talking about Oma Kroner's home, I wondered about my Opa's house. Everyone stopped walking and talking. They looked at me, then back to my Opa who, after a long silence, said, "Ah…., far away from here." His voice made it clear that he wanted to talk about something else.

"Can we all go there sometime?" I directed my question to the entire group of adults hoping one of them would answer. They all looked at each other, then started a different conversation and began to walk back to Neu-Ulm. I didn't understand why my question was so hard to answer. A simple yes would have satisfied me that someday we would go to Opa's birthplace.

Opa Kroner   Mutter Karlheinz

Walter

Marianne

1941 Spaziergang to the city of Pfuhl

Being somewhat stubborn, I would not be quiet until I had an answer. Finally, my great-aunt Marie, Uncle Michel's wife, put her hand on my shoulder and said, "Walter! It's far away so we can't walk there." "How about taking the train?" I asked quickly, with hope for a promise.

"Walter!" boomed Vater's voice. "That's enough now!" His body language was clear; no more questions. To reinforce his point he put his hand on my shoulder, squeezing his fingers so it was just short of painful, which I knew it meant, "Stop talking."

As was my habit, I checked my mother's facial expression. She had a penetrating stare. Her eyebrows would lift upward and her eyes would get larger and look like they were about to pop out, but only after they bored a hole through my head. She did not say a word, but I knew what the stare meant. "Stop whatever you are thinking of saying or doing." I was to be seen, not heard.

I made another attempt a few days later when I visited my Oma and Opa Kroner alone. In addition to his regular job as a railroad switch master, Opa had his own shoe repair business, as well as a dog grooming business. It was okay for me to visit Opa and Oma as long as I told Mutter where I was going. Within ten minutes I was in their ground-floor apartment, where my grandparents and their spinster daughter Walburga resided. I was always welcomed by my Oma, and she would give me a small slice of bread with some jam on it. My intention was not the food. I wanted another chance with my question while Opa was sitting still at his shoe-repair workbench. There, in the family kitchen by the window, looking out onto the courtyard of the apartment complex, was his shoe-repair bench, storage bins, and his stool. I was allowed to sit quietly on a chair next to him and watch. Opa was a quiet man and there really was not much conversation. I would simply stare at every move he was making. He sat on his stool holding wooden tacks between his lips and he would fasten the outer sole to the shoe. He would take a string and draw it over a wax bar before punching holes and sewing leather together. I loved the smell of the glue he used on soles and heels to join leather to leather. Opa, like his son Hans, was a man of very few words. He was a demanding man, frugal, and very hard to please.

As I was sitting there staring at him, I made another attempt with my question. "Opa, when you where little where did you live?" He didn't even look up as he remained silent and continued working uninterrupted. I felt a hand on my left shoulder. It was my Oma, who said, "Come, I want to show you something." Thinking it would be a picture or a map related to my question, I followed her into their living room. There was a huge table covered with patterns, rulers, scissors, and fabrics. It was my Aunt Walburga's seamstress workshop. My grandmother sat me in a corner, right next to the grandfather clock, put both of her hands on my shoulder and in a friendly but serious voice said, "Opa doesn't want to talk about it; never ask him again." She didn't say please, and she said it in a demanding tone. One look at her face and she had made her point crystal clear. Her stare cut right through me.

I worried for days that my grandmother would tell my parents that I had asked again and that I would be really in trouble. After a time, however, I realized that my grandmother did not betray me. I liked her, in fact I loved her, and from then on we would often wink at each other, as if to say we were sticking together.

My curiosity about the issue became even more intense. My questions were almost endless: Why is there such a silence about my questions? Is it a secret everyone has been sworn to keep quiet? I promised myself that someday I would find the answers about my Opa's life.

Labeling People

I wasn't exactly the most well-behaved child in the first year of Volksschule (elementary school). I still had difficulty with people telling me what to do without explaining to me why. My teacher, Fräulein Schmucker, was stricter and more authoritarian than Mutter. Schmucker had black hair and black eyes, dark facial hair between her upper lip and her nose, a face that never smiled, and her legs and arms were covered with black hair. In fact, her facial features looked like they belonged on a man's head. I know these details because we had to constantly sit up straight with our eyes straight ahead. This meant we were either staring at the blackboard, a map, Hitler's portrait, or her. With the exception of the maps, she was more interesting to watch with her stare, unsmiling facial expressions, yellow teeth, and a wart on the left side of her nose. I hated her from the beginning. I despised her after she kept pulling me from my desk by the ear to take me to the front of the class. While there, she would reprimand me in front of the class, hit me on my behind with her one-meter wooden ruler, or worse, smack me on the palms of my open hands. This happened many times.

The worst part of all of this was that I was trapped between her and Mutter. I wouldn't dare go home and complain about the pain, treatment, or embarrassment. If I did, I would get punished twice. Mutter was convinced I deserved any punishment the teacher gave me, no questions asked. The second year was only slightly better because on my report card under "Führung und Haltung", behavior and performance, I received a grade of "ausreichend" which was the equivalent of two on a scale of five, with one being an unacceptable grade. The other marginal grade, a two, was in "Rechnen und Raumlehre", arithmetic and geometry. During the summer of 1941, my mother gave me academic assignments every day as punishment and to make sure that her son would never embarrass the family again. At the end of the second year, Frau Schmucker gave me a three in everything except in "Führung and Haltung," for which I received a five, the best grade. I won my battle with Schmucker. I gave her no opportunity to punish me, reprimand me, or find a flaw in my behavior. If she had it out for me she was going to lose, and lose she did. For the first time, I discovered I could change things.

Walter

Walter's elementary school class of 1942/43. Teacher Fräulein Hermann

Fräulein Hermann was my third and fourth year teacher and it was she who opened up a world to me that I didn't know existed. No one in my family, on either my Mutter or Vater's side had ever gone beyond the required schooling of nine years; except for Vater's one year at the university. Beyond that, one either learned a trade or married. By the time I was nine years old, I discovered that some of my family's friends, several of my father's patients, and one of our neighbors, had studied at universities. I became aware that these people lived better, had nicer things in their homes, and even spoke High German. On one of our walks from school I asked Fräulein Hermann, "How is it decided whether one can go to the university or not?" She explained the German school system to me, starting with the first four years in the Volksschule. Based on one's performance in Volkschule, you could either qualify for the Realschule (secondary school) or the Oberschule (later called the Gymnasium), a preparatory school for the universities. I thought about her detailed explanations and asked her if she thought I could make it to the Oberschule.

"Walter, with your curiosity you can go far." She smiled encouragingly. I asked her, "What do I have to do to get started?" "You have to get the best Zeugniss, report card, at the end of your fourth year and pass a test," she told me. I decided that I was going to make it to the Oberschule, with the intention of using it as a means of studying further. There were too many questions and curiosities to be answered and satisfied.

There were not many books in my home, except for my Vater's encyclopedia, dictionary, atlas, and adventure stories by Karl May, and, of course, the Bible. Karl May wrote adventure stories about the American Indians and this is how America first became real to me, even though it was the Wild West. Frau Unkauf stimulated my reading interests and supplied me on a regular basis with books. Some of these books had to do with countries, while others were animal stories. Frau Unkauf would not only give me books she would discuss them with me later. For me she was a kind of tutor. Since my father would often visit Frau Unkauf's home to repair things and build things, I saw how she lived. Her home was like a museum. There were real oil paintings on the wall, including portraits, landscapes, and still-lifes. I didn't know the artists, but the paintings looked like they belonged in a museum. There was furniture of various design periods including Jugendstil, Art Nouveau, and Biedermeier furniture from the mid-nineteenth century. The best part of visiting Frau Unkauf was that she would answer my questions, she would question me, or she would go to a book and say, "Read this and you will find the answer to your question."

When Vater and I were invited to have lunch at Frau Unkauf's, it was an experience in itself. We were the only guests. There were fine linens, delicate china and crystal glasses, and real silverware. There was a formality the likes of which I had not been exposed to before. There would be candles, flowers, sugar cubes, and a container with cigarettes for my Vater. I knew then that I was going to learn as much as I possibly could from Frau Unkauf. At three in the afternoon, there was Kaffee and Kuchen and the same formal table setting with china, crystal, and all the same formalities. Frau Unkauf was clearly upper class, but she was what I would call an earthy woman - real, genuine, and very caring. She didn't act like other "rich" people.

I knew about rich people. They were the ones who could afford to play tennis on clay courts and send their children to ice skating lessons. They were the people who lived behind locked iron fences with their beautiful gardens. They were the equestrians who would go to the stables near our home and ride their horses to the training areas in their special uniforms. They were the people who could afford to have touring kayaks designed and built by Klepper who toured up and down the Danube. They were the people who could afford to belong to the Rowing and Rudder clubs with their long boats racing up and down the Danube. I watched them all with envy. These luxurious pasttimes were in my world, but behind an invisible wall of wealth not to be penetrated by what Mutter would call "our kind."

I only knew Frau Unkauf as a widow. Her daughter Ursel was for most of the war years studying at a university. I didn't know how or when, but I was going to study at a university no matter what. This was not a rejection of my parents or their education, or their place in society. It was simply an awareness that there was more to this world than in the circle of my existence. Life was so much broader, deeper, and had so many more dimensions. I remember thinking there is a world out there beyond Swabia and I would like to know it.

"Tante" Hansi and her car, 1929

"Tante" Hansi, 1937

My parents had another book that often drew my attention. It was a photo album containing pictures of my Tante Hansi living the U.S.A. I learned about her because of a gift she sent to me, a toy American police car, complete with wind-up motor and siren, steerable wheels, and leather seats. It was a green convertible with gold chrome emblems and rubber tires. It was the toy of all toys, but I had to play with it outdoors because of all the noise it made. I wanted to know more about Tante Hansi. Vater took me to his office and showed me the photo album. Tante Hansi was a friend of my parents who emigrated to America in her early twenties. The photographs were of skyscrapers in New York, Chicago, and the Chicago World's Fair in 1933. There was Niagara Falls, Yellowstone Park, and her home in California. Her name was Janet C. Beck and she lived on 408 Plagu Rubri in Santa Barbara, California with her St. Bernard dog and beautiful car. For years I would read everything I could get my hands on about America, the country that declared War on Germany in 1942. It was then our enemy. I had no idea what all of that meant.

Back in the world of Volkschule, every other week during the school year, the Catholics went to a designated room with their priest while the Lutherans (Evangelicals) met with their deacon in a separate classroom. I knew all about the Bible because my parents had one of those pictorial family Bibles. Before I could even read, Mutter and I would talk about the Bible stories. As a consequence, I always received a grade of five in Religion. One time in Religion class, we were talking about communion and the deacon overheard me whisper to my deskmate, "The Catholic priests are very selfish. They drink all the wine themselves." I was lifted out of my seat and slapped across the face by the deacon. He demanded, "Tell the class what you just said." I refused. I wasn't stupid enough to repeat something for which I just gotten slapped by his huge hands. He didn't force me to say it and decided to tell the class himself. He explained that such remarks are not allowed because it was disrespectful and sinful. I was just about to ask which of the Ten Commandments that was, but I decided against blurting out the question. I was grateful that this event never reached my parents' ears.

About the time I turned eight years old, I became aware of the tendency of people to label others. I could overhear people being referred to not just by their name but by some other characteristic. There were Jews who had to wear the Judenstern, Star of David. There were protestants, catholics - and other religious sects - communists, gypsies, flüchtlinge (displaced people from the east), and prisoners of war. Even I had a label. I was called "Schillemockel," because I wore glasses and had crossed eyes. This meant I was an imperfect blond boy, a marked human being. There was no discussion in my family about these labels. One day, Vater and I were in the garden when one of my classmates walked past and called out in his Swabian dialect, "Hey, Schillemockel." I said to Vater that I hated that name. There was a long pause while he stared at me then he said, "Come with me."

He took me to the tool shed. He held a simple pane of window glass in one hand and a focusing lens in the other. He asked me to hold out my hand and hold it still. He oriented the focusing lens so that the sun's rays would hit my skin, and the heat was so intense it almost burned me. "Can you feel it?" he asked me, as he removed the lens. "Yes," I said, "that hurt."

"Good," he said and replaced the lens with the sheet of window glass. "Now hold out your hand and let the sun's rays shine on your hand. What do you feel now?" "Nothing, except the warmth of the sun." "Good. So what did you learn?" I didn't respond; I just stared. He explained, "The glass is you. The sun's rays are the words that people hurl at others. You can let the rays concentrate on the inside of you and burn you, or you can let the rays go straight through you, where they won't hurt." It was many years before I fully understood the idea of transparency and focused solar radiation.

It was August 25, 1942, around noon, when the city of Neu-Ulm experienced its first real air raid alarm. A siren located on the roof of the jail across the street from our apartment painfully reached our eardrums. Our training told us to run as fast as possible into the bomb shelter. Each apartment block of eight family units had a designated cellar area equipped with benches to sit on during the bombing raids. At the end of the bombshelter corridor was an escape ladder to a cellar window, in case the stairs to the exit doors were blocked. At the other end was a knock-out masonry section leading to the bomb shelter of the apartment block next door - a kind of interconnected tunnel system. Each bomb shelter had pressure resistant doors to prevent a blowout or implosion (in the case of pressure bombs). These alarms were sounded every time bombers were in the vicinity. When the planes moved beyond the city a pre-clear and then an all-clear alarm was given.

At first, the airplanes flew at a very high altitude, appearing as tiny silver objects in the sky. Rarely did we see any German fighter planes pursuing them. Initially, it seemed the airplanes would always fly from east to west, suggesting they were flying from bombing the Romanian oilfields to their home base in England. My brother and I would run up to the upper level of the attic to watch and count the silver metal birds through the roof window. As of 1942, we had not yet experienced a bombing raid; the war was still somewhere else.

Air raids were not the only reminder of a war moving ever closer to Neu-Ulm. Food was rationed and in short supply. Breakfast was limited to one hard roll with some homemade jam. Lunch, the main meal of the day, started with two big bowls of crème of wheat soup or some other type of soup intended to make our tummies feel full, if only for a while. After the soup, there was one piece of meat the size of a slice of bread for the entire family. Mutter and we two boys would get a slice, the size of the end of an adult thumb, with some type of potato, pasta, or vegetable. Vater would get the remaining meat portion. Mutter was very creative with her cooking by finding ways and means of making us feel full. My family was fortunate because of the harvest from Vater's garden, gifts from Vater's private clients, and Mutter's frugality. That meant we had flour, eggs, bacon, canned food, cornmeal, and some meat. Every time Vater came home with a patient's barter, Mutter would divide the food and share it with my aunts and uncles. From the garden, Mutter made canned fruit, jam, and bottled juices. Apples were stored in the rootcellar, as were cider, sauerkraut in a barrel, and potatoes.

One of Mutter's food stretching techniques was the way she buttered a slice of bread. She would spread the soft butter across the slice; then she would scrape the butter off, leaving only the butter left in the voids of the bread. We also wore hand-me-down clothing. Mutter would make clothing for Heinz. Later, she would repair it and adapt it for me to wear. She made my sister's dresses as well as her own. Mutter's favorite time was in the evening when all the chores were done and she could enter her seventh heaven, her sewing corner. We had learned that if we needed Mutter to be in a good mood, we had to catch her when she was sewing.

Mutter also had an energy conservation technique during the heating season. We had a wood-fired kitchen stove and a tall cast iron stove in the living room. Wood, coal, and brickets (pressed coal dust) were the source of energy. The stove pipe was suspended along the wall to extract all of the heat before it reached the connection to the chimney. In earlier times, the bedroom doors where left open so some of the heat could move into the colder bedrooms that had no source of heat. During the war, we hung our pajamas on the heat shield behind the living room stove, and we took turns sleeping with the bedwarmer in our bed. The copper bedwarmer was filled with hot water from the stove and placed at the foot of the bed. The bedwarmer was then moved from one bed to another to warme the sheets. The ucky person for that day was the one who would go to sleep with his or her feet against the woolen protective cover of the bed-warmer.

At least once a week, usually Saturdays, we would go to the Stadtbad where Vater worked, and scrub ourselves down and take our weekly bath. The rest of the time we cleaned ourselves using a warm lavatory of water, soap, and a washcloth. Mutter, who wouldn't go to the Stadtbad, sometimes lit the wood-fired hot water heater in the bathroom to take her Saturday bath. When Marianne was little she could take a bath with Mutter. This was indeed one of my Mutter's only luxuries.

The government demanded that the citizens help with the war effort by donating skis, blankets, gloves, scarves, and anything else useful to the soldiers at the front. Church bells were removed and melted into war machinery. Hitler Youth collected rags, bottles, and metal for the war effort. During harvest time, the youth were expected to help on the farms. During the war, most farms were run single handedly by women whose husbands were fighting somewhere on the front. Women who managed farms were given prisoners of war to work side-by-side with them.

My brother was assigned to work on a farm in Nellingen During the harvest of 1943. One weekend, Vater and I went to the same farm to help with the hay harvest. We worked for 12 hours from early morning until evening and we were exhausted by the end of the day. In the evening, Vater and I were invited to have supper before we returned to Neu-Ulm. Heinz camped with the Hitler Youth and they were fed at camp. We were taken into the dining room where two plates were set out for Vater and me. One slice of bread, a small cube of butter, and some jam was on each plate. My father spread the butter and jam and gave me his portion, suggesting that I could eat it on the way home. With that, he stormed out of the room with me behind him. Later, I understood the dislike between farmers and city folk. Hitler did not allow the farmers to sell their goods at city markets, and city folk didn't come to the farms to buy what they needed. As a result farmers were dependent on what the government offered to pay. There was no love between farmers and city folks, and Vater and I rode home on the motorcycle still hungry and thirsty.

The Hitler Youth Dagger

At noon on March 16, 1944, the painful sound of the air raid alarm sirens tore us away from our daily routine. Instead of running to the bomb shelter, I immediately went to the attic while Mutter and Marianne descended into the bomb shelter. Heinz was a message runner for the Hitler Jugend (Hitler Youth). He had to report to the nearby city water tower for his orders. The first thing I noticed as I opened the small roof window in the attic was the absence of the faint and far away hum of airplane engines. Instead there was a loud, deep, roaring and vibrating noise. At the same time I could hear the anti-aircraft guns with their rat-a-tat-tat-tat sound. No sooner had I made this observation, than I heard a long sustained whistling sound followed by an explosion. Vater had told us that if you hear this sharp whistle it means the bombs are falling further away from where you are, otherwise you will just hear an explosion. I screamed, "We are being bombed," but there was no one to hear me.

Walter's bomb shelter in the basement of the apartment building, without the benches.

I flew down every flight of stairs, with my hands steadying myself against the railing; racing to the bombshelter. Only at the landings did my feet touch the floor. As instructed by Vater, I took my five-year-old sister Marianne, who was sitting next to Mutter, and placed her on the cold brick floor with my body over hers to protect her. The basement bomb shelters had a vaulted masonry structure that was painted white. The shelter was cold, sometimes damp, and filled with various odors coming from the nearby storage units. Each storage unit was defined by wood lattice partitions. Sometimes you could smell the sauerkraut stored in a wooden barrel; other times the fermenting odor from apple cider permeated the basement. With the exception of Marianne and me there were only adult women in our section of the shelter. The men in our apartment unit were either in the war or had assignments with the fire department or the civilian rescue corps. My favorite neighbor, Frau Muschweck, was praying out loud, and periodically she would stroke the back of my head.

At first, there were many whistles with far-away explosions. Then the explosions moved ever closer and soon we could hear falling objects above us. We couldn't tell whether it was our own building falling around us or the debris from a nearby building. The cellar windows blew into our bombshelter and the sound of praying, crying, and screaming became louder. I covered my sister's ears so she wouldn't hear the fear, or have her eardrums damaged. One of the neighbors in our shelter kept screaming "We are going to die, we are going to die." I lifted one of my hands from Marianne's ear and I whispered assurances in her ear. I kept telling her that I was protecting her, she would be okay, and everything would be alright. I knew she would not believe these words, but I tried to reassure her anyway. Vater was never in the shelter. He had to be with the Luftschutz, the Nazi organization that took over the volunteer fire brigade. Vater and I had discussed "angst" (fear) many times in the context of swimming in rivers and lakes. I learned that angst of any kind could kill you, whether it is fear of what a person might do to you, bombing, danger, or misfortune. What we heard falling all around us was Neu-Ulm's concert hall taking a direct hit, one-hundred meters from our apartment building. When the all-clear alarm sounded, we went outside and saw the old parts of Ulm in flames. Smoke was everywhere and I experienced a nauseating odor in my nostrils; the smell of destruction.

On April 20, 1944, Mutter had to relinquish her influence and control over my upbringing. From that day on, the Hitler Youth program, the nazi youth organization, would take over and she was forbidden to interfere. At age ten, boys and girls were required to join the Hitler Youth. Boys started out in the Deutsche Jung Volk (DJV), German Youth People; and, girls started as Deutsche Jungmädel (DJM), German Youth Girls. All other youth organizations and gatherings were declared illegal by the Nazis. However, there was one exception to this rule: the Catholic Youth Groups in Germany could continue to meet and organize because of some special agreement between the Vatican and Adolf Hitler. The joke amongst us Protestants in the Hitler Youth was that Hitler and the Pope were in bed together.

I was getting ready to be inducted into the DJV, the first section of the Hitler Youth. In school, we were instructed that we had to serve in order to save the Fatherland, and I was ready to do my part. Inductions were always on April 20th each year; it was Hitler's birthday. My parents, purchased the requisite summer and winter uniforms and accessories without discussion. The summer uniform included black shorts, tan shirt, long wool socks and the scarf with leather knot. The beltbuckle had the Hitler Youth emblem - a red and white diamond shaped sign with the swastika in the center, held by an eagle. A leather strap slanted over the right shoulder fastened at the back and front of the waistband on the left side. The winter uniform was long black wool pants, black shirt, and a wool cap with the Hitler Youth insignia. Missing was the Hitler Youth dagger that we had to earn through the Mutprobe - the Test of Courage.

The Hitler Youth system was fairly simple. Service was mandatory starting at age 10. Boys aged 10 to 14 were called "Pimpfe." Hitler Youth (HJ) was the formation for boys aged 14 to 18, and they were referred to as Hitler Youth. The age group of 14 to 18 began pre-military training, including learning how to fly, sail, and fight with handguns and anti-tank weapons, as well as anti-aircraft weapons. Others prepared for the signalcorps and similar military services. The last nine months of the Hitler Youth training included service in the Reichsarbeitsdienst (RAD). These boys built tank traps, trenches, roads, and other military defense structures. There were similar organizations for girls organized around the same age groups. Girls became active in searchlight brigades, rescue efforts and non-combat activities.

I became a Hitler Youth member on April 20, 1944, two months before my tenth birthday. On Hitler's birthday, we assembled in our brand new uniforms at the Hitler Youth Haus at the Illerkanal. At the swearing-in ceremony, we swore to serve our Führer, Adolf Hitler, faithfully and selflessly. Part of the promise we made was to be obedient to our youth leaders and to the comradeship of German Youth. I was assigned to a Kameradschaft, a group of about 10 to 15 boys. My Kameradschaft was under the leadership of a seventeen-year-old Hitler Youth, with the rank of Rottenführer, equal to a private in the military. Three or four Kameradschaften were called a Schar - a platoon-like unit. Three or four Schars made up a Gefolgschaft, and so forth. Each of these groups had a leader who had an equivalent rank in the military. I was assigned to the Fanfarenzug - the drum and trumpet corps - and was given my own trumpet. We were indoctrinated and prepared to be heroes for the Third Reich. Within a very short time, many of us, including me, were convinced that we could do our part in the war effort. This included being prepared to die for the Fatherland. I was ready and anxious to do my part.

Pimpfe in Training: April 1942 Hitler Youth assembly in front of the Hilter Youth House.
Photo from "Stadt Neu-Ulm 1869-1994," page 299, by the Stadtarchiv Neu-Ulm 1994.

I was now free from parental control and supervision. Training consisted of Wednesday evening lessons and practice; all-day Saturday training or service duty; and, Sunday morning assembly and parades. It struck me as interesting that we always assembled on the plaza next to the Protestant church, and never by the Catholic church with a similar plaza, two blocks away. Formation always started as church service began and the congregation was singing. The Fanfarenzug was practicing and everyone else was making noise by screaming commands. I was convinced we were supposed to disrupt church services for the Protestants.

We were indoctrinated, trained for camouflage, and we learned to play the trumpet and march at the same time. We learned marching songs and how to march in formation. Service included helping on farms,

August 1940: Neu-Ulm Hitler's Youth on the march.
Photo from "Stadt Neu-Ulm 1869-1994," page 329,
by the Stadtarchiv Neu-Ulm 1994.

collecting metal, glass, old clothing, and anything that could be used in the war effort. Many times, we had to collect money from civilians and gave out tokens in return that could be placed on the lapel or hung on Christmas trees.

Pimpfe in Training. Photo from "Stadt Neu-Ulm 1869-1994," page 331, by the Stadtarchiv Neu-Ulm 1994.

I don't remember our Rottenführer's name but he was a poster child for the Hitler Youth with his blond hair and blue eyes. He even spoke Hochdeutsch instead of our Swabian dialect. Hochdeutsch is the formal German language that one would learn in school. It was usually spoken on formal occasions or on the radio. I thought of him as the "Snake"; his hair was shiny and flat, like a slithering snake's skin, his eyes didn't look friendly, and his smile was anything but genuine. Two of his oft-repeated remarks I shall never forget. The first one was a question, "What is a hero?" He always insisted that a true hero was willing to give his life for the Fatherland. The way he explained it was that one might have hero potential, but not until one gave his life could one be called a real hero. The second remark was about him and his leadership of our Kameradschaft. He told us that he was bound and determined to qualify as early as possible for the Waffen SS, the most elite soldiers in all of Germany. SS stood for Schutzstaffel, meaning special protection squad. It was true that the Waffen SS, as well as the Wehrmacht (the army), picked the top graduates from the Hitler Youth.

The Snake went on to explain, "Your performance under my command will help me get into the SS, so now you know my expectations of you." We had to perform beyond the best of the best in the Neu-Ulm Hitler Youth. I was excited and looked forward to the games, training, and service that would prepare me for my own goal of someday becoming an officer in the Wehrmacht; a soldier, but not a Gestapo agent. My heroes were real soldiers in the navy, army, and Luftwaffe, the German air force.

The Snake would sometimes scream instructions at us, digging his fingers into our flesh at the same time. It was a mistake to show pain. If we did, we had to crawl on our belly half the distance of a soccer field. Looking at him and listening to his speeches stimulated a very negative reaction in me. I didn't like him and my intuition told me he could not be trusted. I had nothing specific to point to, but in my gut I knew this was not going to be a good relationship. I decided that anyone who treats another human being with neglect and cruelty was not a

Mensch. If the SS would take him, then I had no interest in the SS. Besides, I hated the black uniforms of the SS anyway. Yet, I was the underling and I wouldn't dare express my thoughts. I remembered my Vater's advice: "Never show your feelings and thoughts; if you do, you are vulnerable."

We in the Hitler Youth had already been indoctrinated about the enemy, especially the enemy within our own population. We were told there were spies and saboteurs who wished to destroy the great German Reich. We were also told that if we saw, heard, or became aware of anything odd or suspicious, we must (the emphasis was on must) report it to our Scharführer. On one of our Sunday morning assemblies in front of the Church, we were standing around waiting for something. The Scharführer, several Kameradschaftführers and one of the Pimpfe from my neighborhood were engaged in a conversation standing by the nearby war monument. We were all curious of what was going on and we were told that the Pimpf had reported on his father and mother. After a while a car drove up, two Gestapo agents and one military officer got out of the car and joined the discussion. The three drove away again and after what seemed like a half-hour they returned with the Pimpf's father. The father was a professional military officer and had just come home on vacation from the Russian front. He was taken away by the Gestapo and the Pimpf returned to join our formation.

The Pimpf very calmly and with pride explained to us that his father had spoken out against Hitler and that his mother told him to be quiet. His parents argued in front of him and it was clear to the Pimpf the father was an enemy of the Reich. The Pimpf told us that he reported his father to the Scharführer. The Pimpf and his mother returned to their life in our neighborhood and two weeks later there was a death notice in the paper that the Pimpf's father had died on the Russian front.

Now I began to understand why there was no discussion about current events in our house, why there were no opinions expressed, and why I was told "we are not going to talk about this." The life of secrets and concealing things had begun. I understood why there were secrets and so much silence on so many things; revealing secrets was equal to death.

For two weeks in June, my Hitler Youth Kameradschaft went to summer camp. We received leather rucksacks, blankets, bivouac utensils, and camping tools. We learned how to pitch tents, make a fire, cook, camouflage, and search the woods for edible plants. Amidst all this fun, there were two activities where the Snake took us to the edge of the camp for special instructions. Each of us was given a sealed paper sack filled with gypsum dust. We were asked to kneel down, place the sack between our knees, and attempt to break the sack by squeezing our knees together. He explained it was physical training for our adductor muscles. He went on to explain that if we had the enemy pinned to the ground with his face down and our knees putting pressure on the kidneys we could kill a man. This struck me as peculiar because when my brother went through Jungvolk training he never mentioned anything about this type of training exercise.

Another thing that was not part of the normal training of the DJV was training with a rifle. Although there was no ammunition involved, we had to learn how to aim and operate a bolt-action rifle. Other Kameradschaften didn't get this training and from that moment on, I knew my gut feeling about the Snake was correct. I didn't know what he had in mind but I decided to keep my eyes and ears open.

Hitler Youth dagger

At the end of June, the new inductees had to take the Mutprobe - the Test of Courage. All of these tests and games were familiar to me because the older Hitler Youth in my neighborhood would talk about them. The official Mutprobe was to jump from a height of three meters into the water. I had grown up around the Donaubad and Stadtbad and had learned how to jump from the three meter board. The test required jumping feet first into the Danube. The Mutprobe was the last required test we had to pass in order to receive the coveted Hitler Youth dagger. Three boys from my Kameradschaft and I decided we were going to show real courage by diving head first off the three meter board, without telling the Snake. When we stepped back into formation on the shore, dripping wet, the Snake screamed: "You four head first Pimpfe have not passed the Mutprobe!" "Why not?" we asked in unison?

"You disobeyed orders; you were asked to jump feet first." He grinned from ear to ear. "Besides, you three were obviously not challenged; therefore it was not a Mutprobe. If you want your dagger you must pass next week's camouflage test."

Hatred is the best way to describe what I felt. The camouflage test was a much harder test to pass. It involved getting from one side of a city boundary to the other side of town without being captured by the older Hitler Youth boys. The test was scheduled for the following Saturday, with the boundary being the Glacis Park on the western edge of the city to the Augsburger Gate at the eastern Edge. The northern boundary was the Danube and going into the river was immediate ground for disqualification. The southern edge was the Ringstrasse around the city. The Glaci Park extended along the Ringstrasse and it was the favorite hide-and-seek area for this exercise.

I had a few days to devise a plan. I couldn't discuss it with my brother because he was part of the group that was supposed to capture us. I decided not to discuss my plan with my family out of fear someone might let it slip. I took my plan to the casket maker who had his shop and farm by the Illerkanal near to our garden. When I described my scheme to him, he assured me that he could help but pointed out that I could die if we did it the way I originally envisioned it. He described the shortfalls in my plan, and explained the dangers if we didn't take certain precautions. We resolved the problems and he agreed to be ready by the following Saturday.

We assembled at the Hitler Youth House at eight in the morning. There were about twenty Pimpfe and at least thirty older Hitler Youth, including my brother. The older Hitler Youth had to remain inside the building for a while. Each Pimpf, the Hunted, was given a red armband, which if captured was taken by the older Hitler Youth, the Hunters. The zone between the Hitler Youth House and the western edge of the Glaci Park was declared off limits for the Hunters. It was an area for the Hunted to disburse and to get a chance to get started. The Hunted were released at nine while the Hunters were released at nine-thirty in the morning. We had until four in the afternoon to arrive at the goal line - the Augsburger Gate. Those who had not signed in at the goal line by the time limit were as good as captured.

I ran back to the Illerkanal Bridge, but instead of going to the casket maker I ran to the garden. I did this in case the Hunters had spies watching the Hunted disperse and camouflage ourselves.

Having an older brother who went through all of this really helped me form my own strategy. I climbed over our garden fence, crossed the garden, climbed out of the garden and ran toward the Danube. I ran through the woods located in the flood zone towards the casket maker's place. All this time I moved through bushes and thick foliage to make it difficult to observe me. I entered the barn on a side door facing the woods. Once in the barn I saw the four-wheeled cart with one ox already hitched to the wagon. Propped up on the cart floor was an upside down casket; the lower front part was already covered with hay.

"Climb in, put your face against the crack of the floor boards of the cart and I'll lower the casket over you," instructed the casket maker. "What about the manure?" I asked. "If we don't have the manure the Hitler Youth can easily move the hay and will find the casket." He saw my concern. He went on to explain, "I'll cover the rest with hay. Then I will pull up the cart to the manure pile and cover the hay with manure. They will not want to go through the stinking mess," he assured me.

I asked "If they stop you, what will you tell them? If they ask why you go to the opposite side of town with manure, what will you tell them?" I suddenly realized that would be a fair question. "I will tell them that I am delivering this load to my sister's garden in Pfuhl. Do you think that will work?" he said with a smile.

It all went without any difficulty, except for the awful smell and the increasing warmth of the hay cover and the heat from the manure. The boards on the cart floor weren't exactly clean and I realized this cart was used to transport manure. Suddenly the cart stopped and I could hear voices, including those of the casket maker. I couldn't make out what they were talking about. It took forever for the cart to move again.

It must have been twenty minutes - twenty minutes of feeling good about our progress - when there was a loud command "Halt!" The cart stopped and again I heard voices and then suddenly I heard someone poking around the top of the casket. I thought I had lost the game.

The noise level increased and when the casket maker screamed in his Swabian dialect "Ihr Arschlöcher kennet di Mischde alloi ablada; I net" (You assholes can unload this manure yourselves; not me). There was silence. I was beginning to burn up with all that trapped heat and was ready to give up. The asphalt pavement was radiating heat towards the bottom of the cart and stupidly I didn't bring anything to drink. I was soaking wet in my black uniform just from sweating. The casket maker was right; I could die here. It was a good thing we only had a thin layer of mist on top of the hay.

Finally the cart moved again. The casketmaker and I agreed that he would drive past the finishing line at the Augsburger Gate as an added precaution. I wanted to approach the goal line from the back, because I didn't trust the Snake. I was not prepared to take any chances. The casket maker freed me from my smelly sauna prison and he simply said: "Congratulations, and you better take a bath in the Danube before you go home."

I recognized the Snake from the back. I walked up to him, stood next to him and as the stench reached him he covered his nose and moved out of the way, as he stared at me. It was 1 PM when I reported and signed in. I asked if anyone else had made it. I was the first one to reach the finish line. I decided not to wait around and went over to the banks of the Danube. I lay on the grass and, looking in the river's mirror, I saw a most unpleasant view of myself. I was filthy and dirty and I myself had difficulty coping with the aroma around me. I walked into the river in my underwear and started to wash my uniform. The dirt just kept floating away above the river stones, and I finally waded in and cooled myself with the freshness of the river.

I was pounding the water "Yes, Yes, I did it." I was more excited that I beat that bastard Snake, instead of receiving my dagger. I beat him with my own plan with the help of the casket maker. I put on my pants still wet and went home. I shared with my Mutter my excitement that I had passed the test and I was going to get my dagger. She had no interest in my excitement and she showed no reaction. At the following Sunday's assembly and award ceremonies, the four smartasses who dove with their headsfirst into the Danube finally received their daggers. The Snake, instead of feeling proud, took me aside and said, "Ich bin noch nicht fertig mit Dir. (I am not finished with you yet.)"

On the fifth of July, 1944, on the basis of my school report card I had qualified for the Realschule. I was so excited about this news; here was my first step toward a university education. Vater wasn't around to share in the news and Mutter smiling, suggested that it may not be a sure thing. After the Realschule I still had to qualify for the Oberschule but it didn't matter. Fräulein Hermann and I accomplished what we set out to do. She was going to challenge me to always do better, and my job was to meet that challenge. No one could possibly know the passion with which I took that challenge, because as my father once told me: "Don't tell anyone your goals until you achieved them. In that way you won't be as disappointed in yourself; and, others have no reason to think less of you."

For the first time that I could recall, I felt that I was more than a Schillemockel, a marked human being. I felt successful. I became aware of feeling good about myself not because I accomplished something someone else had asked me to do, but because I reached a goal I had set for myself by myself. My parents had never talked with me about setting goals, dreaming, or reaching beyond. My parents' advice was simply to be the best at whatever you do.

It felt good having dreams, goals, imagined possibilities, and the intrigue of something being out there in the world that perhaps someday I could reach. I was on my way to float free of the past; free of the limits set by my heritage, society, and my visual handicap.

Volksschule in *Neu-Ulm*   Kreis *Neu-Ulm*

IV. Klasse

Schuljahr 19 43/44.   2. Halbjahr

1. Führung und Haltung:

      sehr gut.

2. Leistungen:

Leibeserziehung *gut*

   a) Leichtathletik   b) Schwimmen   c) Turnen   d) Spiele

Deutsch: Musik *gut*

   a) mündlich *gut*   Zeichnen und Werken *befriedigend*

   b) schriftlich *befriedigend*   Hauswirtschaft:

Heimatkunde *gut*   a) Handarbeit

Geschichte   b) Hauswerk

Erdkunde /   Rechnen und Raumlehre

Naturkunde: /   *befriedigend*

   a) Lebenskunde   Schrift *gut*

   b) Naturlehre /

3. Bemerkungen: Der (die) Schüler wird zum Übertritt in die Hauptschule für _____ reif erklärt.

Neu-Ulm , den *5. Juli* 1944.

D*ie* Klassenlehrer*in:*   D Lehrer   D Schulleiter

J. Hermann

Unterschrift des Vaters oder seines Stellvertreters:

Walter's 1944 report card stating he was qualified to attend Hauptschule.

The Smell of Death

All hell broke loose in the city and on the radio. Police car sirens blared, seemingly endlessly. Loudspeakers on top of cars screamed. Everyone was hurrying, not stopping at the street corner to talk. The proclamations from the loudspeakers said the enemies amongst us had failed in their assassination attempt on Adolf Hitler. If there was silence in the family before July 20, 1944, there was now almost dead stillness in our home. Even the radio was turned down low, and we heard rumors that the Gestapo had ways of finding out if people were listening to the BBC from the U.K., or to short-wave radios.

The war was not going well. Fear and mistrust prevailed. Everyone, including myself, went through the motions of daily life, but even the noise level at the Donaubad was significantly subdued. We were supposed to be delighted that our Führer had survived the assassination attempt. I heard that those responsible for the plot were killed by the Nazis, but I was dismayed that all of my military heroes were dying too. Oberst Mölders, an ace pilot, and Submarine Commander Günther Prien, both highly decorated war heroes, were reported to have been killed in battle.

On October 14, 1944, we received news that General Erwin Rommel was in the temporary hospital in the Wagnerschule of Ulm. I rode my bicycle to the hospital but no one would let me enter, even into the corridor. Rommel was not only a Swabian, he was a general that had the respect of every German. On the 18th of October, the official announcement of his death was proclaimed in the newspapers. I had read everything I could get my hands on about Rommel and his accomplishments. He was a true Swabian living in Herrlingen, a village outside of the city of Ulm. On the day of his state funeral, I had stationed myself across from the Rathaus where he lay in state. I was standing between two officers at the first line of an honor guard from the Wehrmacht. I remember seeing his widow and his son Manfred following the casket out of the Rathaus. Manfred Rommel was in the Hitler Youth stationed at the anti-aircraft gun tower near our apartment, by the railroad bridge.

The Russian front was weakening; the Allied Forces had landed at Normandy. Wunder-waffen - wonder-weapons - seemed to be arriving too late, and our soldiers on the front did not have sufficient weapons, clothing, food, or supplies. Secrets, shame, and sadness entered my once optimistic and hopeful life. One of my family's friends was Major Krämer who fought in Russia at Leningrad. He lost a leg in the battle and was manning a desk in some military office in Ulm towards the end of the war. As was my habit when my parents were entertaining, I pretended to be asleep while in reality I was listening to what they talked about. One of the remarks Major Krämer always made was: "The problem is that they let corporals make major war strategy decisions." I couldn't get this remark out of my head because major war strategies were supposed to be decided by Generals. I couldn't ask for a clarification, or it would reveal that I was eavesdropping. Later I discovered the corporal was Adolf Hitler - the highest military rank he reached in the first World War.

On December 17, 1944, the third Advent Sunday, 200 British bombers dropped their weapons of destruction on the cities of Ulm and Neu-Ulm. They dropped close to 100,000 bombs onto the twin cities, including pressure-bombs that tore buildings apart, and incendiary or phosphorus bombs that burned anything combustible. They also dropped anti-personnel explosives in the form of pencils, ink-pens, and toys that would explode when one tried to operate them. One of my neighborhood friends lost his left arm when he found and tried to use one of the pens.

The Allied military strategists intentionally protected the Münster from the destruction. Farmers in the field away from the city could see the bombs raining down in an elliptical circle. The Cathedral was untouched and saved. However, seventy percent of the city was destroyed and over 700 people were either burned, suffocated, blown apart, or crushed by falling buildings.

Even before the all-clear sirens sounded, Vater rushed to our bomb shelter and instructed me to run into every bomb shelter on our block and tell the people to check their apartments for incendiary bombs. We didn't know that Vater had crashed into a bomb crater right by our front door with his motorcycle. I raced out of the cellar and saw the strangest phenomenon. It was supposed to be dark, but the sky was bright red, a fire storm illuminating the city. Herr Braun's lumber yard and shop were in flames, and I could feel the heat and hot air of the fire storm. I saw my father dragging his motorcycle out of the crater as I raced next door to Moltkestrasse 27. I jumped down the stairs, opened both pressure resisting doors, and screamed at the top of my lungs my father's instructions. I raced back upstairs and onto Moltkestrasse 29.

As I ran along the sidewalk the street next to me exploded as if little explosives were shooting out of the street pavement. I could hear the anti-aircraft guns with their rat-a-tat-tat-tat rhythm, but the other sound was new. As I jumped into the door cavity I realized that I had just been shot at by a low-flying fighter plane. I ran down to the bomb shelter repeating my warning and everyone looked at me in a strange way. Someone held me as I tried again, but nothing came out of my mouth. My vocal cords had clamped up and I couldn't make a sound. Sometime later, someone took me back to my own bombshelter with tears streaming down my cheeks, but I couldn't hear myself crying. I remember feeling extremely ashamed, I felt that I was a disappointment to my Vater. To be given a task by Vater was always a welcome thing; to do well by him was most important; but, I was not prepared for failure. This event was never an issue with Vater, he only said "It happens and that is why I keep telling you: Angst macht dich tod." (Fear will kill you.)

After I recovered and had my voice back, my Mutter asked me to run over to Ulm, where some of my relatives lived, and check to see if they were safe. I was to find out whether their buildings had been bombed or burned, whether they were alive, and then come home immediately. I checked the apartments at the Arsenalstrasse where Uncle Ernst, Tante Else and my favorite cousin Elfriede lived. Their building was untouched so I didn't go any further and instead raced over to Goethe Strasse where two more families lived. Everything within 100 meters of their apartment buildings was in ruins; however, their buildings were safe, and after ringing their doorbells I found they were also okay.

The sun had just come up and I needed to get across town to where my other relatives lived. I decided to take the pedestrian bridge over the railroad yards as a short cut to the Bahnhofplatz, and from there to the area near the Münster. The train station was bombed out and there seemed to be a direct hit on the train station's bomb shelter. As I approached the Bahnhofplatz, I saw that the ground was covered with human body parts. There were arms, legs, heads, torsos; the dead bodies of adults and children. There were thousands of body parts and they were all covered in gray dust. Was it concrete dust or some other kind of powder? At my feet was a red scarf covering what appeared to be a head without a body. I remember this so clearly because the red scarf was the only color anywhere, everything else was black and gray. I will remember my next thought forever: "so that is what dead heroes look like." I met death; it was silent, gray, and smelled awful. There was the smell of burning human hair; severed body parts where blood was supposed to ooze out, but instead the stumps were just a dark tar-like ugliness. There were body parts where the skin had peeled; and, then there was this strange odor I had

December 1944: Remains of the citizens of Ulm after a bombing raid.
Photo from "Ulm in Trümmern," page 36, by Eberhard Neubronner, 1991.

never smelled before. These body parts didn't belong to soldiers; they were civilian adults and children. I felt lost, out of control, I wanted to scream, cry, curse, beat on someone's chest that was still alive and beg them to make it go away. "Angst macht dich tod," I thought I heard someone speak but there was no-one around. "Fear will kill you". I started to run.

I continued my run to Uncle Eugen's home and furniture shop. He was fighting on the Western Front, but I needed to check on Tante Christine and her three daughters. When I arrived at the Hafengasse I could see Christine with her children searching for their things in the ruins. I asked if they were okay and with tears streaming down their faces they nodded their heads. I raced to my Uncle Jakob's house at Mathildenstrasse. Uncle Jakob was on a submarine in the Atlantic and Tante Marie was home alone. I saw her standing in front of her burned-out home holding a white handkerchief; there was nothing worth saving. She held me for a moment; another one of those rare moments when I was hugged by someone I loved dearly. Tante Marie was my favorite aunt and I felt anger and pain that something had hurt her and taken everything away from her. Here she stood all alone, her husband in the war, their Häusle reduced to smoldering ashes, being lonesome and homeless. I wanted to stay there in her embrace but it really was she who needed to be held as she had lost everything. I didn't know what to do so I said my goodbye. I didn't know how to express my feelings; what would be an appropriate comment? I just walked away staggering over piles of bricks, stones, burning beams, and dirt.

I wiped my face and saw that my hands were black with soot. I didn't realize that all the dirt and smoke would leave its filth on my skin. Before I crossed Gänsetor Bridge over the Danube, I once again went to the river to wash away the filth. The fresh water felt very cooling and stopped the burning in my eyes. As I was hurrying home, my dream of becoming a soldier suddenly became a burden. I didn't want anything to do with military, war, fighting, bombing, killing, hurting, and hopelessness. I still wanted to study at the university, but not to become a military officer.

On my way home, I saw people being carried in chairs with the same gray dust over their bodies, people that were dug out of collapsed buildings and carried in blankets to the hospital. The flesh hung off of people's arms as they walked to the hospital. Building walls collapsed, killing more people still trapped under the rubble. The sky was darkened with smoke and the smell of death was everywhere. I walked into the apartment and Mutter said, "Well?"

I said, "Well what?" I had forgotten why she had sent me on this journey of death and destruction. I gave her my observations and she sat down and covered her face. I knew she was crying. Once again, I didn't know how to respond someone who was hurting, crying, and lost. I sat across the table from her staring at her jerking body. Finally she stood and disappeared into the bathroom; I heard the key turn, locking the door. I silently moved to the bathroom door, placed my ear on the solid door and listened. All I could hear was the periodic sniffle.

I ran to the attic storage room to cry. I knew boys weren't supposed to cry, but I needed to do something. I wanted to be held, touched, loved, and reassured. My Mutter never touched me except in the case of physical punishment. I needed to know that feeling scared, afraid, and hopeless was an acceptable feeling even for boys. There was a hole in the roof, near to the roof window, and the clay rooftiles had fallen into our attic storage room and totally destroyed my American toy police car.

I had just rejected my dream of becoming a military officer; perhaps the dream of going to the university would also disappear. For me, it wasn't the Americans or British who had done this. It was "der Krieg" (the War) that caused it all. It was easier to think of the enemy as an entity or a phenomenon, and not a country or its people. Even though we had lost touch with Tante Hansi, I was sure we would find her after the war and perhaps I could go visit her. I buried my American police car in the garden across the street, close to the fence, and put a notch into the fence post as a clue where it was buried. In that way I could look at the burial spot from our kitchen window, and keep my dream of going to America alive.

For as long as I can remember, Vater had a bronze ashtray cast in the form of a Bavarian mountain climber's hat with the image of an Edelweiss on the side. The ashtray always held one of his lit or unlit cigars. The rim of the hat contained paper-clips. As was true with everything else on, or in, the desk, it was off-limits. A few days after the December 17th bombing raid, Vater noticed his ashtray was gone. He asked who took it, but no one knew anything about the missing item. The bomb crater in front of the house was still a huge hole filled with water. I went downstairs to watch the city workman pump it out, and when the crater was just about empty I saw the bronze ashtray. The workman gave it to me after I told him it belonged to Vater. I cleaned it and placed it on Vater's desk. That evening he wanted to know how the ashtray suddenly reappeared. I acted innocent and did not respond. For weeks it remained a mystery that no one could solve and slowly the question was forgotten. Later I learned that bombs caused implosions as well as explosions. The ashtray must have gotten sucked from the top of his desk out through the window, and then dropped into the crater.

Neu-Ulm in ruins. Photo from "Stadt Neu-Ulm 1869-1994,"
by the Stadtarchiv Neu-Ulm 1994; photo by Heinz Leiwig

The enemy was not yet finished with the destruction of Ulm and Neu-Ulm. The following description was taken from the Neu-Ulm Newspaper dated March 5, 1970, Vol.III, written by August Welte and entitled, "The Zero-Hour," a term citizens of Ulm and Neu-Ulm used to refer to the 107 minutes of destruction on March 1 and March 4, 1945.

"Two more bomb attacks took place that focused on Neu-Ulm. Reportedly, 808 bombers dropped 2,885 tons of bombs to destroy what took the citizens 134 years to build, even though 75 percent of the city had already been destroyed on December 17 of the previous year. Over a period of 45 minutes the bombers dropped 1,950 explosive bombs, 10 bombs in the form of mines, and 100,000 incendiary bombs. Three days later over the course of 62 minutes, 500 bombers dropped an additional 2,000 explosive bombs, 110 mines, and 65,000 incendiary bombs."

"The destruction included the train station, the Catholic Church, the school (the Realschule), the Post Office, and the entire industrial sector. With the exception of a few apartment blocks, the hospital, the Protestant church, and the Volksschule, the city was an endless rubble of brick, steel, and burned wooden structural frames."

My family was lucky; our apartment block was not destroyed. I believe we were saved because we lived only one block from the city hospital with its red cross painted on the roof and walls. For me the end of the Zero-Hour meant there was no more war to be won. What remained was my own battle to survive. I realized that my life of tranquility had been transformed to a life of struggle, fear, and the threat of being killed by high-in-the-sky murder weapons, and a daily existence where everyone was responsible for their own survival.

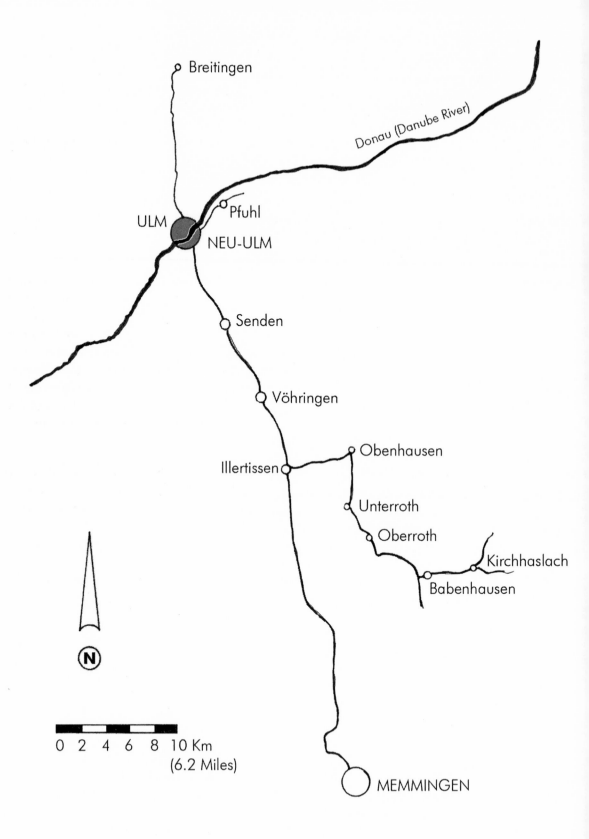

Breitingen

Donau (Danube River)

ULM
NEU-ULM
Pfuhl

Senden

Vöhringen

Obenhausen

Illertissen

Unterroth

Oberroth

Kirchhaslach

Babenhausen

N

0 2 4 6 8 10 Km
(6.2 Miles)

MEMMINGEN

Alone and Lost

On March 6, 1945, we escaped from the city. Vater showed up with a truck and transported Mutter, Marianne, Frau Unkauf, Tante Emi, who lived next door to us with her two children, and me to Babenhausen. There was no discussion, everyone was scared, and somehow I sensed the end was near. My brother, almost sixteen by then, was with the Hitler Youth defending the Fatherland, but neither of my parents knew where he was. He had been ordered to fight in the war at the age of fifteen. We took the kitchen buffet, dishes, clothing, beds, and food to escape from the city. Frau Unkauf's friend in Babenhausen, a furniture maker, agreed to take us in. Babenhausen was a German military command center. In the nearby woods my father's firefighting squad hid their fire equipment to prevent its destruction. Babenhausen was about twenty-five miles south of Neu-Ulm. This worked out well because it meant Vater could still keep an eye on his family and serve his community.

Accommodations at Babenhausen were too crowded, so Vater moved Mutter, Marianne, and me, as well as Tante Emi, Herbert and Helga, to Kirchhaslach about five kilometers east of Babenhausen. Frau Katheininger, who owned the farm and whose husband was fighting on the Eastern Front, was our host. With the exception of a French prisoner of war, Frau Katheininger managed the entire farm alone. We lived on the second floor of the farmhouse and I was instructed to do whatever Frau Katheininger asked me to do. I never understood why my cousin, Tante Emi's son Herbert who was my brother's age, was not in the Hitler Youth and why he didn't have to get his hands dirty working on the farm. The other strange phenomenon was that the French prisoner of war had a room in one of the out-buildings on the farm and he was free to work and roam about without a guard.

Kirchhaslach has a pilgrimage church in the Baroque architectural style. The church's history began in 1386 and it has since undergone many additions and renovations. It was out of respect and courtesy that I had to go to this Catholic church since there was no Protestant church in the village. On my first attendance, I was seated with other young boys in a balcony section. At the end of the service the priest greeted us at the exit door and some of us got punished because we were noisy. The priest's left hand pulled on my ear, while his right hand slapped me across the face. He told me don't come back unless you can be quiet. It was a lovely church, but it needed a loving priest.

Behind the farm on a wooded hill was a huge artillery piece hidden and camouflaged in the woods above the farm. The barrel of the gun alone was at least 15 meters in length. Artillery shells were stacked between tree trunks. I was wearing my Hitler Youth uniform and the soldiers let me climb up onto the gun structure where I could see that the gun was pointed over the village of Kirchhaslach at an opening in the forest on the opposite hill. That opening was where the road to Babenhausen disappeared into the woods. I realized that the Germans were expecting the enemy to come out of that clearing in the woods. This meant that we on the farm below were directly in the line of fire. As I had learned by now, I kept my mouth shut except for the most noncontroversial things.

I learned how to milk a cow, not very successfully I might add, and became proficient in how to drive a team of oxen to tend the fields. I was also responsible for cleaning the cow barn and collecting eggs from the chicken coop. It was about mid-April when Vater rode up on his motorcycle for a discussion with Mutter. I was told that Vater had to go into Neu-Ulm to the fire station and get some things. I was to go with him to help transport something back from our apartment. There were no details; I was told, "Just get your uniform on and go."

It was dark when we rode away and the only light anywhere was the small beam of light from the motorcycle's headlight aimed directly in front of the motorcycle. We rode through Babenhausen, west in the direction of Kellmünz, then north to Illertissen and on to Neu-Ulm. Vater stopped at the fire house and told me to walk to our apartment, get some empty potato sacks from the cellar, and wrap the marble eagle on the buffet in the living room with the sacks. He would meet me at the apartment in about one hour. I knew the eagle was a valuable piece of Italian marble, but I didn't understand why we had to take it back with us.

As I turned the corner from Luitpoldstrasse onto Moltkestrasse, the Snake was ringing our door bell, looking up at our kitchen window. Heil Hitler was my required greeting and he immediately commanded me to go with him because we had to report to the Hitler Youth house. "I can't, my father told me to wait for him." I replied. "Your father is only a Luftschutz officer and I outrank him. I command you to come with me," said the Snake. I had trouble with his comparisons but I let it go. I told him, "Just a minute, let me tell Frau Braun where I am going."

The Snake reluctantly agreed. I rang the Braun's door chime and when she looked out of her kitchen window, I told Frau Braun that I had to go to the Hitler Youth house and to please tell my Vater where I had gone. She told me she would and with that I jumped on the crossbar of the Snake's bicycle.

Once we arrived at the Hitler Youth house there were at least forty people, including Hitler Youth and old people from the Volksturm. We had to load rifles, boxes of ammunition, first-aid kits, food supplies, and leather bags onto carts. There were four-wheeled carts to be pulled by one or two people; two-wheel pushcarts with long handles; and there were three or four large wagons with teams of oxen driven by the Volksturm soldiers. In addition, there were numerous bicycles with leather bags hanging over the crossbars. After we loaded the supplies on the carts, we covered them with tarps. We were instructed to form a single line and follow the ox carts and to keep a distance of ten meters between us. I didn't recognize any of the Hitler Youth or any of the Pimpfe; and, as we moved out I realized that the Snake was nowhere to be seen. In fact, none of the boys from my Kameradschaft were in this caravan. We moved south and in the village of Illertissen we turned east toward Obenhausen. After a while we turned south to Unterroth.

Then it happened again. I heard that sound of the low-flying airplanes and in seconds they flew right over us. There were at least three fighter planes. They passed us, then turned and came back towards us. Then all hell broke loose. Dirt was flying, carts flew in the air, and I dove into the ditch by the street. I heard crying, commands being screamed, and endless calls of, "Help me!" As soon as the planes had passed over us, some of us ran across the road towards a wooded area and I dove into what appeared to be a sandpit. The attack continued along the road, but those of us in the sandpit were out of the line of fire. The planes made two more passes over the caravan. I remember there were three Pimpfe, myself, and one older Hitler Youth digging ourselves deeper into the sand with our bare hands. I looked over the grassy edge and saw bodies lying perfectly still. There was screaming, and I saw arms reaching into the air for help. By the time the planes came back for another attack, I had covered most of my body with sand. After that everything, sounds, airplanes, and screams, faded away from my ears as silence washed over me.

The next thing I remember was that it was dark, and I was alone in the sandpit. I was dressed in my winter Hitler Youth uniform that consisted of black woolen long pants, a black shirt worn over a tan shirt, and a woolen cap into which I had buried my face. It was cold and damp and in the distance I could hear rifle or gun shots. Over by the road, there were still some small fires burning wooden carts and wagons, the remnants of our caravan. There were dead bodies scattered about and several times as I crawled over to the road I called out, "Ist jemand da?" (Is anyone there?) There was silence. How could that be? Surely there had to be someone. I had no idea how long I was out, but all the bodies that I touched were dead. I kept crawling, hoping to find a human voice. I had never felt so alone.

I crouched and ran to the edge of the woods opposite the road. I wasn't sure where I was anymore. I had to keep the road in my sight so I wouldn't get lost. I decided to walk next to the road in the same direction as the caravan. I came to the village sign of Unterroth, circled the village to the south where I had to wade through a small creek. It was ice cold but I was lucky it only came up to my waist. Walking with water in your boots would be a dead giveaway with the squelching sound of every foot step. I took off my shoes, rung out my socks, used my shirt sleeve to wipe the inside of my boots dry before putting myself together again. At the other edge of town I saw a directional sign to Babenhausen. That was a huge relief; I knew where I was. As I approached Babenhausen. It was almost daybreak. I saw what looked like German soldiers and Hitler Youth in the distance. I lay in the grass until daybreak, crawled and circled around the town and on towards the village of Kirchhaslach. I stayed on the side of wooded areas as long as I could keep my eye on the road I was following. I wanted to avoid everybody because I was in a Hitler Youth uniform and I could be taken as a deserter and shot on sight. I didn't want to become a hero. I was alone and lost.

As the sun was coming over the horizon I entered the forest between the two villages, keeping my eye on the road a short distance away. Up ahead I saw an enormous roadblock prepared to be completely closed at a moment's notice. There were tree logs interwoven to form a crib. The space between the logs was filled with huge rocks. The entire structure was at least three meters high, four to five meters deep and extending far into the woods on either side of the road. There was an opening big enough to allow a truck through. On the side of the road was enough material to close the opening. I moved to the road and approached the roadblock. I suddenly realized there could be mines in the woods given the size of the roadblocks; the Germans were expecting the enemy to come from the same direction I was coming. As I walked towards the opening in the roadblock I saw a person up ahead, but with the sun blinding me I couldn't see any details. The sun's rays were a welcome sense of warmth, but I had to shield my eyes because of the low angle of the sun. I thought it odd that someone would wear Lederhosen in April. As the person came closer I recognized him; it was the Snake, but he was out of uniform. He carried a rucksack and looked like a typical Bavarian at the Oktoberfest. I thought this could be the end for me. He knew me. He knew I was on the run, and since there were only the two of us, he could become a hero by shooting me - a deserter.

He recognized me and the first thought that entered my head was the threat he had made, "I am not finished with you yet." There was a deer-horn handle sticking out of the sheath pocket in his lederhosen, so I knew he had a knife on him. I quickly went through a mental checklist of possibilities: I was in uniform; he could have a weapon in his rucksack; he could claim that I was deserting my Kameradschaft and he could shoot me. I tried not to show that I was scared. Shooting would give our position away and would attract attention; he could try to use the knife. For some reason the knife didn't scare me as we had learned how to defend ourselves, but if there was a gun it could be the end. He walked through the roadblock, stretched out his right arm in the Hitler salute: "Heil Hitler. Where are you going?" he asked me with a fake smile on his face. I responded with the Hitler salute, "Heil Hitler. My family lives in Babenhausen and I have to go see my grandmother in Kirchhaslach."

The grandmother part was a lie, but we had lived in Babenhausen so there was a little bit of truth in my statement. He didn't ask me anything about the caravan, or if I reconnected with my father. I realized he was running away. Why else would he wear lederhosen? It was his disguise.However, if that was the case, he was moving towards the American line. We parted without a salute or a Heil Hitler, but both of us walked very slowly past each other in opposite directions. I remember walking sideways so I could keep my eyes on him; he did the same. When I walked through the roadblock I raced into the forest to hide in case he was coming to get me; I had forgotten about the mines. I listened for him, but there was no sound. While hiding behind a tree I picked up a stick and threw it in his direction; no response. I ran out to the edge of the road, tripped, and landed flat on my face in the ditch. There still was no noise or movement. After about thirty minutes, lying perfectly motionless, when all was quiet, I crawled onto the road. I looked in his direction and saw nothing. I ran as fast as I could, took the turn by the church and the Rathaus in Kirchhaslach and on to the last building on the left; Frau Katheininger's farm.

"Where have you been? Your father came by looking for you. You are a mess. Go clean-up." Mutter flooded me with these questions; except she didn't ask how I was, or what happened to me. "I was forced to help out at the Hitler Youth House and transport supplies. Didn't Frau Braun tell Vater where I was going?" "Yes, but how did you get home?" was my mother's next inquiry. "I walked."

I cleaned up my uniform, stashed it into a potato sack, and crawled under my bedcover to shut out the world. I realized that I had come once again near death, but thank God I was saved. That night I took the sack with my uniform in it and buried it behind the farmhouse. I was finished with the idea of becoming an officer, and finished with wearing uniforms or anything else connected to the military forever, or so I thought.

The Making of a Thief

One day, after Hitler's birthday in 1945, which noone celebrated, we were still living on the farm. Mutter woke me early and suggested that I look out of the window. The German army was retreating, moving from Babenhausen through the village of Kirchhaslach. They were retreating in the form of a slow moving continuous snake of beaten-down human beings. Our room at the farm was a corner room and we could look in the direction the Germans were coming from and where they turned up the hill into the woods behind the farm. I immediately raced to the artillery position behind the farm and discovered they had vanished, as had all evidence that they were ever there. I was relieved because that meant the Germans were not going to put up a fight over Kirchhaslach on their retreat in the direction of München. I went back to the corner windows and watched in horror at the sad sight.

There were no motorized vehicles, no tanks or motorcycles. There were soldiers on crutches with bandages over their heads, some with an arm in a sling and some held upright by comrades. They literally dragged themselves through Kirchhaslach. Carts with oxen were carrying those who could not walk. An officer's staff car, fully occupied, raced past the winding line of human misery leaving its dust cloud to settle on the soldiers. The view I was looking at reminded me of a painting I once saw of Napoleon's retreat from Moscow. I was beginning to feel angry, confused, and disillusioned about all of the things I had been taught about Germany: human values, being a Mensch, helping your fellow human being. All of the greatness of German poets, scientists, composers, artists, and generals was overshadowed by this walking shame.

Propaganda pictures always showed the German soldiers being greeted by the liberated citizens of the country they captured - giving them flowers, holding their babies to be kissed, and giving them the Hitler salute. Similar scenes greeted the German soldiers at their return from successful campaigns. What struck me was that this retreating army did not even receive a cup of water or a helping hand from the citizens of Kirchhaslach. There was noone from Kirchhaslach, not even me, standing on the side of the road while the German soldiers were retreating.

Two days later, Heinz returned to the farm. All he said was that Americans had captured Ulm and Neu-Ulm, as well as Babenhausen. I suddenly realized that the Americans must have been close behind me as I traveled to Kirchhaslach. There was no discussion of where he had been or what he had done. Heinz didn't appear much different from the dirty soldiers of two days ago with their torn uniforms. While Heinz waited for the water to heat up for a bath, we saw a village official hang the white flag of surrender outside of the town hall. Within the hour an American Jeep drove into the village, stopped in front of the town hall, and was surrounded by a group of people. Then, the Jeep drove back up the hill from where it had come, back to Babenhausen.

The next day I was awoken by a loud and rumbling sound that came from the direction of the forest between Kirchhaslach and Babenhausen. A tank division of the United States 7th Army was moving towards Kirchhaslach. One could feel the tank vibrations by touching the ground. Out of the forest came a mechanized line of tanks, artillery, trucks, and jeeps each with American soldiers on top of them. There was not a single soldier marching alongside. The lead tank stopped right in front of Frau Katheininger's farm. That is when I noticed that all of the soldiers were black. There was not a white soldier in sight. I had seen my first American, a Neger, as they were called in German. I had seen black people in Vater's photo-album of the 1936 Olympics and I remembered Jesse Owens. I also remembered cartoons and postcards that depicted black people as cannibals, sub-humans, and super-humans. Finally, I came face to face with a real Negro.

People from Kirchhaslach looked out of their windows and waved to the Americans. There was a knock on the downstairs main door. Mutter and I stood at the top of the stair landing looking down into the foyer sparsely illuminated by the small panes of glass in the doors. Two black soldiers opened the door, entered, and closed the doors. I stood there scared stiff, looking into darkness with a little glare from the glass. I saw the whites of their eyes and teeth and there were metal cups seemingly floating in midair. Mutter called to Frau Katheininger telling her, "All they want is water." Frau Katheininger hurriedly came with a pot of water and gave it to them running back into her room and locking the door. The soldiers said something we didn't understand and then went outside. They were heating water under some type of heating element to make coffee or tea. After a while the Amis started to move, a parade of war technology that lasted over two hours. Eventually, toward the back of the column, we saw white-faced American soldiers. The most fascinating part of my introduction to the Americans was their jovial attitude and friendliness. I had no idea where the Americans were going, but they were moving in the general direction of München.

I was awed by the power and strength of the United State military technology moving through Kirchhaslach. The soldiers didn't look exactly clean, but they seemed better equipped than the German soldiers I had seen. I was surprised and impressed by the American soldiers and their friendly and courteous manner in which they related to people. The war in Kirchhaslach was over and yet soldiers knocked on the front door to ask for water instead of storming into the foyer. All of the propaganda and hatred I was taught in the Hitler Youth stood in stark contrast to the reality of what I was witnessing. The Americans shared chocolates, chewing gum, candy, and cigarettes with the former enemy. There was an old one-legged man leaning against a wall at the farm across the street from us. As the soldiers were heating their metal containers, two of them went over to theine-legged man and let him drink out of their cup. Afterwards they lit a cigarette put it between his lips, and stuck a cigarette pack in his coat pocket. It was at that very moment that I decided that someday I would discover America for myself and learn more about this gentle "enemy".

A week later a much louder sound and vibration appeared and within minutes the sky was filled with airplanes of all imaginable types. They were flying so low and in close formation that we could see the pilots hanging their elbows out of the cockpit. I called it the flying metal carpet of hundreds of air planes. The planes were not bombers, but two-engine transport planes that had windows on the side. There were also hundreds of fighter planes and small transport planes. I assumed that they were going to land at München.

On May 7-9, 1945 the German Reich surrendered to the Allied Forces. The war was over and a new struggle for survival was beginning. There was peace, but there was no food, no wood or coal for heat, no infrastructure, and no gasoline. Later Germany was divided into the American, British, French, and Russian Zones of Occupation. On May 10, 1945, Vater came with a wagon and a team of oxen to move us and our belongings back to Neu-Ulm. If we didn't return to our apartment it would be taken over by the authorities, which at that time were the Communists. As we drove through the streets of Neu-Ulm, what captured my attention was not the destroyed city but rather the American troops patrolling the city. They were friendly, helpful, and I saw them give chocolate to children. Mutter, surprisingly, said they were gentlemen, commenting on the way they treated their German girlfriends. Hardly a day went by where one wouldn't hear some wonderful story about Amis being nice, helpful, friendly, and genuine. Yes, we knew all about their interest in young women, but for someone my age that was no different from looking for the best brewery in town. The story about Amis' friendliness and helpfulness was usually told in contrast to the British, French, and Russian occupation forces. Any town in the American Zone was most fortunate. The British didn't have much to give and they had not forgotten the bombing of London. The French, well they and the Germans never did get along, and the Russian were out for revenge, peace or no peace.

Since the Communists, Socialists, and Christian Democrats were now legal parties in Germany, it took a while before the Americans figured out how to create order from chaos. Initially the new authorities were mostly Communists put into office by the American Occupation forces. It took a while before the American Occupation forces realized that the Communists were not interested in democracy. They took from the haves, and instead of giving to the have-nots, they kept most of what they collected for themselves. Everybody in the neighborhood knew who the Communists were except the Americans. My surrogate dog Arko was confiscated by the Communist Police and trained as a police dog. If the occupation forces needed to find non-Nazis, a Communist was a sure thing. It took many months before the problems with a Communist dominated city government and police became apparent and the Americans removed them from office. Not before Vater was arrested, however.

Ulm and Neu-Ulm were essentially a heap of rubble, mountains of fallen bricks, dirt, iron, and broken concrete. Each day people searched the rubble for their belongings and broken things that could be mended. Burnt out buildings with their walls still standing had holes where windows used to be, surrounded by blackened burn marks. Passageways big enough for a tank to move through were the only level surface, but there were no sidewalks. What I saw reminded me of the talk that was going around town. People would tell the story of how Hitler in his campaign speeches in the early thirties had promised Germans that he would transform Germany so that they wouldn't recognize it anymore. He was right. We didn't recognize our Germany anymore; it was almost totally destroyed. The black market dominated the economy and there was nothing one could buy legally. The stores were empty with the exception of a bakery in our neighborhood.

The period from 1946 to 1948 was a time of hunger, begging, and theft. It was also a time when Germans enjoyed the Hoover feedings, a schoollunch program funded by the American government, and the Marshall Plan. It was a time when Vater and Heinz had to go through a de-Nazification program, which meant they were required to do hard labor on rebuilding the city's infrastructure. During that time, I volunteered to clean and stack bricks for the recycling of buildings that belonged to our neighborhood. I also volunteered at the Gärtnerei Hermann where they grew and sold vegetables. It didn't matter how much money one had, there was nothing available to purchase. The black market was the most popular place for commerce. I remember Herr Hermann exchanging a handful of asparagus for a large electric power-drill.

There would be an announcement over a mobile loudspeaker system that on a specified day and location meat would be available. Since there was no rationing system anymore it was first come first serve. Vater would stand in line around four in the morning; Heinz would relieve him at five and I would have to take my brother's place at six in the morning. Mutter would show up shortly before the doors opened at eight. It was not unusual that by the time Mutter arrived at the counter there were only soup bones. Vater's therapy patients, who had previopusly supplied us with food in lieu of payment, had nothing more to give or trade.

October was usually the apple season and one of the great free food supplies were apples that had fallen from trees on the side of roadways. Anyone could pick them up. Usually the fallen apples had worms in them, but that didn't matter. We would clean them, cut them up and Mutter would make apple sauce, or an apple pie if we were lucky. Citizens were also allowed to go into harvested fields and dig for potatoes left behind, or vegetable leaves. It was during that time that my Vater asked Heinz and me to join him in the living room. Vater sat at one end of the table, while Mutter stood near the door. Vater started to cry; something I had never seen him do. When he gained control he informed us that Heinz and I would have to go and find our own food. He suggested collecting apples, potatoes, and anything else we could find. We were asked to go to farms and beg for food. He explained that he would continue to do the same to take care of Marianne and Mutter.

It was painful to see my hero cry, to have him tell us that he could no longer do what he had always done, supply our family as well as his siblings with food. He turned away from us, and for the first time in my life, I went up to him and touched him, trying to show him that I loved him. Such gestures were not normal in my family. Hundreds of times he would reassure me growing up by saying: "You can do this." Now I turned to him, put my hand on his arm and said, "I can do this."

Thus, a daily ritual began where I took my bicycle and drove out into the countryside and into the farm villages, collecting and begging for anything from bread, butter, eggs, bacon fat, and so forth. I also "accidentally" knocked on many treetrunks to help the apples fall to the ground. No one would know the difference between a free-falling apple with worms and one that needed a little help. There was a competition between my brother and me as to who could bring home more food.

During those times, boys in my neighborhood formed a small gang. We had a hiding place in the cellar of a former warehouse, complete with crates, tables, shelves and candles. Everyone else in the gang was doing the same things my brother and I were doing, and sometimes we would bring some of the things to the hiding place, particularly apples and pears. We all realized that it was getting harder and harder to get things from farmers. This was understandable because everyone looked to them as the only places where there might be food. We also collected cigarette butts, stripped them, and placed the tobacco into small cans to give away or take to the black market.

One of my begging trips was to the largest farm south of Neu-Ulm where I had spent many weekends helping during the harvest and other times. I knew the family well, I knew the farm and their house, and I had adopted their German shepherd as another one of my surrogate pets. The first time I went there, I was sure that I would get something to take home. Instead, the owner's wife told me in her most vulgar and meanest way, "You god damn beggar schweinehund, get away from here. I don't ever want to see you again," and slammed the door in my face.

I felt that I had earned a little help and so I planned my revenge. With the fellows in my gang, I planned a robbery of their root cellar. I knew where it was and I also knew how to get into it without a key. There was a trap door for dropping firewood into the wood storage room underneath an arched breezeway. From the wood storage room, you could gain entry into the basement corridor and into the pantry. My first architectural drawing was to sketch the plan, the trap door, and the door that provided access to the stair leading back to the breezeway. Once there, they would be in the open for their escape.

The problem was the dog. My plan was to go to the farm early in the morning and wait until I could see the farm manager and ask him if I could take the dog for a stroll. He had never denied me in the past. I just had to make sure that I chained the dog to the doghouse when I got back. I knew that the farmer's wife would take the milk to the dairy early in the morning and the manager would usually go to the fields or the forest. Once they were gone, the other gang members had to let themselves through the trap door, load the booty into rucksacks and take the door to the stairs and their getaway.

On the agreed upon day, the dog and I went for a stroll down the road and to the woods. The other guys were hiding in the nearby bushes with their bicycles carefully hidden. Within an hour, I returned to the farm and hooked up the dog. I noticed that neither the wife nor manager had returned. I then went back to our hideout in Neu-Ulm. We had lard, bacon, ham, sausages, butter, cheese, eggs, and one loaf of bread, as well as cans of spreadable meat for bread.

The booty was in the hideout and the problem was how to divide it. Each of us could only take home what one normally would get by begging. We divided everything into small pieces that seemed appropriate for a handout. Then we made a list of all the people in our neighborhood that didn't have a man in the house and those that had small children. We divided the remaining booty into small packages in paper bags, cans, and jars, and placed them at the apartment doors of the people we had identified. Bags that went to the elderly, or that had a male in the house, included our recycled cigarette tobacco. We decided the heist would be a one-time event because of the danger of being discovered.

Excellent sources of food were the American kitchen trucks. These trucks would pull into Neu-Ulm's Glaci Park and prepare the meals for the soldiers. At noon, the soldiers would come from various parts of the city, stand in line for their food and sit on the grass to eat. We noticed that some of the garbage cans behind the truck were filled with half empty bags of bread, open cans of spam, and other perfectly edible food. We figured out a strategy to collect edible food from the garbage without being seen by the cooks. Once again we distributed what he had brought to our hideout.

I liked everything I saw about the American soldiers except one unkind act that I still remember. A trainload of soldiers stopped at the Bahnhof in Neu-Ulm. Soldiers got out and children ran up to them asking for chewing gum, chocolates, and cigarettes. I was a lot more cautious and stood aside and watched. Two soldiers had huge leather gloves on their hands and they were tossing an orange back and forth. I had never tasted an orange, and I thought it odd that they played with food. The few of us who stood watching on the sidelines moved our heads back and forth as if we were at a tennis match. One of the soldiers missed the orange and as it was rolling away, a young boy ran after it. The soldier and the boy arrived at the orange about the same time. The soldier took his boot and squashed the orange right in front of the boy's eyes. The other Americans screamed and shouted. I couldn't understand what they said, but I knew they were not cheering. It felt more like they were angry with the soldier who destroyed the orange. He must just have been an angry person because the rest of the Americans were really okay.

My favorite discovery about the Amis occurred during my sixth year at Volkschule. It was the American financed Hoover feedings. Food was prepared in the school kitchen and served to the school children. We brought a small metal container to school and at noon we stood in line for our daily nourishments. There was pea soup with pasta, lentil-soup with bread, oatmeal and fruit, rice soup and meat, bread and tomatoes, dumplings, and hot chocolate. Sometimes there would be oranges, other times ice cream with butterscotch sauce. The best part about Hoover feedings was you could come back for seconds or thirds provided you ate all of your previous serving. I learned to eat real fast so I could go through the line at least twice.

During our teenage years, Heinz and I lived in the same household, but at a distance. I had no feeling of brotherly love or sense of camaraderie. We never played together, primarily because our playmates were closer to our own age. He also had very different interests from mine and at first I just assumed it was the age difference. What struck me as curious was the relationship Heinz had with Vater and Mutter. Heinz and Mutter enjoyed each other. They had interesting conversations, and there seemed to be something invisible flowing between them that I could not see or sense. Heinz and Vater co-existed, but their relationship was always filled with tension. Heinz clearly did not admire Vater the way I did and I had no idea why. Vater would often come home from the garden and complain about the work Heinz had done, work that had to be done over again. I never saw Vater express any love and affection in the way he did to me? When I say Vater showed love and affection toward me it too was invisible but could feel loved. He never hugged me, he never shook my hand in a congratulatory way, I just knew when he was pleased.

Late in the fall of 1946, I learned why there always seemed to be a tension between Heinz and Vater. The authorities announced that free firewood was available, provided we cut our own trees, trimmed the limbs, cut the tree into one meter long logs, and transported them out of the forest. Trees that could be cut were marked. We were told they were damaged, having bullet holes and shrapnel in them. It was the site of a major battle just outside the city of Neu-Ulm. We could take as much wood as we could cut and haul away in one day. Arrangements were made with Uncle Jakob's truck from Mayser's hat factory to transport the logs. Vater, Heinz and I rode our bicycles about twelve kilometers east to a forest near Strass, carrying our own saws and axes. It wasn't long before my brother started to complain about all sort of things, including the muddy and wet ground. Vater said to Heinz, "Halt dei Gosch ond dua schaffe." Meaning "Shut your mouth and work." Unfortunately Heinz would not do it and the tension increased.

Vater and Heinz worked together to fell trees. I had to cut the limbs so that Vater and Heinz, using a crosscut saw, could cut the tree into one meter long logs. Vater explained to Heinz that all he had to do was to pull the saw towards himself, and then Vater would do the same each time the handles were about to touch the tree. Vater had to say over and over, "Stop pushing the saw." The rhythm of operating a crosscut saw never materialized because Heinz kept pushing the saw, making it bind up. Vater angrily told Heinz, "Get out of here and go trim limbs." Heinz by then was sixteen, I was eleven, and now Vater asked me to take the place of Heinz at the other end of the saw. After a few back and forths with the saw I got the idea and Vater and I cut logs all day. When the truck arrived in late afternoon we loaded the logs, and our bicycles on top, and rode home.

It became obvious that Heinz had difficulty working with tools, with his hands, and with Vater. Vater didn't have the patience to teach him, and I am convinced Heinz really didn't want to do it in the first place. He never learned the basics of working with Vater. First you never interrupted the work by suggesting alternative methods. Second, you never complained about the work being hard or difficult. And third, you rested when Vater rested. I learned this when I was seven years old. I think the two of them avoided working together in an attempt to avoid anger and disappointment. I remember Heinz would come home from the garden and complain about Vater, and Mutter would patiently listen. There were times where I heard Mutter talk with Vater about Heinz's complaints, and I thought that was a big mistake. Only sissies ran to mutters and complained about vaters, and I knew my Vater didn't like sissies or snitches.

The Pain of Silence

I had a favorite place by the Danube hidden within a cluster of lilac bushes. It was a U-shaped cluster with a clear view of the river but it provided a visual barrier between me and the promenade above and behind me. This place was my hideaway, a space where I struggled with my thoughts, trying to understand my pains, and dreamed of things that could be. When the war was still far away from Neu-Ulm, the river was quiet, silently following its course. About seventy feet to the west of my hideaway was the railroad bridge over the Danube. Every once in a while a train would disrupt the silence and intrude on my thoughts. It was here where I had conversations with myself, especially when I struggled with my relationship with Mutter. This place was also my crying space as I struggled with feelings of ugliness because I had one blind eye and my eyes were not lined up. I was a Schillemockel with glasses. During the war, I brought to my hideaway my fears, anger, and schemes for surviving situations I imagined or anticipated.

Towards the end of the war, the railroad bridge had been destroyed and its collapsed superstructure created a major blockage and a section of whitewater. The German soldiers had dynamited the bridge as part of their retreat strategy. Passage downriver or upriver was virtually impossible except for one chute between the bridge abutments nearest to the Neu-Ulm side of the river. The American and British occupying forces had rebuilt the bridge temporarily. The rushing water cascading between bridge remnants drowned out human sounds. No one could hear my cries, screams, and expressions of anger. Struggling with what I had seen, heard, and experienced in the first twelve years of my life was not unlike the transformation of my tranquil river into whitewater rapids.

In July of 1946, I finished my last year of Volksschule dropping to a "C" average. That summer, I discovered that I had to share my hideaway. Every time I visited, I had to clean it by removing cigarette butts and used condoms. Kids called them "Parisers" and I had no idea what they had to do with the city of Paris, or how they were used. The Amis had discovered my hideaway and they brought their German girlfriends there. There was no conflict, except for the garbage, since I was never allowed to be out at night. It became a shared hideaway.

For me, a new struggle began that perhaps had a more formative impact on the rest of my life. Once the Nazi era had come and gone, we no longer had to live in fear (or so I thought) and, perhaps we could learn something from our occupation forces, the Americans. Some of the struggles with my Mutter continued as if the war had not changed anything, others were new. For example, I could never understand why other kids were allowed go see American movies or go to the America Haus in Ulm to learn about the U.S.A. Was it because once again there was an outside force that was trying to influence Mutter's children? Her boys had been brainwashed by Hitler and she was not about to relinquish her role again to the Amis? I wanted to know what would happen if I saw a movie made in Hollywood. The worst part was simply that Mutter would never engage in any kind of dialogue about her rules.

My mind was bursting with questions to which no one in my family would give me answers. Besides my usual questions, there were new ones. Questions about Hitler's Germany, the war, the hatred towards Jews, Gypsies, women who dated French prisoners of war (who had their heads shaved), the ridicule of certain religious sects, and why people were forced to wear labels on their clothing - as in the case of Jews and their Star of David.

I had questions about the Pimpf who reported his father to the Gestapo and whose father couldn't possibly have returned to the Russian front "to die in battle." Was he killed like my favorite General Rommel, poisoned on the way to somewhere? Now that the war was over and the Gestapo was gone, why couldn't we talk about these things? Were my parents still afraid? What did I need to be afraid of? If I promised never to talk with anyone else about whatever we would discuss, would my parents trust me? Even this question was not being discussed.

In the case of my Vater not wanting to discuss things, I could only conclude that it had to do with a secret that could never, ever, be revealed; or that it was something he was ashamed to reveal. There were thoughts I had about my own acts that needed to be confessed so I wouldn't feel as guilty as I did. I knew stealing was a sin and I knew that giving stolen things to people who were starving, no matter how well intentioned, was not a noble thing to do because it had been pounded into me that the ends don't justify the means. "Stealing is stealing and that is that," my mother used to say. I knew that breaking and entering into a place to steal food was robbery, and I knew that my own justification of hunger might not make sense to others. This conflict between seeing, experiencing, and feeling the pain of hunger and doing something about it to make the pain go away was and still is a heavy burden. I needed at least to confess so my parents would know and I wouldn't have to carry the guilt by myself. However, all these things were never talked about.

The new police force, mostly Communists who had been appointed by the Americans, went through everyone's apartments to make sure no one was hoarding things. It was also against the law to buy things on the black market. One day, as I took one of Mutter's pies to the bakery to be baked, a common tradition at that time, I passed my Tante Emmie on the street. She looked under the cover at the unbaked pie and asked me what kind it was. I thought nothing of it and told her it was a plum pie. Vater had gotten the plums from one of his clients. Not long after that, the police came and arrested Vater for having the plums, saying he must have bought them on the black market. They would not tell him who reported him. I later informed on my Tante Emmie and told Vater how I knew she did it. I always hated her after that, and to this day I struggle with the jealousy and hate that drove her to report her own brother, knowing he would be punished.

I was stuck in my own home with little compassion, tenderness, or love. I wanted my parents to talk with me about what happened to me when I was kidnapped by the Snake and almost killed by airplanes. It wasn't just me that they didn't talk about. There was no discussion about where my brother Heinz had been at the end of the war either. Did they not care? Was it too painful to relive? Were they ashamed because they couldn't or didn't do anything about it? All I wanted to know was how and what did they feel when they didn't know where their sons were. There were other Hitler Youth child-soldiers that didn't make it. Why was no one in our neighborhood talking about them? Any attempt to broach the subjects was cut off with, "WE WILL NOT TALK ABOUT THIS NOW, NOT EVER!" The stern look on my parents' faces made it clear there was not going to be any discussion.

I had to take my favorite teacher's advice. Fräulein Hermann would never give me the answers. Instead, she would say, "Try to think of another way to formulate your questions." I filed the questions away for later. There were other, more pressing issues, problems, and questions, all of which had to do with what I would do next with my life. I continued with my fantasy about someday finding Tante Hansi. If she could be located, there would be a chance that my parents would let me go visit her in America.

Some things became very clear and firm in my mind as a result of what I had learned in the last seven years. My lesson of survival was that as a person, man, and perhaps a vater, I wanted to always have multiple options for my security. Neither my Opa nor Vater depended on a single source of income; they always had multiple incomes. Having multiple abilities and strengths became paramount for me. Family strength and cohesiveness was the buttress of life during struggles and the road to one's survival. I learned that when there are even the slightest cracks in a family's relationship, they may threaten the stability of one's health and wellbeing. Family bonding, I learned, was a constant endeavor to be nurtured and enriched. Finally, I learned and appreciated that even the nicest people can become beasts in their attempt to survive in a time of hunger and fear. Trying to survive should not be used as an excuse for destroying lives, but as a reason to gather around you those whom you love and trust as a protective and invisible shield.

In 1947, Vater constructed rabbit stalls in the garden across the street and chicken coops in the big garden. The kitchen, with its large soapstone sink, was transformed into a butcher shop as rabbits became our main source of protein. This also marked the time when we no longer had to beg for our food and Vater once again began to take care of our extended family. Heinz and I had to feed the rabbits and clean out the stalls. The pelts of the rabbits were made into slippers, gloves, and other useful items of clothing. Having our own egg supply was a joy, but taking care of the chickens was not. The problem was the rooster who, whenever we tried to get him into the coop for the night, would attack my brother and me. We always complained about this attacking rooster, but Vater never believed us. One time, when the rooster attacked me I hit him so hard I was sure I had killed him, but he recovered and staggered to his roost. A few weeks later when I walked through the apartment door, I noticed Mutter had a grin on her face, signaling that something interesting or funny had happened. She suggested I go into the kitchen and look at Vater. He was busy processing a chicken. When Mutter asked him to turn around and face me I saw that Vater had a hole in his forehead. Evidentally, when Vater had bent down to close the chicken coop trap door, the rooster jumped on his neck and started to peck at his head. At that point Vater grabbed him and twisted his neck, and the rooster became that night's supper. It was Vater's resourcefulness, skill, and talent that allowed my family to survive. Aunts and uncles were equally taken care of by Vater's menagerie and sustaining urban agriculture.

Marianne, Walter and Karlheinz in September 1946, having survived WWII.

Rebel with a Cause

I will admit that I became a problem child. I was a rebel with a cause. My cause was that I wanted to be free to explore this new world: the world without the fear of Nazism, the world that the Americans made possible, and I wanted to get to know them. I was curious. I wanted to go see the Americans; I wanted to sit near their officer club by the Danube and try the brown drink they called Coca-Cola. I wanted to go see American movies. The American occupation forces had a program called German Youth Activities (GYA). The goal of the program was to re-educate the German youth and to engage them in non-authoritarian recreational activities. This included games featuring democratic ideals, free thinking, fair play, and tolerance. There was an America Haus in Ulm where I could find out everything about America, but that place was declared off-limits by Mutter. I could not go and hang around the gates at the American army bases or interact with the Americans. There was a German POW camp just south of Neu-Ulm that Mutter wouldn't allow me to visit. In short, my life was channeled in a very narrow way. We were allowed to accept the American care packages and their content, but that was the limit of interacting with the former enemy. Despite these rules, I no longer asked permission for anything, I simply did what I wanted to do. I had to find out for myself why Mutter thought something was a bad idea. I was the only child that my Mutter had difficulty with. I lied, stole, and probably broke every rule she established. Everytime I asked, "Why?" I was told, "Because I said so."

A toy that was very popular in the spring of 1946 was a push-cart, the forerunner of the soap-box derby car. Two wooden axles with ball bearings as wheels supported boards big enough to sit on. At the back was a wooden ledge for pushing the cart with a stick. The front axle could swivel and a rope was used for steering. It seemed as if everyone in my neighborhood had one of these carts except me. What I needed was the ball bearing wheels, the rest I could find myself. I was told that the only one that had these ball bearings was Hitzler, a boy in our neighborhood who stole them from the former military supply depot in the industrial sector of Neu-Ulm. By now, this place was heavily guarded so I couldn't steal them myself.

Hitzler was one of our neighborhood's bad boys and everyone knew it. To associate with him was frowned upon by Mutter, as well as the mothers of my playmates. However, one day when I was coming back from swimming in the Danube, I saw him and asked, "What would it take to get four ball bearings?" "That depends on what you have," he replied. "Would you take a pack of tobacco?" I asked. He assured me that we could make a deal with tobacco. My reason for suggesting tobacco was that I knew Vater had four packs of American pipe tobacco hidden in the bottom of his dresser drawer. On the day of the planned exchange, however, Hitzler had changed his mind.

"The price has gone up," he said. "I need one pack of tobacco for each wheel." I was shocked, but since I knew there were four in the drawer I decided I was going to steal them. The black-market value of one pack of pipe tobacco was worth four to five pounds of butter, which meant it was better than gold.

We agreed to meet that afternoon. While he was waiting in the breezeway of the Hof, I went upstairs to steal the tobacco. I stashed them in my lederhosen and when I was halfway down the stairs I heard my brother call to my mother, "Stop Walter! He is stealing Vater's tobacco!" My brother was turning me in, I thought. He was just like Tante Emmie who reported on her own brother, or the Pimpf who turned in his father to the Gestapo. My brother was a traitor.

The windows in the stairwell were still broken and cardboard was stuck in their frames. Mutter called me back upstairs, but I was able to hide one pack between two sheets of cardboard. I was caught red-handed with the other three packs.

I learned that my brother came home, saw Hitzler by my bicycle, and asked what he was doing. Hitzler told him that we were exchanging ball bearings for tobacco. I gave Mutter the three packs and she asked me to get undressed. She had discovered that physical punishment through lederhosen did not have much of an impact on me. She also went to the dresser to discover that the fourth pack was still missing. "Where is the fourth pack of tobacco?" she asked me as she was standing there with a leather dog whip. "I don't have a fourth pack," I lied.

The whip was a leather strap about the length of an arm. One end was the thickness of an adult thumb with a clasp to hook into a dog's collar. The other end was tapered to the thickness of a little finger. Mutter swung the whip with all her might, stopping after each stinging strike to ask the same question, "Where is the fourth pack?" Each time I said I didn't know where it was. I figured that if I was going to be severely punished I had to get something out of it. I was still hoping I could trade the one pack for four wheels.

This beating went on for no less than two hours and I was afraid that I might have driven Mutter over the edge. She stopped and told me she was going to see Hitzler and find out if I already had given him one pack. While she went across the street to where Hitzler lived, I ran into the kitchen and took out a knife to cut myself. I was trying to make it look like I had attempted suicide, but only intended to give myself minor cuts. I just wanted the beating to stop; maybe the blood would cause her to stop. In my hurry I grabbed a regular dinner knife with its round tip and tried to puncture my chest where my heart is located. The dull blade wouldn't cut and I was afraid to jam it too hard. I could hear Mutter coming up the stairs so I ran back to bed. The beating continued for a while with the same question and the same answer, "I don't have it."

After about thirty minutes, she stopped and told me that she'd let Vater deal with me. She had never said that before. Mutter had always taken care of her kids and never turned punishment or lecturing over to Vater. I realized how terrible a situation I had created and I had no doubt Mutter considered herself a failure in terms of having raised a son who had turned into a thief. I realized it wasn't just about thievery, it was about stealing the source of food from everyone in the family.

When Vater came home I could hear them talking in the kitchen. He came to my bedroom, sat on the side of my bed very calmly and said, "Mutter told me everything, including your punishment. I am just going to ask you once whether you know anything about the fourth pack. If you tell me you don't know anything about this pack, I'll accept your answer and there will be no more punishment. However, if I find out later that you had something to do with its disappearance I will punish you; and Mutter's punishment will be nothing compared to what you will get from me. Do you understand?" "Yes Vater," I said. "So what do you know about the fourth pack?" he asked.

I paused, looked at him and Mutter, and then told him I didn't know anything about the fourth pack and I didn't have it. To this day I wonder if I would have admitted my guilt if Mutter hadn't been in the room. For whatever reason, I would not admit to something for which I had been beaten mercilessly.

"I'll take you by your word, and that will be the end of it." With that Vater left my bedroom. There was no supper for me that night and I fell asleep.

That night I decided there was no way for me to convert the pack into the bearings. Vater was too well known throughout Ulm and Neu-Ulm and sooner or later word would get back to him about his son's trade. I decided to dump the tobacco. On the way to school the next morning I grabbed the pack from its hiding place between the cardboard. I stuck it in my lederhosen, unsure where to dump it. The path to school took me through a small alley and past a convent's garden. As I took the pack out of my pants, I tossed it into the garden, thinking the nuns would probably give it to someone. I didn't see my sister Marianne coming down the alley and she witnessed me throwing the package. She had heard about the shameful act and knew that it was the fourth pack. I made her promise never to reveal my secret, assuring her that I would do the same for her.

In the summer of the same year, our family life transformed because Vater was home more often. He was no longer fire marshal, he had fewer patients, and the lifeguard organization DLRG had been declared a Nazi organization and, therefore, illegal. He took the whole family on a summer vacation in the Alps, reserving the Mountain Club's cabin as a base camp. Part of that vacation was to climb a mountain called Hochvogel with his two sons. Hochvogel's peak is 2,592 meters above sea level and it would take two days to complete the climb. The whole family, including Mutter and Marianne, took the train to Oberstdorf. Mutter and Marianne took the gondola up to the Nebelhorn while the three men started their climb of the Hochvogel. Mutter and Marianne returned on their own to the base camp.

German Alps, Hochvogel on the right at 2,592 meters above sea level.

Walter and Karlheinz on their way to the Hochvogel in 1946.

We carried our food and equipment to the Prinz Luitpold House at the foot of the Hochvogel, a climb that took seven hours. We camped there overnight and started the final ascent early in the morning. It was a clear day with nothing but blue sky, a perfect climbing day. At the age of twelve I had never climbed a mountain, only steep hills and tracks. Vater gave direction, advice, and explanations as we followed the climbing route identified by markers. In some places steel cables were pinned to the rocks where flat and slippery surfaces had to be traversed. I knew that Vater had been a mountain climber ever since his youth, but I had never seen him in action. Heinz and I learned the rules of living on and climbing a mountain. We learned the importance of teamwork when you put your life in someone else's hands and vice-versa. After five hours, we reached the peak and enjoyed the beauty of the Alps in almost total silence. To the east was Germany's highest mountain, the Zugspitze, at 2962 meters above sea level. With the exception of the Zugspitze, the Hochvogel was the highest peak in our field of vision. The silence allowed us to listen to the music of the wind as its tune varied with its speed. A nearby cross served as a memorial for all of the people who had lost their lives on the mountain.

Vater broke the silence and explained that we had to leave if we wanted to catch the train in Oberstdorf. This meant we had to descend 1700 meters to the valley floor and walk over 11 km as the crow flies in six hours. We made great progress, but at four in the afternoon we had to make a critical decision. If we took the long descent to Oberstdorf we would miss the train, which created a problem because we did not have any hotel reservations; nor did we have camping gear with us. In front of us was an alternate descent, but it was restricted for experienced climbers only. Vater turned to me and said, "You have climbed the Hochvogel. I think that makes you an experienced climber."

The path into the valley was one continuous steep slope of rock with little greenery interspersed. Vater asked me if I was willing to try it and I told him that I thought I could do it. We made it to the bottom and had one hour to make the train. Vater said we could only make it if we marched really fast. If I had walked any faster I would have been running. I had never before or after had this type of bonding experience with Vater. Each of us had the responsibility not to slow the group down. Vater would take my backpack for a while to lighten the load, but return it after a while when he carried my brother's load. Periodically, without breaking our stride he would check with us, whether we were okay, and made sure we had enough liquids in us.

I never felt as close to Vater as I did in those two days. It was a once in a lifetime experience that was worth more than hundreds of sessions of working with him in the garden. I saw Vater as a nature lover, a steward of the natural environment, a teammate, a teacher, and a guide. For him, the mountain was a metaphor for life just like the river. "The mountain will teach you that you are always dependent on someone or something else. On the mountain you will form true and lasting friendships," he would say. He was right. My father had become my friend.

Book Two

WORLD EVENTS 1940-1954

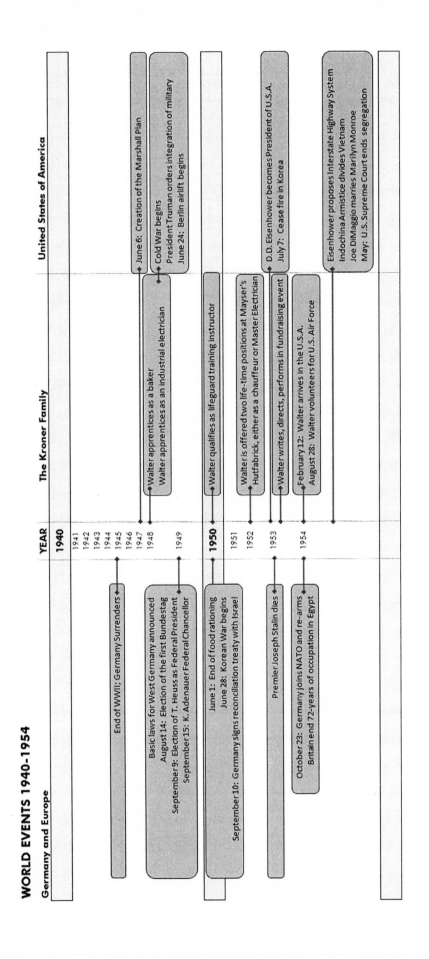

Germany and Europe	YEAR	The Kroner Family	United States of America
	1940		
	1941		
	1942		
	1943		
	1944		
End of WWII; Germany Surrenders	1945		
	1946		
	1947	Walter apprentices as a baker; Walter apprentices as an industrial electrician	June 6: Creation of the Marshall Plan
	1948		Cold War begins; President Truman orders integration of military; June 24: Berlin airlift begins
Basic laws for West Germany announced; August 14: Election of the first Bundestag; September 9: Election of T. Heuss as Federal President; September 15: K. Adenauer Federal Chancellor	1949		
June 1: End of food rationing; June 28: Korean War begins; September 10: Germany signs reconciliation treaty with Israel	**1950**	Walter qualifies as lifeguard training instructor	
	1951		
	1952	Walter is offered two life-time positions at Mayser's Hutfabrik, either as a chauffeur or Master Electrician	
Premier Joseph Stalin dies	1953	Walter writes, directs, performs in fundraising event	D.D. Eisenhower becomes President of U.S.A.; July 7: Cease fire in Korea
October 23: Germany joins NATO and re-arms; Britain end 72-years of occupation in Egypt	1954	February 12: Walter arrives in the U.S.A.; August 28: Walter volunteers for U.S. Air Force	Eisenhower proposes Interstate Highway System; Indochina Armistice divides Vietnam; Joe DiMaggio marries Marilyn Monroe; May: U.S. Supreme Court ends segregation

Thief's Apprentice

My hope of going to America included getting a university education, seeking my potential in the context of freedom, creating my own identity, and the pursuit of happiness. My parents had lost all contact with Tante Hansi, so that hope seemed destroyed. The bloody war was replaced by the Cold War and life was reduced to physical survival. By 1947, the Oberschule and Realschule had been bombed out and were not yet rebuilt. Even though I had already attended Realschule, the only school that was available was the Hauptschule, a secondary school. Hauptschule qualified a young person for Berufsschule (trade school). The economy of Germany did not make free education possible for all qualified students. So, the only possibility for me was to go to the Berufsschule after I graduated from Hauptschule and learn a trade. That meant I had to decide what I wanted to become and then find an employer who would agree to take me on as an apprentice. The employer had to be a Meister (Master), the qualification for teaching a craft or trade.

I decided that I wanted to learn land management so I could become a manager of a large agricultural estate. My justification for this idea was that I loved the outdoors. I had enjoyed working on a farm during the Hitler Youth days, and I loved animals. Animals would never betray you, turn on you, or set out to destroy you. Being around them meant peace and tranquility. I was not sure whether the meager food supply and the periods of hunger after the war had anything to do with my decision. I have to admit that moving out of my parents' apartment was the highest priority related to such a decision. I was rebelling against control and preconceived directions. I was fighting my mother's strict upbringing and I wanted to "float free" of restrictions. I no longer believed that my parents were all-knowing, even though Vater had not influenced me as much as Mutter.

Mutter and Vater quickly talked me out of the land management idea with an argument that I could not disagree with. They said that with all of the displaced persons from the East, there would be no need for apprentices in Germany's agriculture system. Germans who had returned from Poland, Hungary, and other Eastern countries were experienced farmers. I had to admit the job-market was saturated with them and no one was willing to take on an apprentice. During a visit by Frau Unkauf she supported my parents' argument and that settled it for me; agriculture was not a part of my future. Another hope was eliminated.

Sometime later I told my parents that I wanted to become a baker. After their surprise, they asked me to explain my reasons. I rationalized that first, bakers were always needed so I would always have a job. Second, I'd never go hungry. And third, there were a lot of bakeries looking for a Meister. Newspapers were filled with advertisements by widows who owned bakeries but whose husbands had died in the war. They were advertising for a Meister, with the possibility of marriage. While I wasn't interested in marriage, it told me that more and more bakeries would open up giving me an opportunity for apprenticeship.

The real reason was that I had decided I wanted to get out of my parents' home. There was too much to see, to do, and to learn; not the least of which was going to the "Amerika Haus in Ulm" to satisfy my craving for things about America. There were only three types of jobs that required an apprentice to live where he worked: bakers, butchers, and farmers. The farmer option was already rejected and I never liked the cold and wet butcher shops.

In the latter part of 1947, I had surgery on my right eye to align my eyes. I was also blind in my right eye due to the "Lazy-eye" syndrome. From the description, I remember that they had to take out a piece from one eye muscle and insert that piece into a muscle that was too short. It took two operations until my eyes were more or less aligned. The vision in my right eye reached the stage where I could see light and dark objects; however, I could not identify any details. I was slowly feeling better about myself and actually enjoyed looking in the mirror. The fact that I had only one good eye was limiting, but only doctors would know.

Between Christmas and New Years, Vater made arrangements for me to go skiing by myself at another Mountain Club's cabin in the Alps. Since I was supposed to leave right after the Christmas holiday, Vater told me to lay all of my things out before I packed them. He wanted to make sure that I had everything that was needed. A few days prior to the holidays, I had arranged with a friend to get a pack of American cigarettes that I would take on vacation with me. I wanted to try smoking. The exchange of the pack of Lucky Strikes was observed by my brother who had warned me that I would get in trouble if our parents found out. I hid the pack in a plastic soap box holder inside my toiletry case on Christmas Eve. Our Christmas ritual was that Vater would ring the bell and we would enter the room that had been off limits for over a week. In it was the illuminated Christmas tree, and we three children would recite our memorized poems, play practiced pieces of music on our instruments, and then open our gifts.

Prior to the family gathering in the Christmas room, Vater checked my travel supplies. I didn't know at the time that Heinz was present when the checking took place. All I remember is that my brother, with the opened soap dish held up high, came running into the kitchen where Mutter and I were. Heinz screamed, "See! See! I told you so, I told you they would find out." And with that, he held the cigarettes in front of Mutter's face. He seemed to love pointing out to my parents my crimes and misdemeanors. Christmas was a disaster. I had destroyed all of the joy and splendor of the holiday by sneaking behind my parents' back and abusing their trust. In the final analysis, the whole reason for not getting packed before Christmas was that Heinz and I would be given a rucksack as a Christmas present to be shared between us for our vacations. To avoid packing and re-packing Vater, told me to wait with the packing until after we had opened our presents. I also knew Vater well enough that he would have put the soap dish back, without saying anything to anybody, until he could confront me alone and discuss the matter in private. I added insult to injury when I gave Heinz a soccer kick and called him a traitor, the family Gestapo agent, and that he was just as bad as Tante Emi. I think that outburst upset everybody at least as much as the cigarettes. On the way to the train station Vater gave me a dozen eggs, so I knew that he was not angry with me.

When I returned on New Year's Eve to our apartment, my aunts and uncles had assembled for the occasion. I approached the door very silently, and from the laughter and noise I deduced that Mutter's anger had passed.

With the help of my Uncle Christian, who lived in an apartment building in Ulm that had a bakery on the ground floor, my family found a place that would take me on as an apprentice. I suddenly became very unsure about my decision. Nevertheless, I started my apprenticeship with Meister Kilian on January 1, 1948, at the age of thirteen. The bakery was located on Pioneerstrasse in Ulm, with the store facing the street. At the back of the building, but physically connected to the store, was the bakery shop. The shop itself had two large barrel tubs filled with flour, covered by a wooden work surface about three meters long. There were two dough machines and an oven with an upper and lower compartment. Next to the oven was a corridor that led to a room with a hot water storage tank, a lavatory, and a bath tub. The Meister, journeyman, and I had to take our baths in that tub, which didn't provide a lot of privacy. Situated between the shop and the store was the apartment for the Kilian family.

Meister Kilian was a short and thin man of about forty years with thin blond hair. He was softspoken, friendly, and extremely kind and understanding. He had responded to Frau Kilian's advertisements for a Meister with the opportunity for marriage. Frau Kilian had a daughter Erika. Her father had died in the war. Frau Kilian was large and strong and reminded me of what an Amazon woman must look like. She had a loud authoritarian voice and lacked compassion and kindness. She controlled both the store and Meister Kilian. Many times the Meister and I would be working together at the front of the oven, and I would see him crying silently. She spoke cruelly to him, talked down to him, and it felt like he was her slave instead of her husband. The Meister never argued or raised his voice, and even though sometimes the journeyman and I would encourage him to speak up and stop being treated so painfully, he wouldn't.

Frau Kilian even spoke in very unfriendly terms to some of the customers. Once I witnessed a rather cruel act. I was in the store putting fresh bread on the shelves when an elderly lady living in the neighborhood begged for a loaf of old bread. Frau Kilian took her by the arm and pushed her towards the door and told her never to come back and beg again. I asked Frau Kilian who this lady was. She gave me her name and I remembered it. I found out where the woman lived and took some bread and rolls to her. The only person with whom Frau Kilian was friendly and jovial was my Uncle Christian, Vater's brother. We in the Kroner family knew that Uncle Christian had a girlfriend on the side; perhaps there was more between Frau Kilian and Uncle Christian.

The regular workday started at three in the morning and we would be free after three in the afternoon. We made different types of bread, hard rolls, pretzels, and saltless bread for the hospital located two blocks away. At ten in the morning, we had a break that included coffee, bread with wurst (sandwich meat), and cheese. Noon was lunchtime and Frau Kilian would bring our meals to the shop where her husband and we two employees would eat. I always thought it demeaning that she would make her husband sit and eat with the help; it just wasn't done that way. The journeyman and I spent our afternoons playing with the neighborhood kids or going downtown. Saturdays, in addition to making bread, we had to bake the cakes and pies from the neighbors which extended the work day by another hour. Late Saturday afternoon, I would take my bath and go home to my parents.

There were no refrigerators in those days; instead, some people had ice boxes where ice was stored in the top of a cabinet to keep a chamber below cool. My parents had such an ice box, but for some reason the bakery just had a cool pantry, a small vented closet surrounded by masonry to keep things cool. It was on a Monday when Frau Kilian served us a small piece of meat, a slice of bread, and a serving of cooked spinach. It tasted very good, except for the saltless bread. The three of us usually had to eat old stale bread or leftover saltless bread. The following Thursday there was spinach on the lunch plate too, but it had a strange odor.

I tasted the spinach and without thinking I said out loud "This tastes like rotten eggs." I looked at Meister Kilian and I could tell he was embarrassed and didn't disagree. The journeyman simply said he was not going to eat this. Frau Kilian of course heard it.

She came running into the shop and immediately blamed the Meister for not reprimanding me for my behavior. She referred to him as a gutless man, without a spine. And with my plate in her hand she stormed out of the shop and up the stairs. I knew she was going to cry on my Uncle's shoulder about Walter, the badly behaved apprentice. I felt bad for Meister Kilian, but I wouldn't dare say anything. I had already done enough damage.

The following Saturday, when I came home at about five in the afternoon, Mutter greeted me with interest, and a peculiar smile. "So how was your week?" she asked. "Oh, nothing new; same thing every week," I replied. "What did you have to eat this week?" she said. This was an odd question since never before had she asked me what we had to eat.

"Actually we had spinach twice; the first time on Monday and then again on Thursday. But the second time it was leftover spinach and it tasted like rotten eggs," I told her. "Do you mean spinach like this?" she asked. She walked over to our pantry and pulled out a small plate with spinach on it. She placed the plate in front of me and said, "Eat it!"

It tasted even worse than last Thursday, but I was forced to eat it. Mutter explained that I was being punished for being rude and disrespectful for saying what I did. She even agreed that when Uncle Christian brought the spinach to her it was already bad. I understood that Mutter was trying to teach me a lesson about manners and I guess I had a few more things to learn. I wouldn't dare tell Mutter what I was thinking about my Uncle Christian. Now I understood why Vater never had much to do with or say to his brother. I didn't like him either and never have since.

Martin, the journeyman, and I had developed a habit of hiding bread and small bags of flour in our bedroom located in the basement below the bakery shop. These collections were given to the neighbors we knew had nothing, including the lady that had been pushed out of the store. We had to be very careful in doing this and told each recipient not to tell Frau Kilian. Somehow I knew that if Meister Kilian found out he probably would be grateful for the bakery doing nice things for people.

Our bedroom below the oven had two beds, one "nightstand" in between the beds, a desk with two chairs, and an armoire. I was in my room when Martin came in and showed me a wad of money in his hand and told me where the Kilians hid their money. He explained that the money was in a large wooden cigar box behind the linens in their bedroom armoire. The bedroom was directly across the entry to the corridor running between the store and the shop. He went on to describe the setup in more detail. A few days later, he again showed me a handful of money, saying all he did was reach into the box and grab the money because there was no lid. I tried it a few days later and it worked. This stealing went on for awhile and Frau Kilian didn't seem to notice. At first, we took a very small stack of bills amounting to about ten to twenty marks. We usually took the money and bought things we knew neighbors could use. At that time neighbors were still looking for food, dishes, and cookware. We left the "gifts" at their apartment doors so they wouldn't connect them with us.

One day, when Frau Kilian was in the Hof and the Meister was running an errand, Martin and I went into the bedroom separately. We each reached in the back of the linens and took a handful of bills. That same day, we went to the Münster Platz where people would sell personal belongings. I forget how much money we had, but we bought at least eight place settings. When we returned we placed the dishes on top of the armoire in our room. The following Monday, we sensed that something unusual was going on. Frau Kilian and her husband kept leaving the shop and going into their bedroom with the door closed. Martin and I suspected that the Kilian's had discovered the missing money. Frau Kilian raced up the stairs to Uncle Christian.

Uncle Christian walked into the shop with the cigar box in his hands and in his loud obnoxious voice asked Martin and me, "Which one of you stole the bakery's money?" We both looked as innocent as we could and said, "What money?" Uncle Christian and Meister Kilian went down into our bedroom under the oven and started to go through the armoire and nightstand. They lifted up the mattresses and looked everywhere, but didn't find anything. They lifted the dishes down from the top of the armoire and asked whose they were. I told them they were Christmas gifts for my parents, which seemed to satisfy them. I guess they were looking for the actual money, without considering the possibility that we had already spent it.. Uncle Christian informed us that he would take the cigar box to the police.

A few days later we had to report to the police department in Ulm. This was a new type of fear, the fear of being caught as a thief. To be interrogated by the police, as my father would say, was a shameful thing. Even though Martin and I assured each other that we never touched the box itself, I decided I would scrape the tips of my fingers to make fingerprint identification difficult. On the way to the police station I ran my finger tips along the rough surface of the stucco walls of buildings. My excuse would be that I scraped them when I fell after chasing a ball. The journeyman and I agreed that under no circumstances would either of us admit that we took the money. We worked out a signal. After the interrogation, a loud sneeze would mean we hadn't admitted to anything.

While I felt fear, I didn't feel guilt; nor did I have second thoughts about hurting Frau Kilian. As cruel as she was to her own customers, to Meister Killian, and to Martin and me, I felt no remorse. It was she who had to learn that being mean to people had consequences. In my mind, she deserved it.

Martin had to go into the interrogation room first while I sat outside in a corridor on a bench. I could hear the screaming voices of their exchange. I knew that my parents would hear about this because Uncle Christian would tell them. I decided then and there that I was going to walk the straight and narrow and I would never again be seen inside of a police station again. I promised God if got out of this, I would keep my promise. After what seemed like an hour, they led Martin out of the room down the hall to another room. There was no signal I began to panic. Had they broken him? Just as the group turned to go through another door, Martin let out a loud noisy sneeze. During my interrogation, the policemen tried to convince me that Martin admitted to stealing the money and that he also admitted to having seen me steal money. I denied it, kept cool, never screamed, and told them that I didn't care what Martin had said, "I had nothing to do with money disappearing."

We were let go and I decided to tell my parents that I hated my job, I hated the bakery, and I wanted to get out of the bakery apprentice program. There is nothing more boring than getting up at three in the morning six days a week and doing more or less the same thing every day. This was the most basic type of bakery. Other bakeries had a Konditorei that made fine baking goods, tortes, cakes, croissants, pies - work that was artistic. That was not what I was learning at the Kilian bakery. The next weekend at home, I told the entire story about Uncle Christian suspecting his own nephew of stealing and how he reported me to the police. "Well, did you?" came the question. Once again I lied, "I did not, Vater." That was the end of the matter as far as Vater was concerned.

On June 20, 1948, two months after my promise to God, the German currency reform took place. Ten Reichsmarks - the old money - were now worth one Deutsche Mark - the new money. My parents, to the best of my knowledge, had no savings. Every German citizen was given 20 Deutsche Marks to begin a new economy and a new life.

My apprenticeship with the Kilian bakery ended on June 30, 1948, two days after my fourteenth birthday.   I was able to get out of my apprentice contract based on a doctor's certificate. I had been blind in my right eye since birth. The doctor suggested that flour dust could prove harmful to my one good eye. That was sufficient grounds to void the contract.

Surviving in a Whirlpool

On a Saturday afternoon when I was still working at the bakery, Herr Bolz, an electrician, showed up to do some electrical repairs to the oven. I watched him work and remembered Vater's advice, "It is okay to steal with your eyes, watch how people do things, and ask them questions on things you don't understand, or to confirm your understanding."

As I was doing my "stealing," Uncle Christian walked into the shop. We stood there watching Herr Bolz work, and after a while Uncle Christian asked me if I thought I would like this type of work. Since my Meister was not around I said, "It looks very fascinating."

Later, Vater, Uncle Christian and Uncle Jakob discussed with Herr Bolz the possibility of taking me on as an apprentice electrician. I will never know what the three Kroner men did to convince Herr Bolz. I did find out later that he had always refused to consider taking on apprentices. It occurred to me that Herr Bolz's work on the oven was a pretense for him to meet me.

Contracts were signed between the Mayser Hutfabrick (Mayser hat factory), Walter Bolz Master Electrician, Hans Kroner, and me to educate me as an industrial electrician apprentice for a period of three years. (Bolz's Master's Certificate with his photo is shown on the right.) On my first day at Mayser Hutfabrik in November 1948, the morning was spent touring the entire complex. We started in the power plant that had two steam driven turbines as electrical generators; from there I was taken through the entire hat making process. I was introduced to the machinery that mixed rabbit fur onto a wet cone three feet high, through a long process that reduced its size to a fifteen inch felt cone. From there, the cone was formed into various types of hats. After the forming, the hats were moved to a finishing section where hundreds of electrical sewing machines and trimmers were used. The process ended when sandbags were heated on steam tables to be used in the final hand ironing of every hat. Mayser hats had won numerous gold medals in World's Fair competitions.

After lunch, we toured the various power distribution systems, transformers, cable rooms, and the tour ended in the communication control room. The knowledge I had to acquire ranged from power generation to electrical motor repair; from wiring of buildings to communication electronics. Meister Bolz explained to me that I also had to learn shop skills. Included were skills to use the blacksmith shop, machine shop, sheet metal shop, and the carpenter shop. The excitement kept building. I was going to learn how to operate all of this fine machinery and make things with it. However, Meister Bolz warned me that I had to start at the bottom. The factory was being rebuilt because it had been heavily damaged during the war. As a consequence, there were jobs that had to do with digging through rubble and finding electrical equipment that could be rebuilt.

Once a week I had to attend Berufsschule for an entire day. My teacher was Dr. Arndt. Here we had classes in mathematics, practical geometry, natural science, business, electrical and mechanical technology, and so forth. Dr. Arndt was a very patient teacher. I know this because

Walter's electrician's trade school, or Berufsschule. Dr. Arndt, his teacher, is front and center.

I constantly bombarded him with questions about physics, theory, and nature. It was absolutely fascinating and every day I rode my bicycle to work with great anticipation. Neighbors commented to my parents how happy I seemed to be. "We hear him whistling and singing all the time now." They were right. Not a single day was like the previous day; every day there was something new and curious. I was happy and felt good about myself; learning through discovery was an exciting adventure.

There were two other people in Herr Bolz's electrical shop. One was a middle-aged man who did not have any specific trade qualifications, but knew most of the things that had to be done in terms of installations, repair of electrical motors or appliances. He was never allowed to operate the power plant or make the final electric wiring connections, but he was invaluable to the shop. The other man was a former SS officer and licensed electrician. He was also a champion fencer and wore glasses that were so thick you could barely see his eyes. That always gave me difficulty. I need to see a person's eyes when I talk with them, something I could never do with this former SS man. He was not a happy man. I often thought that he was still fighting the Second World War; .

As is custom, I always addressed everyone in the shops, except other apprentices, by their last name. I immediately took a liking to Meister Bolz. "Walter," he started to give me some advice, "from now on instead of calling me Meister Bolz, call me Herr Bolz; and, I am going to call you Balde." "That is ok with me, but why do you want to call me Balde?" I asked. I had no idea what that name meant. It certainly didn't mean anything in German. He looked at me and asked, "Do you know my first name?" I should have known but had to admit, "No, what is it?" "I too am named Walter," he replied, "and calling you Balde makes it a lot simpler around here with others calling me Walter."

Thus began our relationship, which over the course of five years was almost like father and son. I never called him anything but Herr Bolz. Sometimes, he would invite me to do weekend work through his private contacts and we would work on electrical installations in new homes and small businesses. That meant I could make money on the side. This extra money never saw my Mutter's hands. In our family each of the three children were expected to contribute sixty-five percent of our weekly pay to the family budget. I never found out how the sixty-five percent was determined. Mutter kept the remainder in her secret hiding place, saving it on our behalf. If we needed money - to go to a dance for example - we had to ask for it and she would decide how much we needed. If we weren't happy with her budgeted amount, we were invited to stay home. I didn't like it and I also thought it was not very smart. I thought the money should be held in a savings account earning interest, but I knew my mother's attitude about banks.

I actually had two bosses.. One was Herr Bolz and the other was my Uncle Jakob who was the personal chauffeur to Herr Seidl, the owner of the company. Uncle Jakob's four car garage and auto shop was just across the main road from the factory. My bosses expectation of me was perfection. If Uncle Jakob saw me do some work that was less than perfect, even if it was a conduit that was supposed to be buried, he pointed it out to Herr Bolz who would make me do it over again. Perfection, for example, meant a curved bend in a metal conduit had to be a continuous bend and be perfectly level, regardless of whether it was exposed or concealed.

I began playing soccer in secret on the Mayser team as goalie. Mutter would not allow her boys to play any sport except swimming and gymnastics. She proclaimed that she was not going to raise men who, when they got married, created soccer widows, which she herself was for a long time with Vater. She also didn't want to wash our dirty uniforms every Monday. I shall never forget the strength of resistance Mutter demonstrated when three domineering men attempted to convince her to let me play soccer on the Mayser team.

After a while, the Mayser soccer team wanted me as their full-time goalkeeper, which meant I could no longer play in secret. A decision had to be made who was going to be the goalie before the season began. On a Saturday morning, Uncle Christian, who was one of the coaches, showed up at our apartment door to speak with Mutter. I overheard the conversation in the living room, as he attempted to convince Mutter why she should let me play soccer. Around noon, he left in defeat. Uncle Jakob showed up with the same intention about an hour later. I had to attend to my chores and couldn't overhear that conversation, but I was sure that Uncle Jakob could convince Mutter because the two of them really liked each other. When I returned, Mutter informed me that, "Your favorite Uncle didn't convince me either." Vater tried the final effort on my behalf after supper. He talked about the value of teamplay, sportsmanship, health and camaraderie. It was eight in the evening when Vater retreated to the Bräustüble for a beer. The end result was that I was reprimanded for having played behind Mutter's back in other people's uniforms, while using Vater's soccer shoes. The score was Mutter 3, Kroner men 0.

While working at Mayser, I had my evenings and weekends free to myself. I usually did my schoolwork right after class, leaving the rest of my weeknights free. Every Wednesday evening, I trained for the Wasserwacht - the Bavarian Red Cross lifeguard organization. Vater was its director and trainer. As a trainer, I discovered a very gentle side in Vater. This bear of a man could be tough as nails, stubborn, and insistent, but after all was said and done the teenagers around him loved and admired him. Vater was a role model for young men in terms of commitment to the community, giving to others, and putting your life on the line to save others. For me, it was indeed an honor when I could walk or sit next to him.

In the summer of 1949, I joined Vater at the Donaubad where he taught me some very special things about rivers and swimming. "Never fight the river or its currents," he said. "It will exhaust you and you won't have the strength to swim out of danger – Angst macht dich tod." He took me out on the river in an open wooden boat that the fishermen of Ulm traditionally used. One moved the boat upriver along the river bank by pushing the steel end of a two meter pole into the river bottom, propelling the boat forward. To get downriver you used the same pole as a rudder. I learned how to use these wooden boats and hold them perfectly still against the river's current so another person could rescue a swimmer and bring them into the boat.

The lesson I shall never forget was how to keep from drowning in a whirlpool. Vater and I went to the confluence of the Illerkanal and the Donau. There, depending on the depth of the river, you could see several whirlpools. He illustrated the whirlpool in a glass of water, pointing out that at the bottom of the tornado shaped funnel the funnel was smallest. He explained, "You let the whirlpool drag you to the bottom, and when your toes touch the river bottom you crouch and push yourself along the river bottom out of the whirlpool." The only other type of whirlpool would be one where the water gets sucked into a pipe, cavern, or tunnel. However, that type of whirlpool did not exist on the Donau near Ulm.

The next lesson was at the end of the day. The Donaubad was closed and we walked to the confluence of the two rivers. Vater went into the Iller Kanal, floated into the whirlpool, and as he was sucked under he held his arms straight up in the air. He re-emerged thirty feet down river. "Are you ready to try?" he asked as he joined me again at the bridge over the Kanal. "How deep is it where you were sucked under?" I asked. "No more than fifteen feet," came the reply.

I looked at this man whom I knew had saved many people from drowning. I knew he wouldn't ask me to do anything that was beyond my ability. I also knew that whatever happened, he already had figured out how he would save me. Blind faith is the only way to describe my feelings about this man who was my father. I always thought that for two people to trust each other this way was one of the most beautiful feelings of relating to another human being. I trusted this man without a doubt. I went to the same place where he entered the Kanal. Before I entered the water he called to me, "Let the water carry you! You will not see the whirlpool from the water's surface. Just wait until you feel the pull and let it drag you under. Walter, one more thing, never fight the water, and put your arms over your head."

I went into the canal and decided not to swim but just float with the current, my legs vertical to the water's surface and arms stretched out to the side. "Good, trust the water. Let the river carry you," he called out to me as I came close to the confluence.

Quicker than I expected, my body was pulled under the water and I could feel the pull of the funnel. It got quiet and as my toes touched the river stones. I crouched and pushed myself horizontally like an arrow and then swam to the surface. I screamed, "It worked!" When I joined him on the bridge he said, "Good, now try it again. But this time, swim with a breast stroke."

This time it was a different, and stranger experience. First, my body was whirled around at the top, and then I felt not only a pull, but a force that twisted my body. I hit bottom and came up again, but this time it took longer to get out of the danger zone.

"What happened," I asked, confused. "What happened is the same thing that happens to unsuspecting swimmers, but they often fight the water and drown. Walter, the river can save your life if you let it carry you to the shore, or it can drown you if you fight its current. Keep your eye on the shore and just steer with your hands."

I remembered his earlier explanation of how to survive if caught in rapids or a fast current. Float in the water with your back arched and feet straight forward, breath slowly, and steer with your hands on your side. You can stay afloat for a long time and conserve your energy while you let the river run. You do the same if you are caught in seaweed that can entrap your body; float on your back and use only your hands, not your arms, to create movement and for steering.

I began to understand Vater a little more. I realized why he was such a master in lifesaving, a hero in the fire department, and a man who could hold his head up high amidst the guilt and shame of WWII. However, he also was something of a philosopher; not because of the books he read, but because of the way he read nature and created metaphors. He suggested to me that the river was a life-giving force; in fact it was life itself. Problems emerge only when people are trying to control it or redirect the river by creating dams and canals. It was Vater that planted the idea in my head suggesting that one had to let the river flow along its natural course. He ended the philosophy lesson with a question, "Have you ever wondered why I never stopped you from doing what you wanted to do?" I knew then that for him I was his river that he wanted to flow freely.

My last test to be an advanced lifeguard was to rescue my 200-pound father with my clothes on. The test was performed in the Stadtbad and I was dressed in my pajamas. I had to swim from the shallow end of the pool to the deep end, twenty-five meters away. Then I had to hold him as I was trained to do and swim back with him in a rescue hold to the shallow end. I barely reached around his large back. I knew he would try something to test me. I had a strong hold on him and practically dug my fingers into his upper arm. He tried to drag me under, but while his head was under water, I wouldn't loosen my grip, dug my fingers into his skin, and I inhaled making it harder for him to drag me under. He finally gave up. I knew he if he had really wanted to, he could have taken me down with him. In November 1950, I received my lifeguard teaching certificate and became a member of the Bavarian Red Cross Wasserwacht.

For the first time, I had accomplished something that made both me and Vater proud. I could follow in his footsteps and I was sure I could live up to his expectations. This was different from passing some test in school, or winning a race, or saving someone's life. This was succeeding against a very tough opponent who was making sure that tomorrow's lifeguard teachers were the best he could train. At the certificate ceremony, he didn't call my name. Everyone knew that I had passed the test and even Vater told me so. Vater walked from the stage and the Director of the Wasserwacht for the State of Bavaria was next on the program. He announced that there was one more certificate that Hans Kroner was not allowed to issue because it concerned his son. Then he announced my name and asked me to come forth and receive it. It was typical of my father that no one, not even his son, would get anything easy, automatic, or without the approval of others.

I had reconnected with my family, lived at home and contributed to the daily chores and garden duties. In fact, it was the garden where I finally got to know more about my father, not in terms of his accomplishments as a Schwimm Meister or lifeguard, but how he thought and worked. There was never any discussion that could be considered a sharing of feelings. It was all conversations from above the shoulder – his intellect and brain. We worked well together. I was able to do satisfactory work, and he didn't mind my questions. But that was because I never asked questions when he was concentrating on his work. I saved them for lunch, the ride home on his motorcycle, or when we stopped at the Bräustüble.

"Focus on the Giving - Not the Getting"

At seventeen years of age, it was customary that teenagers take ballroom dancing lessons. I enrolled in Rudi Wernhard's dancing school in Neu-Ulm. He was both a German and European ballroom dancing champion. During dance classes, there was one girl who by far was the best dancer in the class. Her name was Helga. The dance curriculum included Sunday afternoon tea dances, a social affair that gave the dancers the opportunity to practice. At the graduation dance, Helga and I won the class dance competition. Herr Wernhard invited Helga and me to an advanced dancing course to train for competitive ballroom dancing. I developed deep feelings for Helga, which I assumed meant that I was in love. Besides being very good dancers, we both were very competitive and trained very hard for the dance competitions. Our time together included conversations about our families and our thoughts, but very little about feelings for each other.

I was devastated when I discovered that I was used by Helga as an excuse to get out of her house so she could be with her secret boyfriend. According to Mutter's rules of good behavior, I had to take Helga home no later than ten o'clock in the evening. Helga, instead of going home, would meet her boyfriend. For reasons that were never made clear to me, she was not allowed to have any contact with him. Helga's parents thought that I was the best thing that ever happened to her, even though I had no idea what that meant.

The night Helga and I decided to go our separate ways was the same night that I saw a softer side of Mutter for the first time in my life. When I came home, I told my mother what happened between Helga and me and I couldn't hold back my tears. She asked me what I was feeling, to which I replied anger, pain, disappointment, and doubt. She asked me about the doubt and I could only explain that maybe I could be a good friend to girls, but nothing more. I explained that we had never kissed, or put our arms around each other, just held hands. I felt the need for more and perhaps it was me that was the reason for the absence of warmth. My mother's words were soft, warm, and filled with compassion and understanding. The only time my mother was physical with me was when she punished me. Even after our tender conversation, she couldn't bring herself to touch my shoulder or to express warmth physically. She simply listened, indicated she understood my pain, and promised me that it would take a while, but before long the pain would go away.

I had many female friends through the swimming team, Wasserwacht, and at the Mayser factory, but there was never anything serious. There were attempts at intimacy, but I was so naïve and inexperienced that I retreated from these relationships to something that was safe from the pain of unrequited love. For some reason, it seemed that I was a very good listener and participant in discussions with female friends. It felt good that they trusted me with their inner thoughts, feelings, and ideas. I was always surprised how freely they spoke with me. I really enjoyed the company of girls and found them fascinating.

In the summer of 1951, I reached a major plateau in terms of education and career. I became a certified industrial electrician, a journeyman, with the opportunity to become a master electrician in the future. I felt a sense of accomplishment that was totally mine. I earned all of it; it was not because my name was Kroner. It was an accomplishment for which my Meister deserved a great deal of the credit. However, Vater was the one who had taught me my work ethic and had always encouraged me to do the best that I was capable of doing. Vater was the one who was responsible for giving me the right foundation on which to build whatever future I chose. Another sense of accomplishment that I felt involved my musical skills. I had learned to play the recorder and concertina. On Christmas in 1943, Frau Unkauf and Dr. Köstlin gave me a violin as a gift. It was a valuable gift and had been in their family for a long time. Immediately I started violin lessons with a teacher who played First Violin with the Philharmonic Orchestra of Ulm. He always said that I should consider studying music, and sometime in 1951 he spoke with my parents about an opportunity he could arrange for me to study at the Vienna Conservatory. He stressed that to get ready for an interview, I would have to spend a year doing nothing but practicing the violin. I was extremely honored and proud that my violin teacher would vouch for me. Mutter said, "I don't think you should become a violinist; they don't make a lot of money and they have no time to spend evenings with their family." Another possible future was shattered, a dam created to block the flow of my river, without benefit of discussion or compromise.

By 1951, my social life focused on ballroom dancing, taking accordion lessons, and of course the Wasserwacht. Ballroom dancing meant you had to have a date, since going alone was really not appropriate. In my case, I always invited my best friend – my cousin Elfriede. We enjoyed dancing with each other as much as we loved talking about anything and everything. We felt a very special connection and there was absolutely nothing we couldn't talk about. At times when I would walk home, after seeing her, it amazed me that another person, and especially a female, would reveal things to me that she had never told anyone, including her parents. Even though she was eighteen and I was seventeen, neither of us had any romantic feelings for each other. Elfriede was involved in a romantic relationship about which I probably knew more than I should have. We trusted each other without reservation and there were no secrets between us. I still remember these feelings of being totally vulnerable, and yet comfortable with the trust between us. In my mind the ability to be totally honest without fear was a feeling that had to be present in a loving relationship.

Elfriede studied to be a seamstress, and soon found a job as a fashion model. In the beginning of 1952, Elfriede mentioned to me that she was going to Switzerland. It was customary for girls who were destined to marry into wealthy families to go abroad to work as nannies, maids, and managers of households. Since she was dating a son from a very rich family, going to Switzerland or England to study was expected.

As she told me this, the old feeling of wanting to go to America returned, except more intensely. I had a skill, something to offer an employer, and I had something to build upon. That night, I begged my father to do whatever he could to find Tante Hansi in America. Vater had some friends who had connections with the Amis, and several people helped him trace Tante Hansi, starting with her last known address. I know Vater really tried to do his best, and even Frau Unkauf used some of her connections to help out. Tante Hansi could not be found and my hope of visiting the United States once again vanished. What was to happen next? I didn't have any answers or immediate alternative dreams. I just knew I was never going to give up searching for a future beyond the present possibilities.

The main focus of my teenage years was serving my community through the Wasserwacht. I give Vater the credit for developing in me a sense of giving back to the community. "Konzentriere dich auf das geben, nicht das nehmen. Focus on the giving - not the getting," was Vater's advice. I didn't appreciate the significance of his words until I was much older.

Gemeinschaft is a German word with no adequate English translation. Literally it means community, but it really has a deeper meaning. Gemeinschaft means there are things in life where the community comes first, and the individual second. One finds many Germans doing things for the Gemeinschaft, whether it is volunteer work, risking one's life so others can be

Marianne   Walter

saved, or taking responsibility for the cleanliness of the neighborhood. For me, the Wasserwacht provided this opportunity. Being a lifeguard was an unpaid position. Training, education, and regional meetings were are all paid for by the individual. Being a member of the Wasserwacht also meant one had to participate in fundraising activities.

My time in the Wasserwacht consumed almost all of my free time. Vater was director and I became the technical director. The Wasserwacht was still in its infancy, and I decided to enlarge its ranks. I recruited my friends, neighborhood kids, and former schoolmates to take the initial lifesaving course. My sister took her training with Vater, and before long all three Kroner siblings were active in the Wasserwacht. On weekends during the fall and winter, I worked getting businesses to become members of the Bavarian Red Cross through their contributions.

We trained and taught lifesaving techniques to others. on Wednesday nights. Each Saturday and Sunday, during the summer, we would go to our assigned lifeguard stations along the Danube. Each group had two people at the lifeguard station in case a runner was needed, while the rest went on patrol, walking along the river. We also would take care of people who injured themselves and, if needed, take them to the hospital.

Sometime during the summer of 1952, I was reading an illustrated magazine that had an article about Australia's immigration program for German workers. The program required that young German immigrants sign a contract to work for their Australian employers for two years. Thereafter, they would be free to live and work anywhere in Australia. I applied to the Australian consulate for this program without telling my parents. By the end of summer, the Australian consulate thanked me for my interest; however, they informed me that applicants had to be twenty-one years of age to qualify. Once again I had to accept rejection.

"Hope is a Waking Dream," *Aristotle*

I had three very close male friends in Germany: Fritz, Max, and Bernhard. Fritz worked as a hatmaker at the Mayser Hutfabrik and we often went on tours and vacations together on his motorcycle. We also formed an accordion band together and played at various social and recreational functions. Max and Bernhard were in the Wasserwacht and lived within four blocks of my apartment in Neu-Ulm. They both were machine tool maker journeymen. We went to dances together, took long walks in the woods, and enjoyed Sunday morning früh-schoppen at the Löwenbräuerei (brewery), on the Island between Ulm and Neu-Ulm. Früh-schoppen means having a beer at mid-morning with some type of snack or pretzels.

Max and I were Lutherans and after church on Sunday we went to früh-schoppen. Mass for Bernhard wasn't over until eleven, after which he would join us. In the fall of 1952, Max and I were at früh-schoppen when I told him about my attempt to emigrate to Australia, after my failed attempt to find Tante Hansi.

Walter in 1953.

"You seriously would consider leaving Germany?" asked Max. "Yes, more than you realize," I said. I explained that there were many reasons why I had this American dream. I told him about Tante Hansi's photo album. I told him about my research about the U.S.A and its independence from needing any resources from other countries. Max knew how strict Mutter was and how difficult it was to stay out late, go to movies, not being allowed to go the America Haus, and not being allowed to associate with Amis. Perhaps the worst part was that she controlled the spending of my own money.

Max, Walter and Bernhard dreaming of going to America in 1953.

I told Max the most important reason was that I needed my own identity. For eighteen years I had been Hans Kroner's son, never just Walter Kroner. I explained that with my father's fame all around southern Germany there wasn't anywhere I could go to be totally independent and free. I wanted to try things and fail without my parents standing over me. I needed to be successful on my own without having to feel any kind of indebtedness to my family. I wanted to be accomplished, successful, serve my community, and I wanted to share what I knew with others. Most of all, I wanted to have a chance to study at a university. I said to Max, "You know my family. Can you imagine me going anywhere in Germany to live, work, or join a lifeguard organization where I wouldn't be in my Vater's shadow."

"I see what you mean," he said. "Max, I have no choice but to leave Germany and set out on my own," I told him.

I adored Vater, admired him, and I knew that he would never do anything to give me an advantage. In fact, I had to work much harder than anyone else in the Wasserwacht to earn whatever certificate I received. He didn't want anyone to think that being his son gave me an advantage. Max agreed that he witnessed this lack of favoritism himself.

Max was quiet for some time, then he spoke in his usually soft-spoken way, "Walter, I have an aunt who lives in Chicago and she has been trying to get me to come to America. Almost every letter she writes she suggests that I, and the rest of my family, emigrate to America." "My God, Max. If I had that chance I would go tomorrow," I said.

There was a long pause. He turned his beer stein around, then he took another bite of his bread stick and stared out the window. The silence was unbearable. After what seemed to be forever he said, "If you and I went together I would consider going." I tried to suppress my excitement. "Why don't you write to your aunt and ask her if she would sponsor both of us. Could you do that?" I asked. "Sure," he said. "I will write her this afternoon."

I swear my heart was beating faster than normal. Suddenly, there was a contact in the U.S. There was hope! Maybe, just maybe, she would agree. Maybe, just maybe, this time I would not be beaten down. However, in the back of my mind was that cautionary voice of Vater, "Desto grösser die erwartungen desto grösser die Entäuschungen. The greater the expectations, the greater can be the potential disappointments."

We changed the subject, ordered another beer and soon after, Bernhard showed up. We never even thought of sharing our conversation with Bernd, as we called him, for Max and I were cautious in this regard.

The Donaubad was closed for the season. Wasserwacht duty on the Danube had ended for the summer, and Vater and I were free to accept an invitation for lunch with Herr Bolz and Uncle Jakob. Neither I nor Vater had any idea what this was about, except that the invitation was extended by Herr Bolz who informed us that Uncle Jakob had also been invited. The meeting was in the Bräustüble at the end of the block on on our Street.

Mutter was curious about the meeting too, and when Vater and I both told her that we didn't know she said, "He, Walter, is not allowed to play soccer. I don't care what they offer."

At the Bräustüble, the three men, who in significant ways had shaped my life, were making small talk while I sat there, my curiosity killing me. There was talk about soccer, people they knew, and once or twice Herr Bolz would say to the waiter, "Bring him another beer," pointing to me. It was painful. What was I doing here? I felt like asking, "Would somebody tell me why I am here?" but that would have been rude. They brought each other up to date on events and friends, and even digressed into their attempt to help me play soccer. They agreed that the Kroners were thoroughly defeated by Dora.

Finally Herr Bolz said, "Let's talk about Hans Kroner's Büble." Büble was one of those typical Swabian expressions denoting favorite son in an endearing way. It was typical. I was Hans' son, his favorite, but they couldn't get themselves to say Walter. It was no secret I was Vater's favorite, just like Heinz was Mutter's favorite. My sister Marianne was the diplomat in the family. She knew how to be the darling to both parents. I was known as "your son," "your büble," Hans Kroner's youngest son, Balde, Junger (meaning younger one, as my brother called me). Seldom was I referred to as Walter, with the exception of my sister Marianne. I could not escape from being anything other than Kroner's youngest son. I lacked my own identity.

The discussion was my next goal. Herr Bolz explained that he assumed my next step was to prepare myself for the "Meister Prüfung," to become a master electrician. He wanted to confirm that this in fact was my intention. I answered, "Of course," without analyzing the question. Uncle Jakob observed that I did have another option if being a Master Electrician was of no interest. My Vater asked what he meant by that. Uncle Jakob explained that in another ten years or so he was going to retire and the Mayser factory would need a younger chauffeur and personal mechanic for Herr Seidl (the owner) and his son. Herr Bolz explained that he too was going to retire in ten years and he didn't feel comfortable turning over his position to the current senior electrician. The long and short of this lunch meeting was that I was being offered two possible jobs: either my Uncle Jakob's or Herr Bolz's position.

I was simultaneously shocked, excited, honored, and quite frankly amazed that such offers were made. I don't remember what I said except I asked if could think it over. They both agreed, and Herr Bolz went on to explain to Vater and me that getting ready for the Meister Prüfung would take at least five or more years. Once I had passed the test, I would then be his assistant before the position would be given to me upon his retirement. It was also explained that either of the two offers had the approval of Herr Seidl, the owner of the company, and all of that would be put in writing. I was speechless and all I could do was hold up my glass of beer and say, "Prost, und vielen dank." (Toast, and many thanks.)

Instead of going home, Vater and I went for a walk along the Danube. Before he could ask me a question I said, "Vater! What do you think about all of this?" "I think you should be proud", he replied. "I am, but what should I do?" I asked.

He told me that the decision was entirely up to me. I explored it with him a little further, wanting to know whether Uncle Jakob's offer should be given preference, because he was family. I shall never forget our discussion that followed. "Walter, it is not about family, it is not about me or Uncle Jakob. It isn't even about Herr Bolz and his friendship with Uncle Jakob," he said. "Why not?" I asked. "Life is like a river. It moves on with you or without you," he replied. "But that doesn't answer my question," I complained. "When the consequences of your decision are truly known, your Vater, Uncle Jakob, and Herr Bolz will be long gone. Only you will know how smart your decision was," he explained.

And then I asked perhaps the most personal question I had ever asked Vater. "How did you decide to become who you are?" He paused, placed his hand on my shoulder, stopped walking and turned towards me. "I pursued that which I thought I was capable of doing, regardless of what anybody else thought," he told me. "Do you mean you followed your dream?" I asked. He shook his head, "Walter, dreams are for sleepers; hopes are for seekers. Such things are not dreams. They are the realities of hopes and possibilities that are out there for you to discover. It's something only you can see in your mind. It's like sitting by the river. You can watch it flow by you, or you can jump in and let it move you." "I think I understand," I said. I paused and then said, "Maybe." "It's your life, it's your decision, and that is all that matters," he said.

I knew my father wrote poetry, mostly to my mother. I knew he read Goethe and Schiller, and somehow I knew that I would remember those words of advice for a long time. When we entered the apartment, Mutter's immediate question was, "Was it about soccer?" We both shook our heads. And then my Vater said tongue in cheek, "Your Büble has something nice to tell you."

I shared the news with Mutter while Vater sat at his desk writing. Mutter asked, "What are you going to do?" "I will think about it," I replied. "How soon do you have to tell them?" she asked. Vater interjected, "It's all up to Walter, and he has time."

That night, as I was envisioning the daily lives of my Uncle and Herr Bolz, I tried to imagine myself forty years in the future. I would walk each day from my häusle to the Mayser factory and back to my family. I would be secure and have a lifestyle significantly better than my parents. I could have my own häusle with a little garden. I would have a very good income. There was however no university education in either option. My life would be centered within the city of Ulm or Neu-Ulm. At that time visiting other countries was a distant possibility, at best. If I took either of those options I would have to give up my dream of a university education, finding my identity, my potential, and my future in America. My choices were clear; a secure and pleasant future or a future that was filled with uncertainty, fantasies, hopes, adventure, and dreams, but no guarantees.

The Discovery of Hope

In 1952, Ulm and Neu-Ulm became U.S. military garrisons. Old military bases were renovated for the U.S. Army and new communities were constructed for the families of American soldiers. Out of the mountains of rubble, bricks were picked out and cleaned and steel was recycled to rebuild the cities. But the sense of community had disappeared. Life in Ulm and Neu-Ulm was filled with tension.

- Apartments and homes had to be shared with strangers because there was an immense shortage of living space. Original citizens of Ulm and Neu-Ulm had to live with strangers in their homes.
- There were hundreds of displaced persons from Eastern Europe living in marginal temporary shelters. People who fled territories occupied by the Russians were seeking a new life.
- Former German soldiers and women returning from Russian prison camps had to be reintegrated into our community.
- Women who had been prisoners-of-war in Russia arrived in Ulm in steady streams with children fathered by Russian soldiers.
- Young German men were kidnapped into the French Foreign Legion.
- American soldiers were allowed to socialize with the Germans.
- America introduced democracy to the Germans in multiple ways and the "Amerika Haus Ulm" was a source of knowledge about America.

Mutter, however, informed us that we were to keep our distance from the Americans as well as many of the strangers in our neighborhood. My parents took in one of my great uncles on my mother's side to live with us to satisfy the "share-your-apartment" quota. Altogether in our eight-apartment section there were eight new adults no one knew.

Although Mutter had her difficulties with Amis, she did express a few positive things about the American soldiers. She said they behaved like gentlemen with shoes that were always polished. She was really impressed that American soldiers pushed their children's baby carriages, something German men never did.

Whether it was housing, food, clothing, or job security, everything was in short supply and the future did not look very bright. An airmail letter in those days took a minimum of five days between Germany and the U.S.A. By the end of October 1952, Max had heard from his aunt in Chicago. I didn't tell Max about the offers related to my employment future. He read the letter to me that essentially said his aunt would be glad to sponsor both of us for immigration into the United States. She told us that we had to apply at the nearest American Consulate for a permanent immigration visa. Max volunteered to request two immigration application packages for both of us so I wouldn't have to prematurely alarm my parents. I have no idea why Max and I never mentioned our America discussion to Bernhard, except that at that time the chances of getting a visa were not very good for anyone because of limited quotas.

In November 1952, Max received two visa application packages in the mail, one for him and one for me. I told him I didn't want my parents to know what I was doing until I knew it was a sure thing. We both completed our forms and submitted them. By February of 1953, Max received some correspondence from the Consulate, but I did not.

Max's correspondence contained bad news. He was born in Poland to German parents, which meant he was a Polish citizen and subject to the Polish immigration quota. Essentially, the consulate informed him that he would have to wait. Included in the letter was a graphic that gave an estimate of how long visa applications would take depending on one's birth certificate. Polish visa applications took no less than two years. German visa applications would take no less than one year to be processed. The letter informed him that his application would be processed under the Polish quota system, unless he indicated that he was no longer interested. Immediately I became concerned. Did this mean the whole idea was lost?

"Max, what are you going to do?" I asked. "I am still going. I want them to process it," he said. I told him he would have to write to his aunt with the news and find out if, under the new circumstances, she would still sponsor both of us even though we would not be arriving together. Max agreed to write to her.

Suddenly, it occurred to me that Max's aunt had every reason to suggest waiting until Max had his visa before she committed herself to sponsor me. I decided to wait until Max's aunt would respond before I made any decision related to my future at Mayser. By my calculations Max should receive a response to his latest letter at least by January.

As was customary, after Wasserwacht training we assembled at our Stammtisch, although Bernd couldn't join us. On the way home Max, in the middle of our conversation with no expression on his face and not breaking his step said, "My aunt wrote me and said for you to go ahead and come as soon as you have your visa." I wasn't sure I understood and confirmed what I thought he said. "Max, are you okay with this? Do you mind if I get to go first?" I asked "No, don't be ridiculous. It makes sense," he replied.

It was sometime in early April of 1953 when Mutter handed me a big brown envelope addressed to me from the American Consulate. She held it up and asked me, "What is this?" "Oh, it is information about America," I casually replied "What kind of information?" she demanded. "The same information that I could have gotten at the America House in Ulm, but you won't let me go there," I told her. There was impatience in my voice and a little bit of anger, and I tried not to think about the fact that I was lying about the contents.

In our family, mail is extremely private. She would never have opened this envelope and neither would Vater. I took the envelope, told Mutter I was going to see Max, and left the apartment. I went to my hideaway by the Danube, and opened the envelope with my pocket knife. I scanned the pages of instructions, and directives, and then I saw a form on which two places were circled in a red. The paperwork informed me that both of my parents had to sign at the marked places before the Consulate could complete my application.

My first thought was "Scheisse (shit)!" I had totally forgotten that being under twenty-one might present some difficulty. The big question was whether or not my parents would sign the release. Just to make sure, I re-read the instructions and conditions several times and there was no exception or alternative.

There never was a time where I had second thoughts about going to America. But all of a sudden it was real. I never previously had to make a decision with so much complexity and risk before. I had to ask my parents to spend the rest of their lives without me, which also meant that I would never be there for them as they were getting older. All of a sudden, my decision felt like a selfish thing to do. It meant breaking the bond between my father and me. He and Heinz didn't get along, and now he would not have his Walter working with him. My brother and sister would have to do all the chores that were always split among the three of us. I was asking them to let me go see the world, and have adventures in new places while they remained behind.

As the snow melt rushed through the rapids and drowned out any sound, I also realized that I was asking a lot of people to help me with my emigration. Letters of recommendation had to be written, Max's aunt had to complete affidavits and get them certified. I had to ask Max's aunt for the airline ticket and her assistance to help me find a place to live and find employment. The most traumatic part of the issue was the possibility that I would never see my family again. Crossing the Atlantic Ocean was so expensive few people in my socio-economic income group could afford it. My parents didn't have a telephone, so I couldn't call them and discuss any difficulty I might have. I certainly wouldn't want to impose on my sponsor. Corresponding by mail would mean that, if I needed advice, I would have to wait two weeks to get a response by airmail. Sending packages across the ocean was expensive and never took less than five weeks. I would be cutting off all of my support structures, setting myself adrift in a strange and unfamiliar world. The key question for me was whether I was ready to live in isolation from my extended family, my home, and my country.

I was convinced that I was ready to live alone, support myself, and start a new life in a new country. I had a skill that was useful almost anywhere in the world. I would have to learn English, but that was a problem I could solve. I felt secure within myself that I was ready to embark on this exciting adventure of going to America. I felt I had the right "tools" to navigate on the river of life in a strange country. I rationalized that if I could survive World War II and all of the dangers it threw at me, I could make it in America.

One thing I was certain about was that Mutter might not let me go because she was convinced I was not ready to live on my own. There was some truth in that, given the lessons I learned while I was a bakery apprentice. Even though Vater and I had created such a wonderful bond between us, I had no idea how he would react. I was hoping that he would not stand in my way of chasing my dream. It was getting dark as I watched little air bubbles dancing across the river's surface and collapsing into the rush of water. The sound drowned out my scream. "I CAN DO THIS."

I went to see Max and briefly told him about the paperwork and that I had to get my parents approval. I shared with him my thoughts, doubts, and conclusions. As I entered the apartment Mutter's question was typical. "Where have you been? You missed supper." That was unacceptable in our family and I apologized profusely.

"Yes I know. I have a problem and I need your help with it." I explored the moment. Mutter, with her inquisitive stare. "What trouble are you in now?" she said. "I am not in trouble. I have a chance to go to America and you need to sign release papers."

My father looked up from his newspaper. It was clear I had both of my parents' attention. I gave them the background, told them about Australia, and the opportunity created by my friendship with Max. I didn't want to tell them that Max had a longer waiting time for his visa. I pulled the form from the envelope and said, "Both of you have to sign a release letting me go because I am not yet twenty-one years old."

My mother bombarded me with questions that came so rapidly I had no chance to answer them. She ended the onslaught of inquiries with "....and, what do you know about Max's aunt?"

"Max's aunt is the sister of Max's mother. You know her and I would think you would agree she is a very nice lady," I said. "But you don't even speak English," was her retort. "I'll start taking lessons right away," I promised.

Mutter continued with her questioning. Actually, they were more like declarations, "You don't have a job. You don't have any money. You don't know anybody else in Chicago. How can you possibly even get started?" I answered, "Max's aunt has agreed that she would help by finding me work and getting me settled so I can be on my own. And if that does not work out I will get a job cleaning streets and I will be the best street sweeper in all of Chicago. I will take my accordion and if I need to be a street musician on weekends I will do that."

"What about the job offers at Mayser?" was Vater's question. "I know that if I took either offer I would be able to have a secure future, my own häusle, and a place for either one or both of you to live with me in your old age. I just believe that I can do more with my life than walk out of my house, through a little garden, to the factory and back each day. I believe there is more to life and I want to know what that is," I told him.

"What are you going to tell Herr Bolz and Uncle Jakob?" asked Vater. "I will tell them the same thing you told me; I have to discover the reality of my hopes."

Mutter brought out a small plate with some bread, sandwich meat, pickles, and a glass of sprudel (carbonated water). I ate in total silence. Vater returned to reading his paper. Mutter sat at her sewing machine making a new dress. I don't remember where my siblings were. I went to bed, trying very hard to listen to the whisperings between Mutter and Vater. There wasn't much I could hear except towards the end of their discussion I heard Mutter say: "Look, it is just another one of his crazy ideas. You know he'll change his mind; you know he won't go through with it. Just sign the papers and let's be done with it."

The next day Mutter asked me to fill out the forms and told me that Vater and she had agreed to sign the release. There were no words of compassion, confusion, doubt, or hopes that I would change my mind. My mind is totally blank on what I said in response, but I am sure I must have said Danke (thank you). I didn't want to appear too excited. Excitement could be interpreted as disregarding my parent's feelings and ungratefulness for what they had done for me. I was torn between my inner excitement about the pending adventure and my gratitude towards my parents.

There were other items in the brown envelope. One explained the detailed steps of the visa application process and the things that were required before I could get my visa. Two major steps stood between me and my visa. Max's aunt had to complete a detailed form and provide specific data on her financial capacity to be responsible for me in case I became unable to support myself. The second step was that I had to pass a physical examination given at the American Consulate. Once I passed the examination, I could have my visa within two or three weeks.

Max's aunt completed her Affidavit of Support on the twelfth of May, 1953, and returned it to me so the entire package could be submitted to the Consulate. I think my parents felt a little better when they saw that Max's aunt had a net worth value of $75,000 (roughly $600,000 in 2009 dollaars). It was the waiting that became a problem for me. To overcome it, I decided to fill my time with additional activities so I wouldn't have time to think about the visa.

Memories by a Bridge

I signed up for English language night classes. I also busied myself by planning a major fundraising effort for the Wasserwacht, of which I was the youth program director. The Wasserwacht needed a motor boat. I decided we needed to put on a variety show to raise funds. I wrote the scripts, organized a youth singing group, wrote several skits, designed contests for the attending audience, and created the Wasserwacht youth orchestra. Vater had doubts about its success and suggested we select a small assembly space. I had to fight long and hard to convince him to rent the largest assembly hall in Neu-Ulm. I had no justification for my conviction except hope. All through the summer and fall of 1953 the fundraising event called Bunter Abend (Colorful Night) evolved.

I spent a week touring Switzerland with four of my Wasserwacht friends during this period. It was my first time out of Germany. Later in the summer, I discovered the most beautiful place in Germany, the famous Königsee at Berchtesgaden, Germany, with my friend Fritz Rau from the Mayser factory. These events, together with the planning of the show kept me busy and made the wait for my U.S visa bearable. It was during that time that Max and I told Bernd about our plans. Bernd asked Max if he would approach his aunt with the question of sponsorship. Within several weeks the news came that Bernd would be sponsored and that he should apply for the visa too.

The letter from the American Consulate specified that my medical examination was scheduled for December 28, 1953. It further indicated that if I passed the examination I could have my visa within two or three weeks. Arrangements were made with my great-uncle Michael Mayser, who lived in Munich, for me to spend the night with him on the day before my Consulate visit. For a while, everything went rather smoothly until the doctors discovered that I was technically blind in my right eye. I had never even thought about that being a handicap for immigration, but suddenly being all alone in an institutional building with that issue was devastating. It meant the potential destruction of my hopes. There were conferences, discussions, and reviews until some invisible group of men decided it was appropriate to continue with the examination. When they finally told me that I had completed the exam, I had doubts about getting my visa. One of the doctors showed me out of the facilities and said in English, "You will be okay." That short statement convinced me that I had passed the exam and I started to plan my emigration to America. On Monday January 4, 1954, I received my permanent immigration visa to the United States of America.

"When will you leave for America?" asked Mutter. "I think it will take at least three weeks to write to Miss Ziesack and arrange for the airline ticket. I am going to ask Miss Ziesack to schedule my departure flight for January twenty-five," I said. "You will not leave before my birthday," she said in a way that left no room for negotiation. "Okay. In that case I will ask her to make the arrangement for my departure on February 11," I replied. Mutter's birthday was February 10 and she agreed with that arrangement.

Vater immediately started to build a lightweight wooden box so my personal belongings could be shipped via freighter. It was hard deciding what to take and what to leave behind. Besides clothing, I took my accordion, important books related to physics and electrical engineering, my photo albums, and sewing kits so I could darn my socks.

Bunter Abend, 1954.

On Sunday, January 17 1954, "Bunter Abend" was a huge success and we raised a sizeable amount of money in support of the Wasserwacht. Loudspeakers had to be placed in the hallway of the building because there weren't enough seats. Vater admitted in an interview with the local newspaper that he had not given the Wasserwacht Youth Group enough credit, and that he was very proud of me.

Walter's accordian performance at Bunter Abend, 1954.

There was one tense moment related to my going to America. Max Kühling, a school friend of my father who had emigrated to America, and his wife returned for a visit to Neu-Ulm after 25 years in the U.S. My parents invited them for dinner and there were, of course, discussions about my forthcoming emigration. They described a Chicago and a life in America that made my Mutter as tense as I had ever seen her. They painted a picture of crime, drugs, prostitution, and alcoholism all being the norm in Chicago. At one point she turned to me and said, "Don't think that after you wind up in the gutter over there that you can come home."

My Vater, in a manner I had never witnessed, pounded on the table and in his loudest voice said, "Woman, don't speak such nonsense; Walter can come home any time and under any circumstance." I had never seen Vater this angry or intense. It took a little while before things calmed down, but I think both of my parents needed to say what they were feeling.

There were bon voyage parties with my friends and cousins, aunts and uncles, and Herr Bolz's family. Everyone agreed that I was indeed lucky to have the chance to go the U.S. For me, having a chance to live there presented a life of hope, whereas living in Germany in 1954 was a life still filled with doubt as to whether or not Germany would ever fully recover economically or culturally. Not until after 1956 did it become apparent that people in Germany could create a positive and hopeful future once again. On the night before my departure, my aunts and

Bon voyage party with cousins and friends: Bernd, Klara, Werner and Elfriede.

uncles were celebrating Mutter's birthday at our home. Elfriede's parents told me she wanted to see me before I left, so I went over to Ulm to say goodbye to her. We had, over time, shared our innermost secrets. We promised each other that no matter what happened we would always be there for each other. I wasn't quite nineteen at that point and I had never had a significant relationship with a woman. But the closeness I felt to Elfriede stirred my heart. Some day I hoped to find the same kind of honesty and caring with my future wife that I shared with my cousin.

Bon voyage party with the Wasserwacht: Margo, Bernd, Hans, Max, Walter, Robert and Anton.

On the way back to Mutter's birthday party, I wanted to say goodbye to my hideaway. It was cold. Ice had formed on the river's edge, and I had to be careful going down the small hill on the slippery slope. The way the world was at that moment, it was clear to me that I might never see this place again. Coming back to Germany was not an option I thought I would have. I sat on my favorite spot and touched the branches above, now naked after the leaves had been blown away by the autumn winds. Without the leaves, I

Bon voyage party with the Bolz Family
Top row: Jakob, Marie, Frau Bolz, Herr Bolz
Bottom row: Helga, Walter, Mutter

had only the darkness to make me invisible. The sound of the rapids remained unchanged, and as I stared into the rushing water, I remembered that I had once almost drowned in this river that I loved.

I was sixteen at the time and I had spent the day on the Danube working as a lifeguard. Towards the end of the day, after most people had departed from the grassy lawn of the river's edge, about six or seven of us decided to see if we could cross the Danube through the rapids. Heinz Prinzing, a ten-year old boy from the neighborhood, was always hanging around with our Wasserwacht group. Prinzing, as we called him, decided he wanted to come along. We swam across the river, walked towards the railroad bridge on the Ulm river side, and entered the rushing waters from that point. The plan was to move between the large blocks of stone towards the Neu-Ulm side, and then jump into the only passable part of the river and let the river carry us down stream until we could reach the riverbank, back where we started. None of us had anticipated the power and force of the rushing waters and we tried to hold on to the edges of rocks and find secure footing before we made another move. Progress was slow and I brought up the rear. We could hardly hear ourselves screaming instructions to each other. We were very close to the passable chute when Prinzing slipped, lost his grip, and was slammed against another large slab of stone. The force of the water on his small chest seemed to prevent him from screaming, or at least we didn't hear him. Prinzing kept sinking below the water and periodically his head would bob up to catch air. I went as close to him as possible, but could not reach him. I screamed to one of the other guys to help me and one of them came to my position. We had to reach Prinzing and pull him towards us which meant one of us had to loosen our grip. The other guy found good footing and I gripped his wrist as I asked him, "Can you hold me?" He signaled yes.

A picture of the rapids during a Wasserwacht training exercise.

I gave up my footing and instantly was slammed into the same rock that Prinzing was pinned against. I kept going down below the water, hanging on to the arm of my buddy. I could see Prinzing in front of me still blowing bubbles, and I grabbed him by his hair and pulled him to the surface of the water. Prinzing hugged me around my neck with his arms, and clamped his legs around my lower body. I lost my safety grip and went under with Prinzing. I gulped air and let the current push me past the side of the rock, only to be slammed into another one. Moving sideways my body once again absorbed the impact of the torrent. I had secure footing on the last rock from which it was possible to jump into the chute. I screamed my intentions to my friends, letting them know what I was going to do. I would jump into the chute and float down river holding on to Prinzing. I wasn't sure whether they could hear me. I screamed at Prinzing to start taking deep breaths, to get as much oxygen into his blood-stream as possible. I wasn't sure if I jumped into the chute with him whether my lungs could give us enough buoyancy to keep us both afloat. I started my own breathing exercise, screaming at Prinzing to do the same. I then told him that I was going to push into the chute with him and for him to hold onto me, just not as tight, and we would let the river carry us downstream where I could get us to the riverbank.

I screamed at Prinzing, "Are you ready?" Just as he answered, I pushed us into the fast-moving sluice. We were submerged and moving rapidly. I could see Prinzing blowing little bubbles out of the side of his mouth. I barely managed to get our heads above water. I kept us vertical until I could feel, with my feet, the soft stones of the river's bottom. "Let go Prinzing." He wouldn't release his hold.   As soon as I could support myself against the river's bottom, my friends jumped in and pulled Prinzing away from me. They carried him to the grass and tended to him. He had swallowed a lot of water, but he would be okay. The idea of trying to cross the Danube at the rapids was just another one of those events in my life where I now admit I had more guts than brains.

It was a close call and I was so exhausted I could not move. My Wasserwacht friends had already started to clean my wounds and apply ointment and bandages. The ambulance arrived and both Prinzing and I were transported to the hospital one block away. We were given a clearance to go home with our bandaged bodies. The onslaught of questions by Mutter (Vater wasn't home) were answered very simply: we had to save someone from drowning at the railroad bridge. I didn't tell her anymore than was necessary and by the time Vater came home it was just another event in the life of a lifeguard on the Donau.

I was beginning to shiver as I said goodbye to my hideaway and to my favorite body of water – the River Danube. It had taught me much, and it had brought me immense pleasure. While my parents and friends were not very physical, my river embraced me; it had held me much like a mother holds a baby in her arms. I could trust my river for it would keep me afloat as long as I kept my lungs filled with air. It cooled me during the hot summers, and even its anger and torrent was a thing of beauty to behold. I will never forget the special bond I developed with the Danube, and to this day I feel a deep connection to all bodies of water.

A Painful Parting

Early Thursday morning, the day after Mutter's birthday, Mutter, Vater, Uncle Jakob, Tante Marie and I drove to München in Uncle Jakob's Volkswagen Beetle. In the luggage compartment was one big suitcase and two of my briefcases. The plan was to meet my great uncle Michael for my last German meal at the Hofbräuhaus in downtown München. Then the six of us would go to the airport. Vater's homemade container had not yet been shipped, waiting for last minute items that I might need. Saying goodbye was hard. I said auf wiedersehen to my two aunts and then Mutter. I could tell she was fighting back tears; it was her ramrod straight posture, which was the body posture she always took when she was fighting back her innermost emotions. The goodbyes to my two uncles were typically male; no emotion, just their advice, "Remember you are a Kroner."

Painful good-byes: Mutter, Great-Aunt Marie Mayser, and my favorite, Aunt Marie Kroner.

Uncle Jacob, Walter, Vater and Michael Mayser.

As I walked over to Vater, he couldn't hold back his tears. It was the second time I had seen him cry and it was the most painful moment of the departure for me as I was the cause of those tears. I was breaking the bond between us. He shook my hand while placing his other hand on my shoulder. That was as physical as he could be. We never hugged each other; it just wasn't done in those days. Letters that I received from home informed me that Vater would hardly talk with anyone after I left. This period of silence lasted for six months. He suffered in silence the loss of one of his sons.

On February 11, 1954, just before two in the afternoon, I walked to the airplane dressed in my best dark brown suit, white shirt and bow tie, woolen scarf, and a heavy but brand new woolen overcoat made by my Uncle Ernst, the tailor. In my hands, I held a large leather briefcase and a small zippered case file that contained all of the important papers I would need for my future. Walking across the tarmac, I was followed by a photographer Vater had hired to record the event. I waved to my family who were standing on the balcony of the terminal and paused at the photographer's request as I climbed the stairs to the aluminum belly of this mechanized bird. I remember the stewardess taking my hat, coat, and suit jacket to store them away. My two carry-on briefcases and my hat had to be stored in the overhead compartment. There were two seats on either side of the isle. I had a window seat on the four engine DC-6 SAS aircraft that held 44 passengers. I estimated there were about ten to fifteen people on the flight from München to Düsseldorf, Germany; the first leg of the journey. The next stop after Düsseldorf was Hamburg. From there we crossed the Atlantic Ocean with a stop in Gander, Newfoundland. After Gander, it was Idlewild Airport in New York where my feet touched American soil for the first time. The journey in this propeller driven airplane took a total of twenty-six hours. I didn't know it at the time, but Scandinavian Airlines Systems was the first airline after the Second World War to have transatlantic flights from Europe to the U.S. The plane lifted off the ground as promised at two in the afternoon and the bodies of my dearest family members faded from view.

Besides my personal belongings in the overhead compartment and a suitcase stored in the belly of the plane, the assets that I brought with me were ten dollars, a piece of paper containing the name and address of Max's aunt, and the three words of English that I had memorized: yes, no, and thank you. had started to take night classes in English and Mutter was under the impression that her son knew enough English to get started. The truth, however, was only known to me. I wanted to date a young lady who wasn't Lutheran. She lived in a displaced persons camp and she was a young Gypsy girl. I knew my mother would not approve. In order to spend time with her, I skipped my

Walter's goodbye at Munich, Germany February 11, 1954.

English classes so we could meet instead for the two hours. It helped that she worked at the Mayser Factory; at least there we could see each other at lunch, coffee breaks, and ride ou bicycles together on our way home.

I had my English-German dictionary on me at all times so I could converse when I had too. had learned some new English words when I was trying to understand what the U.S. Consulat had written on my papers. I learned I was Caucasian, male, blond, with hazel eyes, five fee and seven inches in height, and weighed one-hundred sixty-five pounds. It was strange to b referred to as coming from the Caucasus; I had to check that for myself. To me, I was a Germa who had trouble visualizing his height and weight in terms of the British form of measurements

Being on an airplane for the first time in my life had its difficulties, most of which were becaus the voice over the loudspeaker was not in German. The stewardess, however, would periodicall explain things to me in my own tongue. I didn't want to look at the person sitting next to me, trying to prevent the possibility of a conversation and the embarrassment of not speakin English. I had a perfect excuse; I needed to look out the window to see for the last time a plac I called my home, my country. I had never looked down upon the earth from this altitude. had been on mountain tops and on top of the Münster in Ulm, but that was only 161 meter (530 feet) high. My bird's eye view revealed mountains of rubble, empty buildings whose free standing walls with empty window openings had a strange appearance. There was no colo just shades of gray. I could imagine what the American pilots and navigators must have see on their journey to end the war. It was a visual and emotional relief when softer earth and fores colors finally brought tranquility to this visual onslaught.

I was on my way to America - free to seek my future, my own answers to a boundless curiosity, and most of all, to approach life without prejudice. I was sure that if one had no expectations, one could not be disappointed. I argued with myself that the less prepared I was the more open I could be to whatever life presented to me. Having no prejudice and no preconceived images could actually be a freeing kind of thing. This was my plan, to stay open and willing to take in what I would experience without prejudgment. I felt good about myself, strong, and ready to take on whatever came my way. One of my goals, which I revealed to very few (taking Vater's advice), was that somehow I was going to find a way to get a university education. My Vater had the same dream, but he had to settle for less. No matter what I had to do, I was going as far as I could educationally, and the only thing that could stop me was my intellect. I already had decided that I was willing to start at the bottom, wherever that was. However, I was not going to stand still or get comfortable, unless I achieved my hope, as Vater would put it. I was no fool; if I learned anything from surviving WW II it was that there are many roadblocks, detours, and people who will stand in your way. I knew there are people who will stand on my shoulders to keep their head above water, only to drown me. As I was looking at my own reflection in the porthole of the airplane, I was reminded of Mutter's saying, "Before you critique others, grab your own nose." If I wasn't careful, I could be the one to destoy my own hopes. Most important to me was that whatever I accomplished in America would not be because of my last name, or as a favor to my family. Making myself truly independent meant I had to do it alone. I realized, however, that I was already indebted to Max's aunt for sponsoring me and for giving me a loan for the airplane ticket.

I was daydreaming when I realized we had come in for a landing. The stewardess explained that I could leave my belongings on the plane and that we were just deplaning to take on fuel, supplies, and additional passengers. I took my two briefcases and suit-jacket and followed everyone else into the lobby of the Düsseldorf airport. The place was nice, clean, with comfortable furniture, but very little else. I have no idea how long I was sitting there before I became aware that the loudspeaker announcements were all in English. I was waiting for an announcement in German for my flight to Hamburg. It must have been close to an hour when a stewardess walked up to me and asked if I was Herr Kroner. I told her yes, and she asked me to follow her. My airplane was already on the runway ready to take off. A few men were pushing the mobile stairs to the side of the airplane and the door was reopened to let me board. Instead of my overcoat, hat, and suitcase flying to America without me, I rejoined my personal belongings, thanks to the stewardess, who had alerted the airport that one of their passengers was missing.

I quickly became worried. I was not as well prepared for my journey to the new world as I thought. This could have been a disaster since my parents didn't have a phone and I did not have enough German money on me to travel back to Ulm. The school of hard knocks began and the kid from Neu-Ulm suddenly understood that he had a lot to learn. I felt embarrassed as I took my seat and apologized with "Entschuldigung," (excuse me.)

By the time we landed in Hamburg it was dark and all I remember was landing on a carpet of thousands of lights with the reflection of the plane's lights shining on the wet pavement of the tarmac. We were refueled and then we were on our way into the night. I remembered a lesson Frau Unkauf once told me: "Life is like playing chess; you must plan many moves ahead to make sure you control where you are going." Another piece of advice from her was, "Always seat yourself so you can see the exit." I began to understand much better what she had tried to tell me. The darkness into which we were flying was also a black abyss into which I was falling. I still thought not knowing was better than not going; I was convinced I was doing the right thing.

Sometime after leaving Hamburg, we were served open-faced sandwiches. It was interesting; a hard roll was cut in half and an assortment of "stuff" was arranged around the bread. There were new words on little containers. Some I could figure out, while others would have required a search through my dictionary. I didn't want to be that obvious about my ignorance, so I guessed. Mustard I couldn't figure out until after I opened an envelope to discover it was what I called Senf. Cheese was a little easier because the aluminum foil wrapper made it look like Käse. There were cold-cuts, and most of the other items I could deduce easily. The droning of the aircraft engines put me to sleep. Finally the brightness of the lights in the cabin was dimmed and the stewardess showed me how to adjust my seat back.

Landing in Gander, Newfoundland was uneventful except that its terminal was nothing more than a metal shed with some folding metal chairs and a coffee pot in the corner. It looked more like a repair shop and we were told we had to deplane because of refueling. It didn't take very long and once again we flew into darkness.

With daylight came the view of the east coast of the American continent. Soon I saw the skyscrapers of New York. I was about to set foot onto the land of my adopted country, my dream, my hope, the United States of America. What happened next can only be described as if a movie were running at ten times its normal speed. All I remember is being escorted by a SAS stewardess out of the terminal and into a taxi. In Germany, if you sat on a bridge over the autobahn in 1954 you would probably have to wait for fifteen to twenty minutes before you saw a car on the superhighway. Here I was in a taxi with the world whizzing by me in the form of buses, cars, taxis, trucks, signs I couldn't read, and endless noise. The scale of everything was huge. Buildings were taller, streets were wider, and highways were like long asphalt tapes on the land.

The stewardess was going with me to help me board the next plane that would take me to Chicago. We were on our way to LaGuardia Airport, also in New York City. Wow, I thought! A city with more than one airport! I was impressed. The next airline was Trans World Airline, TWA. From the waiting area,q the stewardess pointed to my airplane, a TWA Super-Constellation Skyliner. It was a peculiar airplane in that it had three tails; it sort of looked like a big fish. It too had propellers and I soon discovered that none of its stewardesses spoke German.

When I finally arrived at Midway Airport in Chicago, Illinois, it was night, somewhere around six in the evening. After twenty-seven hours of travel I had arrived at my final destination. The stewardess asked me to stay in my seat and she would come and get me. Sometime later she escorted me off the plane and said something to me that I couldn't understand. Her hand motions, however, clearly indicated that I should stay right there at the bottom of the stair. I placed my hand on its rail and placed my feet exactly where she told me to stand. The last people that deplaned, judging by their uniforms, were pilots and navigators. Nearby was a fenced off gangway with a metal roof, but there was very little illumination. Visually the place was noisy with lights reflected on the wet tarmac. The entire airport was a sea of lights, but it was remarkably quiet. Max's aunt had indicated in her letter that she would meet me at the airport and take me to her apartment. There was no human being in sight, much less within shouting distance. I couldn't even call out for help if I wanted to because no one was there. I didn't dare leave the designated waiting place for fear of making an error and missing whatever was to happen next.

As a result of this fear, it felt like I stood there for a very long time. I was probably there for about thirty minutes, although it seemed like over an hour. In the distances I could hear running steps, saying to myself, "Oh, good it must be the stewardess coming back for me." But the person I saw running did not have a stewardess uniform on. What appeared was a woman in her mid-fifties, a little older than Mutter. She was wearing a black hat, with a see-through net over her face, and calling out my name. She introduced herself as Aunt Marie, Max's aunt. She spoke excellent German and apologized for being late. I had never seen a picture of Max's aunt and I was hoping and praying that this person was in fact Max's aunt.

We picked up my suitcase and, for what felt like another hour, drove from Midway Airport to 4330 North Sacramento Avenue, Chicago, Illinois. The drive felt like one continuous movement along a band of illuminated streets filled with advertisements that I couldn't understand. Wherever there were lights there were people. I thought how different a city this was from those I had known, even big cities like München. In Germany, stores were closed at night. People were at home, not shopping. I caught myself comparing, which I swore I wouldn't do. There is a thin line between comparing and judging, and making decisions on what is better or worse.

I walked into my sponsor's living room and about ten people greeted me with "Welcome to America." With the exception of an elderly lady and her daughter Lois, everyone spoke German. Lois, it was explained to me, worked as a fashion model. The elderly lady was Lois' mother. There was a young German couple, Herbert and Margot, who had a baby and rented one of the apartments my sponsor owned. Herbert was an optometrist who had learned his skills in Germany. My sponsor explained to me that one of the guests was staying over for the weekend in the room that was planned for me. She told me to put my suitcase in the hall closet and I would have to sleep on the sofa until Monday when her friend left. It had been thirty-five hours since I last took a bath and I didn't feel comfortable asking to take a shower. Instead, I excused myself, went to the bathroom, and washed myself in the sink. Then I shoved my dirty undershirt into my briefcase and put on my used dress shirt.

The table was set for dinner and I was given the honor of carving the turkey. I had never eaten turkey, or even seen one, much less carved one. But I was in America now, I thought. I would try anything at least once. I learned that my immigration day was the same day as Abraham Lincoln's birthday. Not a bad coincidence, I thought. I knew who he was from reading about America.

From the left: Lois's mother, Margot, Lois, and Walter.

After dinner, I volunteered to wash the dishes, to which there was no objection. Lois, through interpretations, said she would help me. What happened during the dishwashing period was a shock for me since I was basically uninitiated to the ways of a woman. We couldn't converse because neither of us could understand each others' language. Lois began a touching-fest that began by her rubbing her hand up and down my arm, at least the part that was not in the dishwater. As she dried the dishes, she had to pass back and forth behind me to put them away. I could feel her body rubbing against me ever so gently at first, and by the time I was finished washing the dishes I received what I would call a full body press. I had only kissed a few girls, and then only after many dates, so I never had something like this happen to me. What was worse, I had no idea how to respond. I certainly didn't reciprocate. My level of discomfort turned to fear. I needed to get out of the kitchen. My life in Nazi Germany had taght me not to trust strangers, and I found myself surrounded by them.

When everyone reassembled in the living room, the lights were turned down low there was a boxing match on television. It was a strange setting. There was an ugly lamp with an integrated planter that cast a glow on the wall behind the TV. That was the only illumination in the room. I sat on one end of the couch and Lois sat right next to me in a lounge chair. As everyone stared at the television, she laid her arm across the back of the couch and frequently rubbed my shoulder, moving her hand up the back of my neck, being careful that others couldn't see what she was doing. Periodically, when I looked at her, she smiled and winked at me. I became even more uneasy for two reasons. First, I thought men were supposed to be the initiators. Second, I didn't know what was an appropriate way to ask her to stop what she was doing. I couldn't even excuse myself and go to my room because I didn't have one. People had to leave before I could go to sleep on the couch I was sitting on.

When everyone had gone, my sponsor brought out bedsheets, a blanket, and a pillow so I could make my "bed" on the couch. Besides me, there were three other people sleeping in the apartment: the weekend guest; Lois' mother; and my sponsor who, as a registered nurse, was taking care of Lois' handicapped mother. I had only slept intermittently during my twenty-eight hour trip and I was exhausted. I lay fully awake and scared, however, because Lois' behavior was very strange to me. I could manage warm welcomes, friendly gestures, and hugs and kisses as greetings, but her behavior was beyond all of that. She had touched me more in the course of two short hours than I had been touched by all of the girls I had ever known combined. I fell asleep thinking that I was not well prepared for coming to America if this was how strangers behaved. Exhaustion finally put me to sleep and my last thought was about an invitation from Herbert and Margot to go shopping with them the next day.

Saturday morning Herbert and Margot took me grocery shopping and introduced me to two new and wonderful experiences. First, they ordered a pineapple milkshake for me, a taste that I had never experienced. I thought I could drink pineapple milkshakes forever. Second, we went to a German butcher shop where they ordered meat and cold cuts. At one point I asked Margot why they bought so much meat; it seemed like a month's supply. She told me what they were buying was for one week. I decided right then and there that I would catch up for all of the shortfalls in protein during my teenage years. They bought hamburger meat, steaks, roasts, ribs, and many different sandwich meats like leberkäse, gelbwurst, schwartenmagen, salami, weisswurst, nackte, and fleisch-salad. I felt like I was in heaven even though I had not tasted any of it yet.

Herbert, his wife, and I formed a comfortable friendship. I was glad there was someone closer to my age to whom I could go if I needed something. The car was filled with groceries, an amount that seemed unbelievable for a family of three. Before getting out of the car Herbert turned to me, handed me a piece of paper and said, "If you ever need me these are my phone numbers." I read the paper and on it were his home number and his work number. I thought it strange. I knew where he lived; why would I need both of his numbers. I thanked him and he said, "Just in case." He explained that my sponsor was also his landlord and they wanted to remain on good terms with her. I could sense there was more to this than he would tell me.

I spent my second full day in America writing letters to my family and friends in Germany, but I did not mention anything that would worry Mutter. I knew her first response would be, "See I told you so; you are way too young." Lois' mother was watching television, in fact that is what she did all day after my sponsor lifted her out of her bed, dressed her, and sat her in her chair in the living room. I had never seen a TV so it was no surprise that I was fascinated by the images while trying to understand what was being said. In one day I learned three different meanings for the word "strike." No sooner had I learned the meaning of a strike in the context of bowling, then during a baseball game the same word was used with a totally different meaning. And then, I became more confused when the TV show "Strike it Rich" came on. My sponsor gave me all three definitions and that was the first word of English I learned after my arrival in America. I realized that English was going to be a very difficult language to master.

That same Sunday, evening I asked my sponsor if we could talk. I wanted to know where and how I was going to get a job. I wanted to pay back my debt for the airfare expenses and for that I needed to earn money. She dismissed the entire thing by telling me I didn't have to worry about my debt right then. If I wanted something to do there was plenty of work in her apartment complex. She walked away and I was unsure of my immediate future. I didn't mind working in her apartment complex, I just wanted a day job that paid and I could work for her at night for nothing.

Chicago

My first Monday in America began with my sponsor showing me around her apartment complex. She introduced me to some of her elderly tenants and explained that I had to collect their garbage and place it in the garbage cans located in the basement. Then she took me to an apartment that had just been vacated and she explained that the walls had to be washed and painted. She would bring the paint after lunch. Monday evening, I unpacked my suitcase in a room

Walter's first home in the United States at Sacramento Avenue and Irving Park, Chicago, Illinois.

that had a single bed opposite the door, a nightstand, a small dresser, and a closet that was peculiar. I learned that, in America, they construct closets as part of the building as opposed to using armoires. There wasn't any room for a desk or chair, just enough to get out of bed and get dressed.

I was happy that I could show my gratitude to my sponsor by working for her as a janitor and painter. I remembered telling Mutter that if I had to start cleaning streets, that is what I would do and I would be the best street cleaner Chicago had ever seen. Well, I already had been promoted from street cleaner to personal and private janitor, laborer, and painter, not bad for one day in America. This arrangement became a regular routine for three weeks.

The three-story complex had twenty apartments. She explained to me that if she didn't like her tenants she kicked them out, fixed up the place, and got new ones. That didn't sound fair to me, but I didn't want to question her method. I just filed it away and connected it with Herbert's remarks. My sponsor was single, had immigrated from Bomberg, Germany, and became a U.S. Citizen in 1934 in Fond Du Lac, Wisconsin. She identified herself in her affidavit as "a property owner by occupation," and that her yearly income from rentals was estimated at $12,300 ($95,000 in 2009) plus a weekly salary of $70.00 ($550 in 2009) as a nurse. From our conversation I surmised that in the past she must have made her money as a nurse.

After my first week in Chicago my sponsor helped me to enroll in night school in a beginner English class. There were people from all over the world in this classroom and I no longer felt alone with my difficulties. There were two married couples who recently had immigrated from Germany; however, they were planning to return to Germany. They had expected to live in luxury because their uncle was a rich man. Their uncle however, paid their one-way ticket, found a place for them to live, gave them one month's living expenses and told them they were on their own. Whenever they talked about America they complained about everything, including their uncle. I disliked people like them. They were like leeches on a human body.

After about three weeks of constantly asking my sponsor to find me a paying job she finally made the arrangement. I had to promise that in the evening and on weekends I would still work for her. I told her as long as I could go to school to learn English I had no problem with working nights and weekends. A close friend of hers was a co-owner of a small manufacturing plant, and he was in charge of the machine and spot-welding shop. Premco Manufacturing on Clark Street employed me as a spot welder. On my first day at Premco, my boss who spoke German said to me "This is not Germany. Here in America you can quit anytime you want to, and you are not required to give Premco any advanced notice. However, Premco can fire you anytime we want and we don't have to give you notice either." A worker's loyalty to the employer must be a German phenomenon, I thought, if what the boss told me was true. In any case, I filed it away as I did so many things as my learning process continued. I acknowledged his remarks and started to work. The spotwelder was located in the machine shop mixed in with punchpresses and stamping machines. Doris, a young German woman in her mid-twenties, was operating a stamping machine. She had emigrated from Hamburg, Germany three years before. Her husband continued living in Germany and I could never figure out why he didn't join her. I asked Doris if it was because of money and she said the money was waiting in the bank when he was ready to come. I didn't want to probe anymore. Doris was a well dressed woman, blond, with a friendly, trustworthy face and a genuine smile. Most of all, she was very helpful. Our boss did not tolerate conversations in the shop, so we would frequently talk at lunch, on our coffee breaks, or after work.

Each day at work, a short stocky man around fifty years of age would come into the shop to empty trash. Doris introduced me to him; his name was Bud. Bud's clothes were dirty, he looked like he needed a bath, but I held my hand out to shake his. He was standing there with his head hanging down looking at the floor, not wanting to touch my hand. I reached over and grabbed his hand and shook it to conclude the greeting. He looked up and with a barely visible smile shook my hand back. Doris translated my German which essentially told Bud that it was nice for me to meet him. The boss walked in.

"What in the hell are you doing. We pay you for working not for talking," my boss yelled. "I am sorry," was my response. Doris continued working. "And you Bud, you better get out of here," the boss warned. After Bud left, the boss gave me a lecture in German, "Us Germans don't associate with scum, filth, and lazy no good dogs like Bud."

I was about to burst out with anger when I saw Doris' look at me and shake her head as if to say, "Don't!" I had come to America to get away from the labeling and demeaning of people. The boss was an old German stuck in the quagmire of his old values within a free country. Maybe America needed a de-Nazification program too. He certainly behaved like a Nazi. As far as I was concerned, one judged people by their actions and words and not by their cleanliness, work, status, income, or family. I remembered my father's lifelong motto from Goethe's work: "Edel sei der Mensch, hilfreich, und gut." "To be human: Be noble, giving, and good."

If I learned anything from the war it was that all material things, all precious art, money, even the luxury of being able to take a bath, could be lost in a flash by decree, dogma, and destruction. In my mind the only things that had lasting value were family, friends, love, and knowledge. At lunch, I went to find Bud and discovered that his work station was in the factory's boiler room. I pointed my finger at him and then at my mouth trying to ask whether he was eating lunch. He held a candy bar in one hand and a soup can with a wire handle in the other. The soup can had coffee in it. I gave him half of my sandwich and my apple and we sat quietly together on the dirt floor of his place with a bare light-bulb providing a dim light. Every once in a while he would lift his chin glancing at me. Whenever he came to empty my garbage container he now started to look at me and nod his head as if to say, "Hi." Doris told me that what I did was very kind and admirable and something no one in the factory had done. She also warned me to be careful what I said to my boss.

I continued with my responsibilities at my sponsor's apartment building by working nights and weekends. I usually went to bed by midnight, and worked all day Saturday. Sunday I reserved for myself, to which my sponsor did not object, except she wouldn't allow me to play my accordion. I felt grateful that I was in the U.S. and employed. I was thankful for being able to return favors, and very appreciative for being able to live free in my sponsor's apartment and share her food.

The Fear of Entrapment

The telephone in the kitchen of my sponsor's apartment rang and she spoke English to the person on the other end. She turned to me and told me that Lois was inviting me to go to a movie next Saturday, and she thought it might be beneficial for me to learn English.

"Do you want to go?" she asked. How could I say no without appearing unkind? "Yes, thank you, but I don't know how to get to where she lives," I said. My sponsor explained that she would write down the instructions and assured me that I would not have a problem. Neither Lois nor my sponsor had an automobile so we all used the bus. "What time do I have to be there?" I asked.

After some discussion, they agreed that I should arrive at Lois' apartment by six in the evening. We would eat something before the movie. I told my sponsor that I wanted to take a little gift and some flowers to Lois. I gave her the money and she made the arrangements.

On the proposed Saturday I followed the instructions for the bus trip, and arrived punctually at Lois' apartment. I knew I was in deep trouble when she opened the door. Lois was standing there in her negligee with a lace-type robe over it. After an awkward hello, I held out the flowers in one hand, and her gift in the other. I fumbled frantically for my dictionary, but before I could get it out of my pocket she had taken my arm and led me through the door, which she closed behind us. She explained through the dictionary that she was not feeling well enough to go to a movie. She would prefer that we stay in her place and have dinner. All of our conversations took a very long time because we each had to look up over half the words we wanted to say and show the translations to each other.

I apologized, thinking I had arrived too early, and she still needed to get ready, which turned out not to be the case. My guard went up and my intuition told me there was danger ahead. What woman would receive a gentleman the first time in her apartment in sexy intimate attire? My mind could not rationalize the old saying, "Andere Länder andere Sitten. Other countries other customs." Fear, confusion, and helplessness would describe my feelings at that moment. I realized that the earlier event, while she and I were washing dishes on the day of my arrival, was not just a friendly form of greeting. This was a woman relating to a young man in a form, style, and with an intent that was unlike anything I had read, seen, or experienced before. Part of the problem was that I could only compare Lois' behavior to the females I had known in Germany. I also was afraid that I might offend Lois by my behavior. A gentleman would have left and excused himself, except I didn't know whether such a rejection would be considered insulting in America.

We had some wine, and conversed about my family, her family, and her job in a fashion store. She had a very small dog that she obviously loved since it sat on her lap whenever she sat at the table. Dinner was nice but not impressive. It consisted of a fried chicken drumstick, green peas with a dab of melted butter, and potatoes in a casserole. During dinner, I seemed to capture her attention when I told her what my father did for a living. When I told her he was a physical therapist and masseur, she asked me if I knew how to give a massage. I told her that I had watched my father give massages, but what I knew was by observation only.

It must have been around ten o'clock when she told me that she had to call my sponsor. At the end of their conversation she handed me the phone. My sponsor explained that it was getting late and Lois was worried about me traveling by bus alone. Lois did not feel well enough to accompany me home on the bus, so she proposed that I spend the night. I said "Okay," but my brain screamed, "Caution, these two women may be planning something."

Later in the evening, Lois made preparations for me to sleep on the sofa in the living room. Lying on the sofa with the lights out I could see through the door opening into the kitchen where the lights were still on. She appeared in the doorway in her negligee without the robe and I could see, through the negligee, the outline of a beautiful body. She asked if she could talk to me. I indicated that it was okay. She said, "Why don't you come into my bedroom and give me a massage." I declined and told her I didn't know how. She reached under my covers, took my hand and led me into the bedroom. There the two of us were joined by her dog. Being in bed with Lois was uncomfortable enough. Sleeping with a dog was not my idea of a night's rest. I felt trapped. I had no instructions for the return trip, it was late, and I didn't know how to call a taxi. I was scared beyond description. I have to admit that part of me was curious and excited about the possibility of something that never had happened in my life. I was a virgin in every sense of the word. But the other part of me was afraid because I had no experience with what I thought Lois had in mind, and I was worried about what my sponsor would think if she found out that we had slept together.

I was as uninformed about women, sex, and intimacy as a teenager could possibly be. My education came from what kids called "The Doctor Book" that all German parents had. When my mother tried to talk with me about the birds and the bees for the first and only time, I was fifteen years old and too embarrassed to have my mother explain to me where children came from. The only thing I knew was that a man would lie on top of the woman and that is where the awareness stopped. Anatomical images in the Doctor Book didn't tell me very much and those graphic sections through the human body, revealing the body's anatomy, didn't have any sensuous or informative impact on me. My father had given me words of wisdom on how to be a gentleman, but he had not taught me anything about intimacy or sexuality.

There was no intercourse, just fondling. I soon became excited and the explosive release surprised me more than Lois. As she felt my wetness on her body and on her bed sheets, she became furious. I was supposed to save myself for her, she pantomimed, pointing down to herself. She transformed into a bitter and ugly person, ripped the sheets off her bed, pushed me out of her way, and took the sheets to the bathroom where she washed them. Sheets hung all over the bathroom to dry. I went to the couch totally confused and scared, wondering what would happen the next day. I was absolutely convinced that the entire thing was part of a plan to trap me. Could I be forced into a marriage with Lois? What if she became pregnant, although I didn't know the intricate details of that process? The worst part of this was that I had no one to talk with about the event.

The sheets were still hanging in the bathroom Sunday morning as I brushed my teeth with my finger and her toothpaste. I asked for instructions how to get back to Sacramento Avenue. When I returned to my sponsor's apartment there was a brief conversation of whether I had a good time, which I answered affirmatively. I couldn't even write home to my parents, friends, or favorite aunt. I was stuck with an event, a piece of information, and a worry that wouldn't go away. I also became aware of how inexperienced I was about sexuality and that beyond French kissing and fondling I knew absolutely nothing. Why would a woman get so angry when after all of her caressing there was this event the likes of which I had never experienced? It was different from when I played with myself. Was this an insult to a woman? I had no idea and no way of finding out.

The Trap

Monday morning at work, I asked Doris if she had time after work to talk with me. During lunch I called my sponsor and told her that I would not come home for supper. I had to do some things and would be home by eight. I had this gut feeling that I could trust Doris with what was troubling me. After work, she suggested we go someplace where we could eat and talk. I told her everything and all the details. I asked her what she thought.

"Walter, you did nothing wrong. I have no idea why this Lois would react the way she did, unless she wanted to get pregnant," Doris said. "What do you mean, get pregnant?" I asked. I knew I was in totally unfamiliar waters. I had never received basic sex education.

"Do you know what it takes to make a woman pregnant?" she asked. I could feel myself turning red, wishing I had not brought up the subject. "I am sorry. I didn't mean to embarrass you. My suggestion is to stay away from Lois," she advised.

"But she is a friend of my sponsor and she comes to visit her invalid mother at my sponsor's apartment," I said. "You have to decide how long you want to stay with your sponsor," Doris said as she stared intently at my face. "I have to stay there at least until I have paid for my airplane ticket," I told her. "No you don't; you only owe her the money. You could sign a piece of paper that says what you owe her and how you will pay it back; even include a deadline. You can live anywhere you want right now; you are in America," she told me.

I didn't understand that part of freedom until Doris explained it further. Doris emphasized that America was a free country. My sponsor did not have the right to make me an indentured servant; I was free to go. While this was good news, I had no idea how, when, where, and what I would have to do to make this work. The only comforting advice that Doris gave me was that not all American women behaved the way Lois did. She assured me that my feelings of danger and entrapment were real. Besides, she went on to explain how Lois was way out of my league and I was at a disadvantage. I felt myself relaxing. I had at least one person who, in what she told me, made sense and gave me something to think about. Before Doris, left she asked me if someday I wanted to go dancing. She didn't know about my passion for dancing, and I said that would be a great gift.

When I returned to the apartment, my sponsor was waiting for me and inquired where I had been and who I was seeing. I was honest and stupid enough to tell her, "Doris works with me in at Premco. She is German and she asked me if someday I would like to go dancing." My sponsor turned red in her face as she said, "You cannot go! You cannot see anyone that I don't know. I am responsible for you. I own you until you pay me back the money I spent on you." "Are you saying I have to have your permission for anything I want to do until I become a U.S. citizen?" I asked.

"Correct, or at least until you are twenty-one years of age. I am not going to sit by and take the chance that you get in trouble and I have to pay for everything. I can also call the immigration office and get them to send you back to your mother," she threatened.

I ignored the last comment thinking she wouldn't do that. "What if I introduced you to Doris so you could get to know her? I asked. I thought it was fair that she meet my friend since she was responsible for me. "I don't have the time to meet new people. I have enough trouble with the new people I have just met," she told me. With that she left the room.

A little later my sponsor came back into the room and said if I wanted to go on dates, to the movies, or dancing she would approve of me going with Lois because she knew her and trusted her. In my head the sirens went off again and I realized that I was in danger. Maybe my fear of entrapment, or possibly being forced into a marriage, I thought, was real.

I had suspected that my mail was being openedfor some time, even though the envelopes were sealed when I got them. I decided that I had to confirm my suspicion. On the following Saturday, I stayed around the entry court, waiting for the postman. As soon as he placed the mail in our mailbox, I looked for a letter for me. Lucky me, there was a letter from my parents.

My sponsor had a ritual every Saturday. She dressed up as if going to a festive occasion, but she actually just went to the bank, hairdresser, and shopping. When she dressed up she always ran the lipstick outside the edges of her real lips, to make her mouth look larger. After my sponsor had departed, I went to the kitchen to steam open the envelope. I didn't even read the letter, nor did I remove it from the envelope. I simply marked the pages in their overlapping arrangement, against the inside of the envelope. I glued the envelope shut and Monday morning when I went to work I placed the envelope in the mailbox.

On March 29, 1954, when I came home dinner was on the table. The letter from my parents was leaning against a glass of milk. I carefully opened the letter with my knife saw that it wasn't even folded back correctly, nor was it placed back into the envelope as it was originally. The lines no longer lined up, and there were two different folds where only one should have been. I had proof she was reading my mail, which in my family was simply never done.

Usually, in the morning I had breakfast before my sponsor woke up. I wrote a note and placed it by her breakfast plate. The note said, "Please excuse me, but I don't like it when someone opens my mail and reads it. After all, it is personal."

That evening everything was normal and my sponsor didn't say anything. It was the same on Tuesday and I was beginning to worry that my note to her got lost. However, on Wednesday evening when I arrived at the apartment there were people wall-to-wall in the living and dining room. I recognized some of her friends while others were total strangers to me. Lois was not there, nor was her mother, and Herbert and his wife were also absent. My sponsor had re-arranged the living room furniture and she had placed her favorite chair in the corner so she could preside over the event. I walked as usual to the kitchen to eat dinner; this time the table was empty.

"Get in here you ungrateful son-of-a-bitch," screamed my sponsor. I went into the living room standing in the opening to the dining room. "Sit down." As she pointed to the chair that Lois' mother usually sat in. "I want to talk with you, you Schweinehund. Her outrage was expressed in a mixture of German and English profanity, and by the loudness of her voice there was no doubt she was livid. "Okay," is all I could say.

"How dare do you accuse me of opening your mail and reading it. I would never do such a thing." With her friends around her, she had an audience and I was surrounded by stares, mumblings, and heads shaking sideways, as if I had done something terrible. "These people here are my friends and they can be a witness about my honesty."

I responded, "I have proof that someone in this apartment opened my mail, and I doubt that Lois' mother would do such a thing," I said. "What proof could you possibly have, you stupid bastard, you no good, lazy leech." "I set you a trap and you fell into it," I responded. That was the best way I could express it, but it probably was not a good way to put it. "What trap? What are you talking about?" she demanded.

I went to get the letter from my room and showed it to her so all the guests could see what I did. I explained how I did it, what I did, and then all hell broke loose. "You set a trap in my own home, you ungrateful bastard, you dog of a swine. I'll have you deported. You don't belong in America," she screamed.

I apologized to her and told her I was not angry with her. It was just that I felt my mail was a private thing. "I have to be fearful of my life with you," she said. "The next thing you are going to do in my own home is kill me. My life is in danger with a bastard like you. I have to get rid of you. Get out of here you pig. I don't want to see you in this building again, ever. I'll send you back to your mother. Tomorrow I'll have you deported," she ranted.

I had never been so scared, not even during WWII. If she sent me back to Germany that would be the ultimate disgrace. I would bring shame on my family name. Worst of all, the years of hope and dreaming of being in America would vanish before I could even enjoy my new country. There would be nothing that I could do to rectify the shame of deportation. I went to my room, took my briefcase, and stuffed some underwear, socks, some pants and shirts into it. I placed all of my important papers and money in my zippered briefcase and walked out of the apartment. I had to leave all my other belongings behind, including my accordion, with the hope of getting them later. On March 31, 1954, forty-eight days after arriving in America, I became a homeless person.

My dream of becoming an American seemed about to be shattered. I could not let my sponsor do this to me; I had to persevere somehow. I knew America was for me. I felt an affinity for this country more in my gut than any quantifiable argument. I suddenly understood why immigrants clustered together in ghettos. Even there they would find "bad apples," as Mutter referred to ethically challenged individuals. I simply had to survive the threat of being deported no matter what it took. I could not put Herbert and Margot at risk by going to their apartment. I was too ashamed to contact the childhood friend of my father, Max Kühling who lived in Chicago, and who had visited my home before I emigrated. I was afraid that they would write to my parents about this fiasco.

Homeless in Chicago

I waited at the bus stop on Irving Park and Sacramento Avenue where I normally caught the bus to work. I had no place to go and I didn't feel comfortable calling Herbert's apartment at this late hour. I decided to spend the night, and maybe the weekend, in the Premco factory if I could get in. When I got there, the doors were locked and none of the ground floor windows were open. Breaking in was out of the question. It was cold and all around me were factory buildings and shops with masonry walls with soot covered windows. Garbage was strewn in the alley between Premco and the abandoned factory on the other side of the alley. I walked back to the bus stop where I knew there was a street light and where I could look up phrases in my dictionary. I wrote them on a piece of paper and then repeated them out loud so I would not forget them.

Bud, the janitor at Premco, was living in the boarded up building across the alley. I knocked on the wood panel over the window, spoke my name and said the words I had memorized, "Bud, my sponsor kicked me out; and I need a place to stay. May I stay with you?" He pushed the plywood panel outward where once a window existed. I could see the white of his eyes move back and forth. Bud removed the panel all the way and took my two briefcases so I could climb through the opening and down to the boiler room floor. I thanked him. It was dark by the time the plywood panel had been placed back over the window.

"May I stay?" the next memorized question I directed at Bud, even though I could no longer see him. Then the light came on. Bud nodded his head up and down. As I was struggling to look up some more words in my dictionary, he touched my arm, lifted his head straight up and looked me in the eyes, something he never did, and waved his hands as if to say don't say anything and don't worry about it. In his hunched over position he quickly moved about, put a number of wooden boards over some unused laundry sinks, gave me a potato sack filled with crumbled-up paper, and touched my head and the sack as if to say, "Put your head here."

Hanging from the ceiling was a single light bulb and various cans and buckets. There were wooden boxes stacked below the two hopper windows arranged as stairs to climb out the windows. The old brick floor was covered with layers of dirt and sand so that each step could be heard as one walked around the boiler room. Maybe this was Bud's burglar alarm system. The ceiling was a vaulted masonry structure, below which were pipes and conduits running in every direction. A former workbench served as Bud's kitchen table with wooden boxes serving as containers for soup cans, cereal, and bottles. A hot plate was the only appliance in the room. It was plugged into an outlet at the end of a cable that he had strung across the alley to Premco's boiler room. In one corner of Bud's place was his bed, a metal bed frame and an old mattress resting on a sheet of plywood. A few pieces of clothing where hanging here and there and I could have sworn I saw a rat scurry across the floor. I felt ashamed that I had to depend on someone who needed help from others. Instead he was helping me. I promised myself that I would never tell anyone in Germany about this embarrassing series of events. No one was to find out, because I knew that none of my relatives had ever reached this low a level of existence. When all was very quiet and Bud was asleep, I could hear rats scratching and chewing on things. It gave me the creeps and sleep came slowly.

The next morning it was early when I left the cellar room with Bud because he usually was the first person into the factory to feed the boilers and get things opened up. I washed up in the workers' locker room and put on some fresh underwear under yesterday's shirt and pants. I met Doris at her bus stop and told her what had happened and that I had been kicked out of the apartment. I also told her about staying with Bud.

She stopped in the middle of the sidewalk, pulled me to the side, and stared at me for what seemed like an eternity without saying a word. I couldn't read her or interpret her expression and I wondered if I had made another mistake. "Are you willing to tell a lie?" Doris asked. "Lie about what?" I asked her.

"Tell the boss you have a doctor's appointment this afternoon. Tell him you are worried because of your limited English and you would like for me to go with you." She went on to explain that instead of going to the doctor we would go to the Immigration and Naturalization Office and to the Post Office to see whether my sponsor's threat was real. "Let's talk some more at lunch."

I located my boss on the factory floor and told him I had to see a doctor and Doris was not only willing to take me to her doctor, but willing to go with me for the translations. He asked me what the problem was and I acted embarrassed as if I didn't want to talk about it. The boss surprisingly agreed to let Doris go, but neither of us would get paid for the time off.

Doris knew where to go and we started at the Post Office. Essentially we were told by the official that what my sponsor had done was a crime and that I could take her to court. I had no interest in this; I just wanted to make sure I didn't commit a crime. At the Immigration Office, Doris told the officer everything I had told her, the letter, the boss being a close friend of my sponsor, and my sponsor's threat of having me deported. The questions and answers were many and Doris had to do a lot of translating. His final instructions were simple, but difficult to implement.

His voice became gentle, the words spoken slowly, and he looked me in the face while Doris translated. "First of all, your sponsor cannot do what she threatened you with, unless you have broken the law; and you haven't." "Second, my strong advice is for you to get a new job, and make sure that you have an income so you can afford to live on your own and get out from under her control." I asked, "What if the police show up and arrest me?"

He gave me his card and told me to call him if there are any problems. He explained that any person arrested is entitled to one phone call. "You will call me, okay?" he said. Once again his speech slowed down and his tone became soft and compassionate. "Don't give them the card, just ask them for a telephone. You then call the number on this card and if there is no answer, call the number I have written on the bottom. When I answer you only have to give me your name and then I want you to give the telephone to the policeman. I will find out where you are and I will come and get you. Do you understand?" he asked. "Yes, I think I do," I responded gratefully.

And then the official said something to me that was like music to my ears, even though it came from Doris' translation. "I am sorry that this is the way you discovered America. I assure you, we Americans are not that cruel. He stood up, extended his hand and said, "Welcome to America and good luck." Thank you sir," is all I could say.

Doris was concerned about me staying with Bud. "Walter, I would let you move in with me, but I am living in a one-bedroom flat and I am not allowed to have someone else in my room." "Thank you, but I don't expect that from you. I would appreciate if you could help me find another job," I told her.

I had to quit my job at Premco because I didn't trust my sponsor anymore and I was too scared that she would have me arrested under some false accusation that would be cause for deportation. If I was arrested, while living with my sponsor, or at Premco, it would be a hopeless situation for me. I had to free myself from the clutches of my sponsor and her friends.

"Do you have plans for next Saturday?" asked Doris. "No," I said. "Okay. In that case we will go job hunting. I'll check the papers for you."

We went out to eat and before we parted I decided to call Herbert. I told him everything and said I needed to get my things out of my sponsor's apartment. I asked Herbert if he would meet me at the drug store near to the apartment and help me get my personal belongings. I told him that every Saturday morning my sponsor went to the bank and I would be able to clear my things out then.

Herbert said, "Call me when you are at the drug store around the corner from the payphone. I will come with my car and put your things in the trunk until I can safely take them to my apartment." "Okay, till Saturday morning then," I said. "Walter, you must not tell your sponsor that we helped you because I have no doubt she would kick us out of the apartment." "She'll never know, and thank you Herbert."

That night my mind was in a turmoil. I knew Bud was worried about my comfort, even though we exchanged no words. Once again, I felt my life was in danger. Once again, I was hiding. And once again, I needed to struggle to survive. Before I left Germany, I was confident that I had the emotional, spiritual, and physical strength, my "tools," to navigate the river of life. I was not prepared for my present predicament. I had never expected to be sleeping with rats.

Bud heated some water on his hot plate and handed me a cup of instant coffee. The coffee cup was from Premcor's front office I knew Bud took it just for me. I lay down on my plywood bed and crumbled paper pillow ready to go to sleep. Bud put a blanket over me. It smelled awful, but I wouldn't even think of rejecting his kindness. "Thank you Bud, for the coffee, the place and the bed. Good night, Bud." "Good night, Walter." It was the first time he had spoken my name.

By Friday, I had assumed that my boss would have heard from my sponsor about me having left the apartment. However, there was no indication that he knew anything about the situation. Instead, he asked me to help him take apart a punch press so he could re-order some new parts. It was something I was good at and by mid-day the machine was disassembled and laid out in an organized manner.

It had been eight weeks since I started at Premco, where I was paid ninety cents per hour. This was below the minimum wage paid elsewhere in Chicago according to Doris. For six weeks I had asked my boss for a ten cent per hour raise. I had found out that the person who worked on the spot-welder before me on a good day produced only 120 assemblies. To increase production, I designed and built a jig that made it easy to align the assemblies that had to be welded. Six days after I started on that same machine I was producing between 200 and 220 assemblies per day. I thought the increase was worth ten cents per hour more. I asked again for a raise, but my boss kept making excuses saying he would make a decision soon. At that point I decided to quit my job the following Monday morning.

I left Bud's place early the next morning because I needed to make sure I saw my sponsor leave for her Saturday ritual. I stayed far enough away on the tree-lined street so I could see her emerge from the entry courtyard. She was walking towards the bus stop, but I had to make sure she actually got on the bus. The worst thing that could happen would be for her to have forgotten something and walk in on me. I still had my key and let myself into the apartment. Lois' mother smiled when she saw me, but I couldn't understand what she was saying. I packed my things and said good-by to her. As I put my arms around her, kissed her cheek, and told her I was leaving, she cried. I am not sure she understood my words, but I feel that she could sense the moment. I wrote a note to my sponsor telling her I was moving out and that I would pay the five-hundred dollars I owed her as soon as I could. I also wrote that I would call her soon with my new address and phone number.

My suitcase in one hand, the accordion case in the other, I went to the drug store and called Herbert. I ordered coffee at the soda fountain and waited. It couldn't have been more than thirty minutes before Herbert walked in. We transferred my belongings into his car and he asked me whether I had time to talk. "Where are you living?" he asked. "You don't want to know; and I don't want to lie to you," I told him. I told him about Doris and that she was going to help me find a job. I also gave him Doris' telephone number in case he needed to reach me. "Herbert, I could use some help with finding a place to live. If you know of a place I would be very grateful if you would tell me," I said. "What are you looking for?" he asked. "I want an inexpensive place that is clean and furnished," I told him.

Herbert agreed to help me find a place. "How will I get in touch with you?" I told him to call Doris in the evening with any information he had. "Walter, I am sorry this is happening to you, and I am sorry that I couldn't warn you about your sponsor. Believe me, she is a very mean and controlling person and you want to quickly disassociate yourself from her," he said. "Why do you live in her apartment building if she is that bad?" I asked. "I have a family, it is the least expensive apartment we could find, and for the time being we don't have very many options," he replied.

We agreed that when I had a place to stay I would call him to get my suitcase and accordion. I went back into the drug store, called Doris and told her that I was ready to meet her and go job hunting. We agreed on a place to meet and she assured me that she had several job possibilities lined up.

Doris helped me fill out application forms and answer the interviewers' questions. She also allowed me to use her phone number and address on my application forms. All together we interviewed with at least six manufacturing companies. When we were finished, I invited Doris for dinner, but she had other commitments.

Rescued in Chicago

The next day, Sunday April 4, 1954, was the worst day of my first fifty-two days in America. For some reason my senses were in a highly attuned state. Everything I smelled seemed much stronger than before. Street noises were much louder than I remembered, and I could swear that the wattage of the single-light bulb in Bud's space had increased. My mind was racing from thought to thought, from one fear to another, searching for solutions. I felt that I was in the clutches of an invisible beast who could force me into marriage with Lois through threats, or have me deported back to Germany. One thing was certain. If her friend, my boss, was scheming with her to keep my income as low as possible, I would be indebted to her for a long time and she could control me. I also wanted to put money aside to pay for room and board in the future and I was afraid my sponsor might demand money for sheltering me since I arrived in the U.S. I had to make more money. All of these fears were amplified by the fact that I was unfamiliar with U.S. laws and with the exception of three friends, I was virtually alone. I also worried that my boss would withhold my pay since I owed the money to my sponsor.

Sitting in Bud's "living space," inhaling the fragrance of cigarette smoke, rotting food, dampness, and stale cigarette butts, tears came to my eyes as I remembered the threat Mutter made: "If you wind up in the gutters of Chicago, do not think that you can come home." Her fears had come true, but it was not because of something I did. I was homeless, but not because I was a drunk or drug addict. I was here because I was ill prepared to live in a new world and in an unfamiliar culture. My knowledge of the English language was marginal at best, and I realized I was very naive about human nature.

My analysis of the situation continued: What if something happened to me, like an accident that required medical attention? I had no address; I had no insurance; I had very little money. Several times the thought occurred to me that it would be a mistake to quit my job without having another one waiting. An inner voice reminded me of the chess lesson; make sure you can see several moves ahead. I didn't want to be found by the authorities while I was homeless out of fear of deportation. As a last resort, but only if it was a matter of life and death, I decided I would contact Mr. Kühling, the old school friend of Vater. At that point, however, I placed all of my trust and hope in my friends Doris, Herbert and Margot.

Bud was gone for most of Sunday. When he returned that evening it didn't take him long to see the condition I was in. He took a clean pink machine shop towel, wetted it and handed it to me with a motion that suggested I should wash my face; which I did. He walked over to the workbench, took a bag and handed it to me. I took out the contents and saw that it contained a bottle. I handed it back, shook my head, and said: "Thank you Bud; thank you very much, but I can't......" I was not going to find my solution in alcohol. I don't know how many times that night, in the darkness of the boiler room, tears ran down my cheeks in silence I just kept wiping them away with the pink shop towel.

Monday morning, Bud opened up the Premco factory, as usual. I went with him because I desperately needed to take a shower and put on new clothing. I didn't put on my working uniform because I still planned to quit. I stashed my personal things in my locker and went outside to wait for Doris at the bus stop. As soon as we made eye contact her face transformed with a big smile and she gave me an enthusiastic wave. While she was making her way forward to the exit door of the bus, she was moving her lips, but I could not make out what she was saying. As she stepped onto the sidewalk she said, "Just as I was walking out the door this morning I received a call from Russakov Can Company. They want you to call them as soon as possible. They have a job for you." "What else did they say?" I asked. "Not much; that they looked at your application and they are prepared to offer you a job as an inspector." "Inspector of what?" I asked excitedly, anxious to get the details. "How much will they pay?" "Look Walter," she explained, "he gave me a phone number that you should call. That is all." "Thank you Doris, I really appreciate this."

I took the piece of paper she offered. The news was so exciting that I forgot all about the problem of communicating with the personnel department at Russakov Can Company. Doris looked at me quizzically. "Are you going to quit today?" she asked. "As soon as our boss shows up," I told her.

We didn't want to walk into the factory together. Neither of us wanted our boss to know that Doris was helping me. We made arrangements to meet for lunch and also after work so we could discuss what I should do next.

I went to the front office and asked to see my boss. He came out into the dimly lit hallway and asked what I wanted. I said to him, "Do you remember telling me that I could quit at any time without notice?" "Yeah, I remember; why? Are you quitting?" he asked. "Yes, right now; and could I have my last week's paycheck?"

There was a long pause. He walked back and forth and then asked, "Did you say you are quitting this morning?" "Yes Sir. Right now." His face turned as red as the shop towels. Then he screamed at me, "You cannot quit. I have the punch machine parts all over the place and you are the only one who can put it back together." He kicked and banged on the wall, swearing using a combination of English and German. People came out of their offices wondering what was going on.

Inside I was jumping for joy, but I didn't let it show. I was pleased he had lost his cool. I reminded him, "You had six weeks to consider my request for a ten cents raise and you wouldn't tell me when or if I could expect it. Instead you have given me nothing but excuses," I told him. "You God damn Germans are all alike! I'll never hire another German; all they are interested in is money," he screamed. "But you are also German," I reminded him.

He stopped his rage and stared at me, and the office staff disappeared from the hallway. "Get out of here." "What about my paycheck for last week?" I asked. I stared at him as if ready to do battle. "If you have any money coming to you, you can pick it up next Friday afternoon," he said angrily. "Thank you," I said. I went to my locker, took my belongings, and left Premco Manufacturing.

Afterward, I called Herbert's apartment, but he had already left to go to work. Margot told me that they found an inexpensive place for me and gave me the landlord's name and number. I met Doris for lunch and told her about the parting conversation. During lunch, we called Russakov Can Company and made arrangements for me to meet with the gentleman whose name was on the piece of paper.

By two o'clock that afternoon, I was standing in a furnished second floor room at 1852 West Berenice Avenue in Chicago. The landlord was a German immigrant and a friend of Herbert and Margot. He explained the arrangements. I was to share the bathroom at the end of the

hall and the kitchen with three other men. The first floor was occupied by the landlord. The rules were simple: no overnight guests; no loud noise or radio after ten p.m.; and, everyone had to clean up the bathroom and kitchen immediately after use. The kitchen was in the basement. The place was nothing fancy, but it was spotlessly clean and the kitchen was fully equipped. I didn't need to buy linen, towels, or kitchen utensils; all of it was included in the rent. The idea of cooking and eating in the basement didn't appeal to me, but it was better than Bud's place. I don't remember what it cost me for rent, but I had nothing to compare it to and I assumed that it would be reasonable since the landlord was a friend of Herbert

We shook hands and the landlord asked me, "When do you want to move in?" "Can I move in this afternoon?" I asked. He asked me what I had

Free at last! Walter's first place of his own in Chicago was a second floor room in this house.

to move and I told him that Herbert would bring my things to me. I asked if I could use his phone. I called Margot and asked her if Herbert could bring my things as soon as it was convenient. As the day came to a close, I met Doris at the Premco bus stop and shared the good news. I gave her my new address and the landlord's phone number.

I met the personnel director at Russakov Can Company on Tuesday and he included in the meeting one of the employees who spoke German. He showed me the workplace and explained how at the end of the production line things had to be tested. Testing included checking the quality of threaded holes, the adequacy and the quality of the paint job, and similar things. The company manufactured large explosive bomb containers, gasoline tanks for jeeps, and other military hardware. My pay per hour was one dollar and seventy cents; almost twice as much as at Premco. The personnel staff person asked me, "When can you start?" I asked, "Would tomorrow be acceptable?" He laughed and showed me my locker and the remaining facilities. The German worker helped me fill out the papers I had to complete.

Walter and Herbert on the beach at Lake Michigan, Chicago, Illinois.

Tuesday night, it must have been ten o'clock, the bell rang in my room. Herbert was downstairs with my suitcase, accordion, and a cardboard box. I told him I didn't have a cardboard box. He explained it was something from his family, a welcome gift. There was food, soap, hygiene items, napkins, coffee, tea, and a coffee brewer for my room. Herbert pulled a small bottle of Schnapps and two glasses from his coat pocket. He poured the liqueur, handed me a glass, and said, "Welcome to America, Walter."

Book Three

WORLD EVENTS 1955 - 2004

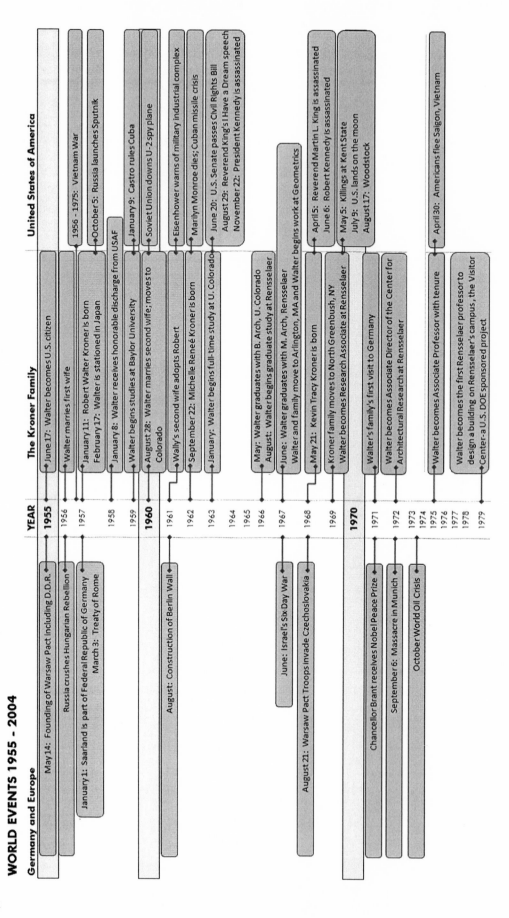

Germany and Europe	YEAR	The Kroner Family	United States of America
May 14: Founding of Warsaw Pact including D.D.R.	**1955**	June 17: Walter becomes U.S. citizen	
Russia crushes Hungarian Rebellion	1956	Walter marries first wife	1956 - 1975: Vietnam War
January 11: Saarland is part of Federal Republic of Germany / March 3: Treaty of Rome	1957	January 11: Robert Walter Kroner is born / February 17: Walter is stationed in Japan	October 5: Russia launches Sputnik
	1958	January 8: Walter receives honorable discharge from USAF	
	1959	Walter begins studies at Baylor University	January 9: Castro rules Cuba
	1960	August 28: Walter marries second wife; moves to Colorado	Soviet Union downs U-2 spy plane
August: Construction of Berlin Wall	1961	Wally's second wife adopts Robert	Eisenhower warns of military industrial complex
	1962	September 22: Michelle Reneé Kroner is born	Marilyn Monroe dies; Cuban missile crisis
	1963	January: Walter begins full-time study at U. Colorado	June 20: U.S. Senate passes Civil Rights Bill / August 29: Reverend King's I Have a Dream speech / November 22: President Kennedy is assassinated
	1964		
	1965		
	1966	May: Walter graduates with B. Arch, U. Colorado / August: Walter begins graduate study at Rensselaer	
June: Israel's Six-Day War	1967	June: Walter graduates with M. Arch, Rensselaer / Walter and family move to Arlington, MA and Walter begins work at Geometrics	
August 21: Warsaw Pact Troops invade Czechoslovakia	1968	May 21: Kevin Tracy Kroner is born	April 5: Reverend Martin L. King is assassinated / June 6: Robert Kennedy is assassinated
	1969	Kroner family moves to North Greenbush, NY / Walter becomes Research Associate at Rensselaer	May 5: Killings at Kent State / July 9: U.S. lands on the moon / August 17: Woodstock
	1970		
Chancellor Brant receives Nobel Peace Prize	1971	Walter's family's first visit to Germany	
September 6: Massacre in Munich	1972	Walter becomes Associate Director of the Center for Architectural Research at Rensselaer	
	1973		
October World Oil Crisis	1974		
	1975	Walter becomes Associate Professor with tenure	April 30: Americans flee Saigon, Vietnam
	1976		
	1977		
	1978	Walter becomes the first Rensselaer professor to design a building on Rensselaer's campus, the Visitor	
	1979	Center - a U.S. DOE sponsored project	

144

Timeline

Germany and Europe	YEAR	The Kroner Family	United States of America
	1980	Reneé Kroner enrolls at Marymount College	
October 10: Peace demonstration in Bonn	1981		March 31: President Reagan survives assassination attempt
	1982	Reneé Kroner goes to study in Italy	
	1983		
	1984	December 23: Hans Kroner dies	May 5: President Reagan visits Bergen-Belsen and Bitburg Concentration Camps
	1985	December 5: Dora Kroner dies	
April 4: Chernobyl nuclear accident in the Soviet Union	1986	Kevin Tracy Kroner enrolls at Vanderbilt University. October 7: Walter represents USA in an exchange program of building scientists with Romania	January 29: Shuttle Challenger explodes
	1987		
	1988	April: Walter receives NYSERDA support to form the Rensselaer Lighting Research Center. May: Walter becomes Distinguished Professor. Walter attends Futures Conference in China	
	1989		
October 3: East and West Germany are unified	**1990**	February 28: Walter and Jean Stark interview for a major research project at Johnson Controls	
August: Gorbachev's Putsch fails	1991	Walter obtains Liebich gift in support of developing affordable housing	War by Allied Forces against Iraq
	1992		
	1993	Walter attends World Futures Conference in Helsinki, Finland	
	1994		
	1995	Walter delivers keynote address at International Congress on Intelligent Buildings, Tel Aviv, Israel	April 20: Oklahoma City Bombing
	1996		
	1997	July: Walter buys "New-Ulm on the Hudson"	
	1998		
	1999	Walter and Jean visit Königsee, Berchtesgaden, Germany	
	2000		
	2001	June 9: Walter and Jean are married. June 12-28: Honeymoon on the Island of Kassos, Greece, Spyros's family's summer home	September 11: World Trade Center attacks
	2002		
	2003	April 9: Olivia Jane Hoagland, Walter's first grandchild is born	March 21: Start of second Iraq War
	2004	Walter's 30-50-75 party organized by Jean Stark. Walter retires from Rensselaer	

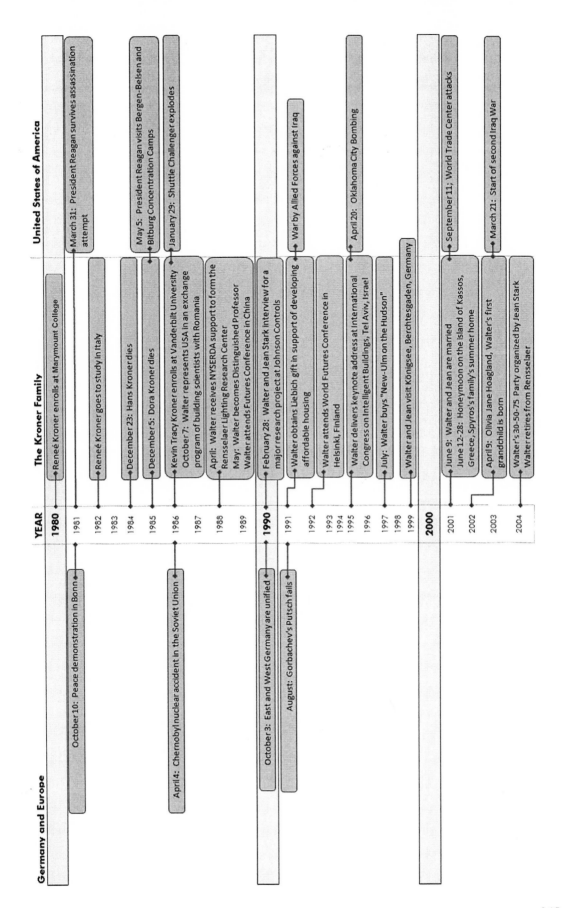

Free at Last

It was too late in the evening to play my accordion, but I wanted to celebrate. My sponsor did not allow me to play the accordion in her home. For the first time since coming to America it felt like I had truly arrived. I was free to come and go as I pleased. I did not have to report who I was with or spoke to, or tell someone about my plans for the weekend. Best of all, I no longer lived in fear of what my sponsor and her friends would do to me. I no longer had to seek approval, or confirm that what I was thinking or planning to do was acceptable. I sat in the darkness of my room looking towards Irving Park Avenue. I couldn't see faces, only lights, some floating freely in the darkness. I heard the sounds of people talking, cars moving, and sirens blaring; all creating a beautiful eclectic symphony. I am sure some people would consider these sounds a bothersome noise, but for me it was a symphony.

Now it truly felt like that I had reached one of my goals: the hope of building a life in America. I didn't think of my sponsor as German or as American. For me, she was a bad apple in a basket of good ones. The rest of the first week was taken up with getting settled in, opening a bank account, and notifying my sponsor about my new address. I contacted the Kühling Family, Vater's former schoolmate, and gave them my address. I didn't tell them anything about my previous experiences or about being homeless. Down the block and around the corner was a bar that on Friday and Saturday nights had a piano player. At one point I spoke with the musician and told him about my accordion. He invited me to bring it and my sheet music some night. We started to play together and by the second or third week I was making extra money accompanying him on the piano.

One of the greatest features in the world that I discovered was the American movie house. I learned that I could buy one ticket, enter the movie at eleven in the morning, and sit through repeated showings until the last showing near midnight all for one price. To this day, I maintain that I learned English by watching the same movie over and over again.

Herbert had introduced me to the taste of pineapple milkshakes. I loved them and every time I went to the ice cream place two blocks from where I lived, I ordered a pineapple milkshake. It was all I knew how to order. One time I pointed to a dish another customer was eating and said I wanted one just like it. It was a strawberry sundae and it became my new favorite ice cream dish, at least until I learned the names of some others. One Sunday morning, I decided to get up early and write down everything I would need to say to order breakfast in English. Besides the soda fountain and the bar where all I had to say was, "Beer please," I had never gone out anywhere else. For about two hours I memorized everything that I had to say, then I proceeded to the restaurant down the street. The hostess seated me and handed me a menu, which I never opened. When the waitress came to take my order I recited my learned script, "I would like to have two eggs with bacon, potatoes, toast with butter and jelly, and coffee with cream and sugar." I felt so proud because she never asked for any kind of clarification she just kept writing.

"How would you like to have your eggs?" she asked. I couldn't understand what she said, however, I guessed that it was a question. I said, "What?" "How... would... you... like... to... have... your... eggs?" She emphasized each word, speaking slowly and clearly. I must have looked puzzled, so she proceeded with a series of words that sounded like a series of choices.

All I could think of saying was, "The first one." She looked at me like I was from Mars, wrote something on her paper, and left. When the eggs arrived they were scrambled. I had never eaten scrambled eggs. I had wanted them sunny side up, but I had not memorized that description. It was quite a while before I ventured out into the world of American restaurants again.

As time went by, the more I discovered what I didn't know, the more embarrassed I felt. Some of the workers at Russakov Can Company gave me the name "greenhorn." For a while, I thought it was an endearing nickname. However, I finally realized that greenhorn is a term to describe immigrants. After I discovered a thesaurs, and synonyms, I found ten different meanings for greenhorn. The one that best described my situation was apprentice or learner. I didn't overlook another synonym for greenhorn that also applied to me: neophyte.

One Friday, right after we received our paychecks, one of the young men at Russakov offered me and another German worker a ride to the bank to make our deposits. He had an appearance not unlike the Snake and was known throughout the factory as a women chaser. He bragged about how many women he had over the course of a weekend and about some of the things he did with them. I didn't much care for him, but the ride to the bank in a red Chevrolet convertible was a tempting offer. The roof tarp of the car was stashed away and we looked like big shots driving through Chicago. One or two blocks before the bank we were pulled over and surrounded by four police cars. The other German and I had our identification checked and we were asked to be seated in one of the police cars. The police disassembled the interior of the Chevrolet and from under the seats, behind the door panels, and concealed compartments in the trunk they pulled revolvers, rifles, and ammunition. After convincing the police that we were not friends and didn't know the blond young man, we were told that we could leave. It was a close call; almost being arrested for possession of illegal weapons of which I had no knowledge. Yes, neophyte was an apt description for me.

I discovered an entire German community of social clubs, and neighborhoods where all the stores had signs in the window announcing, "We speak English," and even movie houses that showed German movies. I was invited numerous times to join German families on their outings or to visit their summer places. I also met Germans who had been in America a long time, but their English didn't sound correct compared to Americans. I discovered many Germans belonged to German clubs and only shopped in German stores or went to German movies. What surprised me was how critical they were of the U.S.A., the American life style, and American women. It's as if they took from the community and didn't give anything back; a selfish sort of lifestyle in my mind. As a result, I decided I was not going to frequent German businesses, clubs, movies, or associations. I wanted to become American, not a German-American. I didn't feel that I was rejecting my past, I simply wanted to embrace my future.

In the meantime, Doris and I saw each other regularly and she found a small apartment for herself in a duplex, soon after I moved to West Bernice Avenue. We became regulars at Saturday night dances at Chicago's Aragon Ballroom. I had never seen such a phenomenal palace designed for dancing. One entered the grand lobby at the street level with coat checks on either side. At the end was a grand staircase that led to a large landing from which stairs led further up to the right and left. Gilded ceilings, opulent chandeliers, and soft rich carpeting provided acoustical noise control. On the second floor, one entered a dining area that followed the edge of a circular dance floor, edged by a colonnade. The design resembled a Mediterranean piazza surrounded by two story buildings. The ceiling was a dark blue with blinking lights simulating stars. Moving across the ceiling were clouds. To this day I have no idea how they created that effect. At the far end of room was a huge stage with a red velvet curtain, behind it the Big Band orchestra.

I was in seventh heaven. I loved ballroom dancing and Doris and I moved across the parquet floor to the rhythm of the big bands as if we had danced together all of our lives. Many evenings by the time I escorted Doris home on the bus and then took the bus home, it was two in the morning before I would go to sleep. Soon the late night trip wasn't needed anymore; she invited me to spend the night. I knew she was married. Even though I never pried into her personal life, it became obvious that her husband was not coming to America and she was not going back to Germany. I sensed she was tired of waiting.

Reality included having to go to the coin laundry and figuring out how to do my wash. I darned my own socks for a while until I discovered that I could buy new ones for very little money. I had to learn how to cook and many times I wrote to Germany to ask Mutter for her recipes. I loved the American invention called dry cleaning. Having someone else do my washing, dry cleaning, ironing, and folding was wonderful. Life had a liberating, discovery-filled feeling, and I felt safe with Doris. The inspector's job was a little bit boring once I had figured out the procedures, but they paid well, treated their workers with respect, and provided wonderful locker rooms with showers and a lunch room that was clean and had vending machines, although I always brought a sandwich for lunch. By June I had saved the five-hundred dollars I needed to pay my debt to my sponsor. With Doris' help, I forwarded a certified check with a heartfelt thank you note in the envelope.

Somehow the Chicago River didn't impress me. It was more like a non-moving body of water that rose with the tide of Lake Michigan. The Lake, on the other hand, did leave a lasting impression because of its size, the waves, and endless shoreline. I spent many hours along its shore, swimming in its cool water. I visited the area where the Chicago World's Fair was held in 1933. Tante Hansi had sent pictures of the Fair to Vater and I had stared at the photographs of the buildings for hours as a child. Very few of the Fair buildings remained. However, it felt wonderful to walk on the actual grounds that had been imprinted on my memory.

The first time I decided to tour the Chicago loop by myself, I mapped my route and took the bus downtown. It was a Saturday and the street was hectic, overloading my senses. I tried to understand the city and read its signs. I visited the Merchandise Mart and was overwhelmed by its seventeen story height, its volume, but also its soot covered façade. I had difficulty imagining that this building was filled with business and retail facilities. The Wrigley Building with its marble façade seemed to tell the story of getting rich by selling chewing gum – something Mutter would not allow us to chew. The Wrigley building, however, was much cleaner and healthier looking. The Old Water Tower reminded me of European Renaissance architecture with its castles and palaces. I remember that walking through the concrete and masonry canyons of Chicago left me with a stiff neck from staring at the immense height of all the buildings.

I had never witnessed such intensity and density. The range of aromas in the city ranged from freshly baked bread and fresh flowers, to the unfamiliar and not so pleasant smells. The sounds of car tires squealing, the steel wheels of the elevated train clanging against the steel tracks, construction noise, and music blaring from speakers were all unfamiliar. I had never before felt this intense form of energy created by noise, moving objects, and people talking and screaming. I had so much to learn and discover. When I returned to the street corner where I had left the bus, I discovered it was a one-way street. I had no idea where to find the bus going in the opposite direction. I didn't know how to get back to my place near Irving Park, which was around the 4000 North area. I had my dictionary, a pad of paper and a pencil, and a map of Chicago where the street names were so small I could barely read them. After walking in several directions I still had no clue how I would get home. I wrote my address on a piece of paper, walked up to a policeman who was standing in the middle of an intersection, and in my broken English tried to tell him that I was lost and needed to get home. I don't remember what he said, but after looking at my paper, he took me by the arm led me out of the intersection, along some sidewalks, and stopped at a bus stop. He wrote a bus number on my pad and touched the brim of his cap. I guessed as a sign of goodbye. The bus driver, after seeing my pad of paper with the address, took care of the rest by telling me where to get off, which bus to change to, and where to get off at Irving Park. The bus driver handed me a bus schedule that Doris and I used to map future journeys through the city, especially when I would be by myself. Once again I felt ill-equipped, but in no way discouraged.

The news from Germany was not so good. Although I had never written to Max about my experiences with his aunt, I did write about them to some of my friends in Germany. Unfortunately, word of my mistreatment reached Max and as a result he stopped writing to me. I wrote to Max to apologize for not telling him directly and I explained to him what happened. I never received a response. I realized I had lost a dear friend.

GI without a Country

My doorbell rang one rainy Chicago day in July of 1954. I looked out of my bay window from the second floor and saw two men standing at the front door. They were wearing raincoats and felt-brimmed hats with dark bands. I went downstairs and after they made sure that I was Walter Kroner, they told me they were from the Selective Service System. I asked them to wait and knocked on my landlord's door to seek his help with the translations. I only partially understood what the SSS men said, but after all was said and done, I learned that in another month I would be eligible to be drafted into the Army.

I had received a permanent immigration visa to the United States of America. However, there was a condition od which I was made aware: I would lose my German citizenship six months after entering the United States. That was a big surprise to me because it meant in another month I would have no citizenship at all, I was a man without a country. I asked them how they could take me into the military when I wasn't even a U.S. citizen. They explained that I could apply and receive my U.S. citizenship within one year after joining the military. I then said, "Do you mean that if I am sent to Korea before a year is up I could die in that war as a man without a country?" The SSS men agreed and said, "Yes, that is possible." These gentlemen, who looked like they had just walked out of a Chicago gangster movie set, gave me their cards and informed me that I had to report to their office no later than August 22, 1954. I would then be inducted into the U.S. Army.

Even though the Korean War had concluded, the risk of being sent to Korea was still high. The Cold War was beginning. The idea of being drafted into the Army did not appeal to me. Citizen or not, crawling in dirty trenches, living in foxholes, and existing under extreme outdoor conditions was not for me. I had been there, done that, and barely survived. I wasn't keen on doing it again. Doris and I discussed the situation and the only other options were: (1) going back to Germany, or (2) volunteering for either the U.S. Navy or the U.S. Air Force. Going back to Germany was out of the question. I was where I wanted to be. Even though America wasn't yet "my country," I didn't mind serving in the military, just not the Army. For me the Air Force was much more futuristic, fascinating, and at least sounded exciting and "cleaner."

The following Saturday, I went to the Recruiting Office on Chicago's North Avenue and inquired about volunteering for the Air Force. After a few questions they informed me that they were not sure they could take me because of my English language difficulty. However, if I didn't mind taking a test they could base their acceptance or rejection on the test results. I indicated that I would be glad to take the test and scheduled a place, day, and time of the exam. I don't remember the location of the test, but it was a big hall with desk chairs and there were about twenty or so young men there to take the same exam. It was a multiple choice test where you marked a box to indicate your answer to the question. I could feel my life slip away as I attempted to understand the questions. I could read words like 'the', 'that', 'when', 'how', 'where', 'this,' etc. But the important nouns, adjectives, and verbs I couldn't understand. I decided that I was simply going to mark a box for each question and take my chances.

At the suggestion of my recruiter, I showed up two weeks later at the recruiting station to see how well I had done on the test. I sat across the desk from the recruiter as he pulled out my file and read the results. His facial expression changed from a friendly smile, to a serious look of concentration, and then to a wide grin. "You passed the test!" he said. "We can recruit you into the Air Force." I wasn't going to tell him what I did to obtain these test results. It would be the

Air Force's problem, not mine. I filled out the papers and he gave me a packet to take home. The envelope contained instructions detailing when and where I had to report. On the day of my recruitment, I would be sworn into the United States Air Force. The only part I understood fully was that I had made a commitment to active service in the Air Force until August 1958, and I would be in the reserves until August 22, 1962.

I went to see Doris and shared the news. I gave my notice at Russakov Can Company and made arrangements to leave my personal belongings with the Kühling family. The evening of August 21, 1954, Doris and I went to dinner and then spent the night together. The next morning she walked me to the bus stop. We talked, we kissed, and talked some more. I was hoping the bus that was taking me to my train would be late. It was then that Doris said to me, "It feels like I am saying goodbye to a husband, but I could never be married to you." "Why not?" is all I could ask. "Walter, a woman needs to feel sexually fulfilled in the same way a man does. I have never felt that way with you." The bus came, tears welled in her eyes, and I was confused and devastated as never before.

What followed was a blur until I stepped off the train in Geneva, New York. My basic training was at Sampson Air Force Base near Geneva, New York. I had no idea where that was and didn't have a map to look it up. Basic training was eleven weeks long and I had no idea what would happen after that. The one nice surprise was that I met another recruit who was a German immigrant who spoke excellent English as well as Hungarian, German, and French. I nurtured our friendship because I knew I needed him much more then he needed me. The other reason our friendship evolved was because the rest of the recruits on the train were rude, and some were even dangerous characters. There were just too many knives, razer-blade cutters, knuckle-bars, and similar weapons. Later we discovered that many of the other recruits elected to join the military instead of going to jail. At Sampson Air Force Base, Flight Number 6525 was known as the "gangsters from Chicago."

The train ride took us through the night and the pounding of the steel wheels against the joints in the train tracks set up a monotonous rhythm. Staring into the reflections and darkness of the railroad car windows, I could not get what Doris had shared with me out of my head. The most devastating and painful part of her message was that I had let her down. I knew how to be a gentleman, and when to bring flowers and little gifts. I realized I knew how to treat a lady in every way, except one. As my brother repeatedly pointed out, I had many girl friends. He was right, but they were just good friends who happened to be female. From them, I had learned that girls enjoyed it when a boy listened to them. I also discovered that girls were interested in all of the details and feelings that surrounded an event. As I thought more about my relationship with Doris I realized we had never had a deeply personal, intimate conversation. I was confused and the only person I knew who could tell me what a woman wanted from a relationship was my mother, and I couldn't possibly put my questions to her in a letter.

I feel very comfortable with women. I find them fascinating and beautiful. I have a tremendous amount of respect for them and their view of the world, which I find is so often different from the male perspective. Growing up in Germany I had learned the importance of manners, courtesy, and how to be a gentleman in all matters and situations from Frau Unkauf and her daughter, Dr. Ursel Köstlin. From Doris, I learned that a man must give back to a woman the same kind of pleasure he receives from her. It was a painful lesson, but one I wouldn't forget.

I was deeply troubled by Doris' comments for a long time, particularly since she had become a very important person in my life. I have no idea what I would have done had she not been at the place where I worked. If there was one person in Chicago for whom I would have done anything, it was Doris. And now it is too late for us. She told me at the bus station that there was no hope for our relationship. I had no idea where the river of life was taking me, but one thing was certain. Someday I wanted to find the right person, marry and raise a family. But there was something I had to do first. I had to learn how to nurture a relationship. I was worried, however, that I might not be capable of developing the ability to do that for it had eluded me thus far.

I remembered my father's motto, "Be noble, be giving, and be good." The secret was concealed in the realm of giving to a woman. The phrase took on a whole new dimension for me. But how could I give something of which I did not know? "Geneva, New York. Everybody exit at the forward door."

We had arrived and a new phase in my life was about to begin.

An American at Last

After I arrived at Sampson Air Force Base, my head was shaved, I picked up my uniforms, had my medical examination and shots, and then settled into the hurry-up-and-wait life of the military. There was screaming, hollering, commands, and insults hurled at us new recruits. None of it bothered me. I had already experienced it all at the age of ten. At the end of the first day we were asked to empty our suitcases and bags onto our mattress. We had been assigned bunks, footlockers, and a place to hang our uniforms. We were asked to stand at attention while our Technical Instructor (TI) checked our personal items. A young soldier followed the TI with a sack in his hand. Things that were not allowed or, in the opinion of the TI, not needed went into the sack. The TI picked up a small blue book with a lock on it from my bunk. It was my diary given to me by my sister.

"Is this yours," he asked loudly so others could hear while he put his nose within an inch or two of mine, holding the diary in his outstretched arm. "Yes sir." "Why do you need a diary in the Air Force? Are you planning to write down secrets?" he asked. "No sir." "Where are you from?" "Chicago, sir." "I know that you idiot. What country are you from?" "Germany, Sir."

He asked me how old I was, what city I came from, and when I had arrived in the U.S. In a voice that everyone in the barracks could hear he said, "So what we have here is a little Nazi boy soldier from the Second World War. Were you in the Hitler Youth?" "Yes, sir." I responded truthfully. "Well young man, I'll find out just how tough you are." He moved on to other recruits, throwing my diary onto my mattress.

Basic training had all of the demeaning qualities one can imagine, and then some. The TI tried to break me, at least emotionally. He assigned me to Kitchen Patrol (KP) duty three days in a row, allowing me only two hours of sleep after twenty-two hours in the dining hall. After I spent countless hours shining my boots so they shone like a mirror, he scraped his boots over the shine, destroying it totally, and told me he thought I could do better. As he did it he looked in my eyes as if to challenge me. I smiled directly at him and said, "Yes sir. Sorry sir. I'll do better." "Are you being a smart ass?" he yelled. I maintained my smile, "No sir."

There were other tense moments, primarily because of my language difficulties. Towards the end of basic training, I had to take tests that would allow the Air Force to assign me to my next training program. During one of the tests I asked the proctor if I could request the Office of Secret Services because I spoke German. He said there was a place I could write my inquiry on the form.

As it turned out, the only careers I qualified for were cook, supply clerk, air police, or administration. I chose administration, hoping that would be the fastest way for me to improve my English. I found out that because I was not a citizen, and with my limited education, I could not qualify for the OSS, officer training, or any assignment that required being cleared for a secret security clearance.

After Basic Training, my travel papers directed me to my new duty station Bryan Air Force Base in Bryan, Texas, my new duty station. I arrived there in November 1954, and while there I took high school educational courses. I took my GED test in the spring and received my high school equivalency diploma. I had achieved my first goal in a series of educational challenges I had set for myself. The diploma would allow me to apply to colleges or universities. However, that goal was still far from my reach. Learning the Air Force's administrative procedures, filing system, and typing were the first skills I had to master if I planned on getting promoted in rank. As it turned out, being well organized came naturally and I was appreciated by my superiors.

I spent many hours in the Enlisted Men's Club learning square dancing. It was there that I met Bee, who was ten years older than I. She was a good dancer and very attractive. She worked as a saleslady in a retail store and lived with her sister whose husband was on an overseas assignment as an Air Force pilot. Bee was part of a square dance group that always came to the Club. Neither of us owned an automobile, so to date her I "rented" a car from a sergeant who lived off base. After a date, I would return the car to the sergeant who would then drive me back to my barracks. After a while this became a logistical and financial inconvenience.

Bee was very shy and seemed to have no goals of her own. Whatever I suggested that we do was always okay with her. She was totally giving, never asking, never expecting. Whatever I wanted was what she wanted. When she and I discussed my concern about not being able to satisfy a woman, she assured me that I didn't have that problem and she was happy. I didn't believe her. I was convinced she was not able to teach me or reveal to me the secrets I wanted to learn. I decided that I needed a relationship with a woman who was strong, had her own opinions, and most of all, her own set of needs and desires I needed someone to challenge me; otherwise it just felt like I was taking advantage of another human being. The relationship ended soon after I transferred to my next Air Force Base.

In the interim, I heard from Bernhard, my friend from Germany, that he and Max had made it to America. Bernhard immediately went to live in a hotel until he found a job and a place to live. Max also had a permanent immigration visa, and he brought his mother and his niece with him under a six-month visitor visa. I assumed that Max's aunt paid for the journey of all three.

On June 17, 1955, I was issued a U.S.A. Citizen Certificate, witnessed by two Air Force Sergeants who had accompanied me to Austin, Texas for the citizenship test and to witness my swearing in ceremony. My dream of becoming an American citizen became a reality and I no longer was a man without a country. While I was still living in Chicago in my one room apartment, I knew in my heart and soul that I was meant to be an American. I was, and still am, very proud of my German heritage, but I knew that if I wanted to move beyond a pre-determined future in Germany, I had to have the freedom to find myself in the U.S. I couldn't point to facts, figures or events that supported my intuitive sense, but when I first arrived in America I knew that I had arrived in the place where I belonged.

While preparing myself for citizenship I discovered the "Freedom of Speech" section of the Bill of Rights. It made me feel even more convinced that I had come to the right place. It said I had the right to speak freely and to share my feelings and thoughts. I learned only much later that I took this right too literally. However, one of the greatest compliments I have ever received from an American friend was, "Walter, with you no one has to guess how you feel, think, or where you stand. You are not afraid to speak and you speak with passion." I didn't worry about what others thought about what I said. I focused on being honest and sincere. I felt America was a place where I did not have to be afraid that something I said would be held against me or lead to persecution, imprisonment, or get me in trouble. In the early years of my U.S. citizenship I was convinced that these feelings were correct. I was still incredibly naïve.

By September 1955, I was promoted to Airman Second Class and received the Good Conduct Medal. In the same month, Lieutenant General Fred M. Dean came to the Bryan AFB to interview airmen who had volunteered for the position of personal clerical assistant to the Commander of the Flying Training Air Force, General Dissosway. General Dean explained to me that I was far too young for General Dissosway's position because he had a daughter about my age. Since the advertised position's duty station was the General's home, it wouldn't work out. However, he went on to explain that he himself had put in a request for a personal clerical assistant. He asked me if I would be interested in working for him. He explained my duties: I would be his chauffeur, driving his private car when he was not using the transportation provided by the motor-pool. I would be expected to cook his breakfast and help him cook and serve drinks when he was giving parties. I would take care of his laundry and dry cleaning, act as host to his guests and friends, and work with his private secretarial staff. The position required that I be single and available on a twenty-four hour basis. I knew that he was interviewing other airmen at other Air Force bases. However, within three weeks I was transferred to the Flying Training Air Force Headquarters in Waco, Texas to serve under General Dean. My first task was to replace my regular issued uniforms with gabardine cloth uniforms, the fabric used in uniforms worn by officers.

It was a choice assignment. I had my own apartment in Waco within walking distance of General Dean's house. Unless we were traveling, working at headquarters, or attending official military functions, I could wear civilian clothing. I was paid a housing subsistence and given a food allowance. At headquarters, I was introduced to the General's staff and his secretarial support staff. I was also given a secret clearance and a series of critical phone numbers in case I needed to reach Headquarters on behalf of General Dean.

The general was above all a gentleman and a person without prejudice. He treated everyone with respect, regardless of rank, and that quality endeared him to me immediately. I knew him during his bachelor years and there were many lady friends who often times had to be chauffeured to go shopping or taken to and from the airport. General Dean shared his house with another bachelor officer, Colonel Rector, who was with the Flying Tigers during WWII.

General Dean and I discovered a mutual admiration for the Field Marshall Erwin Rommel, one of my WWII heroes. The general indicated that Napoleon and Rommel were the world's greatest war strategists and were always studied in the War College. Since Rommel was Swabian, General Dean was interested in having me describe the Swabian character, its culture, including the village of Herrlingen where Rommel lived. We had some fascinating conversations and more than once General Dean would say, "That explains things; thank you." I think he knew Rommel better than anyone.

I had the opportunity to meet many interesting people including the General Staff of the Vietnamese Air Force. The first Indochina War had concluded and South Vietnam was a Republic. General Dean was about to entertain South Vietnam's Air Force leaders. In preparation for a major party in honor of the Vietnamese guests, the general and I spent almost a full day preparing special Vietnamese dishes and drinks. I will never forget the two of us sitting in his kitchen peeling buckets of shrimp most of which went into a dish that used lots of curry. I had never tasted curry, but I found it was delicious. In those private moments I learned a lot about the Air Force, politics, and America's relationship with Vietnam, including the influence and interests of large industrial powers in that small country.

I would go to the General's house every morning, prepare breakfast for him, and if need be, awaken both Colonel Rector and the General. The General and I would have breakfast and plan the events or assignments for the day. Sometimes the motor pool car would pick him up, leaving me free to clean the kitchen, the house, make his bed, take care of his clothing, and take care of his private car. After that, I would run errands for him, get additional assignments from the General's secretaries at headquarters, or if the General was traveling, I was free for the rest of the day. During parties at the General's house I functioned as bartender, server, and if someone needed to be taken home, as chauffer. When the General entertained his dates at the house, I acted as cook, server, and cleanup man. He would tell me when I was no longer needed and at what time they wanted breakfast.

Once again, I existed in an environment that was socially, economically, and educationally very different from the world I knew. I watched, listened, and tried to learn. While night classes were out of the question, it never occurred to me at that time to consider correspondence courses. I also had far too much fun and freedom for my age. Being in the military and living like a civilian, driving the General's car, and going places where enlisted men didn't normally go was simply too exciting to alter the pattern.

I made some very interesting observations at the social events in the General's home when people from the military, politicians, and industrialists were together and had a few drinks. I quickly realized that what I read in the newspaper was not necessarily a full and total explanation of the truth related to current events, war, or conflicts. I wasn't educated enough yet to make sense out of these contradictions, but I started to learn that I shouldn't believe everything I heard or read in the press. When I brought this up with the General he said, "Behind every story there is yet another story, and even if you put them together you will not have the full picture. Figuring out the voids in the 'picture' requires creativity."

There was a young lady working in the pharmacy that I frequented and we became friendly. We often went out for dinner, a drink, or a movie. At that time, even the military did not have cell phones, which meant I had to stay close to my phone at home. Much of our time, therefore, was spent in my apartment where she taught me some of the secrets that had eluded me for so long. With her I discovered that intimacy did not require words, but was a language of its own.

What struck me about our relationship was the absence of a commitment. It was friendship, but it was also lust without expectations. When we were together it was fun, joyful, free, and downright liberating. She was my teacher, I was the student, and we both enjoyed the curriculum. I finally learned how to love a woman. She vanished from my life as quickly as she entered, and left without saying goodbye. I had stopped for lunch at the drive-in that we frequented and was told by the car-hop that my girlfriend's husband was looking for me. My chin dropped, leaving my mouth open in a frozen and speechless moment. I hadn't known she was married. All I knew was that she was living with her parents. I went directly to the pharmacy to confront her, but the owner told me that my girlfriend's husband had just returned from Thule Air Force Base in Greenland, and they had left town. Once again, I felt uneducated because of my inability to sense dishonesty and deceit. On the other hand, I was grateful for what I had learned. I hadn't expected a commitment or a promise from her, but I had trouble with the thought that she had lied to me.

That same day, I received a long letter from Bernhard telling me about Max's situation. He described how three months before Max's mother and niece's visa expired, his aunt, our sponsor, threw all three of them out of her apartment building. When Max came home from work his mother and young niece were sitting on the sidewalk with their personal belongings. Max was forced to take three jobs in order to make enough money to send his mother and niece back to Germany before their visas expired. Bernhard went on to explain that Max had a really tough time with the situation and didn't want to get in touch with me because he was ashamed for having doubted my honesty.

To Hell and Back

In March of 1955, while I was still dating the girl from the pharmacy, I met someone new at a party in one of the local dance clubs. During the course of the evening, I learned that she lived with her mother and stepfather, attended high school, but was about to graduate. Based on our conversations I had the feeling that she was seeing someone else, but I couldn't be certain.

It wasn't very long after our first meeting when I awoke one night to find her standing by the side of my bed. It must have been past midnight. I had locked my door, but it was an easy climb onto the balcony of my two-room apartment. She explained that she had "borrowed" her stepfather's car because she wanted to see me. I discovered very quickly she wore nothing but a pair of slippers and a loose fitting dress. I saw her several times after that night but I had decided to end our relationship because I was not comfortable with her. For some reason, I just felt I couldn't trust her. Her behavior seemed strange for me and doubts started to creep in my mind as to how I am perceived by others. Was I a dumb sucker, a naïve pushover, or simply a greenhorn?

Before I had a chance to end our relationship in a gentlemanly way, she surprised me. In May of 1956 she informed me that she was pregnant. I told her I wanted to go to the doctor with her, that I would pay her medical expenses, and that I was sorry for having made her pregnant. Based on the doctor's explanation and by my calculations, it was possible that I was the father.

In the culture in which I grew up, it was the respectful and responsible act for the father to marry the woman that carries his child. He was to give the child its family name and he was to help raise the child. I was ashamed that I had brought this embarrassing event onto her and her family, as well as my own family. It didn't matter that I didn't love her in the way I imagined two people should in order to make a lifetime commitment. I was going to be a responsible adult, father, and husband. I immediately proposed that we get married, a suggestion she received happily. Although she was not a very religious person, we went to the minister of the local lutheran church to which I belonged. We explained that we wanted, and needed, to get married. Together with the pastor, we set the wedding date for June.

What amazed me was how my future wife managed the situation. She wasn't embarrassed, there were no feelings of shame, and there was no concern about whether we had the means and fortitude to raise a child. The fact that she would receive part of my Air Force salary was all the security she was concerned about. We had no furniture, household goods, or possessions. It was clear to me that I had to immediately buy a car to have transportation for my family. Through a friend, who was an auto mechanic, I bought a 1949 Chevrolet convertible and had a 1954 engine installed. It was a sharp looking car with chrome embellishments and white sidewall tires.

I had to inform General Dean about the latest developments. Working for him required that I be single and without family responsibilities. I arranged to discuss my situation with him after one of our morning breakfast sessions. To this day, I remember sitting in his living room on Polynesian bamboo furniture with thick beige cushions with a green leaf pattern. I apologized for bothering him with my personal situation. He was very understanding and asked to be briefed on what happened. I acknowledged that being married eliminated the possibility of continuing to work for him. He asked me whether I was sure I wanted to get married, explaining that I could take responsibility for the child without getting married. I wasn't sure that I fully understood what he was trying to tell me, but I assured him that I wanted to do the responsible thing. He then asked me a question that surprised me, "Are you sure that you are the father of this child?" I had no idea how to answer that question. I assumed that the expecting mother would know who fathered the child and she told me it was me. I lied, "Yes, I'm sure." I think I wanted it to be true even though I had doubts given her tendency to lie and the fact that I thought she was seeing someone else.

"Do you know to which Air Base you want to be assigned?" asked the General. I had no idea, but she wanted to be reasonably close to her family. The General arranged my new assignment at Vance Air Force Base in Enid, Oklahoma. The base was within the Flying Training Air Force (FTAF) command.

My next difficult task was to write to my parents. I couldn't tell them that we were in love because at the time of conception it was just friendly sex. I didn't want to tell them that she lied to me about her age. It was in the doctor's office that I discovered she was six months shy of being seventeen, and not eighteen as she told me. For me it didn't matter. All that was important was that we needed to be adult, loving, and create a happy world for the baby. One troubling aspect of her home life revealed itself when she and I went with her mother to visit her grandmother in Texas. Her mother asked me if I had a problem with her spending time with another man besides her husband. I avoided responding to the question. While my future wife and I were visiting with her grandmother, her mother went for her rendezvous with this man. Later we met up with the two lovers at a bar. They asked me if I would have trouble keeping the secret to myself. I assured them I was not going to talk about it. I did have trouble with the affair, however, because I felt my future mother-in-law set a very bad example for her daughter. I decided I needed to take my wife away from all of that.

On the night before our wedding I discovered I was about to make an enormous mistake. She had already lied to me about her age and she generally treated me badly and with disrespect. I discounted it, however, blaming the pregnancy. The wedding was to take place in the living room of the pastor and I had made arrangements for Bernhard to be my best man. Bernhard flew in from Chicago for the occasion and was staying in my apartment. The evening before the wedding I stopped at my bride's house to see her. Her mother explained that she was not home, and she didn't know where her daughter was or when she would return. The conversation didn't feel genuine, so I parked my car in the parking lot across the street where I could see the comings and goings at her home. Around midnight the police started to drive around the parking lot, so I decided to leave my car and walk over to her house. I hid in the grass by the side of the house. A car drove up around three in the morning. She stepped out of the car and a young man walked her to the front door. They stepped inside the living room and I rushed in behind them. I grabbed the man by his neck and literally lifted him from the floor, pressing him against the wall. I screamed something at him, but all I remember is that I was outraged and out of control. "Anger will kill you," came my inner voice, and I dropped him to the floor and walked away. She started to scream. Her mother came from the bedroom and told the young man to leave.

Then my bride-to-be directed her anger at me for laying in wait and for checking up on her. She volunteered that the two of them had sex and she emphasized that they enjoyed it. I went home with tears streaming down my face and with feelings of fear, helplessness, and total confusion. I realized I had just opened the door to hell and seen a glimpse of my future. However, for me the wedding had to take place because of the baby, and at the previously agreed upon hour my bride, her mother, and the bridesmaid showed up at the Pastor's house. After I told him about the night before, Bernhard suggested we skip the event. Nevertheless, we showed up and the wedding took place. We went to a motel for the first night and I was not in the mood to consummate the marriage. She, on the other hand, acted as if nothing had happened and suggested that sex would make me feel better.

We moved to Enid, Oklahoma, where I was assigned to the pilot training administration office. We lived in a trailer away from the airbase, and in order to make ends meet I worked nights and weekends at a gas station. One day, we received a food basket from the Red Cross. I took the basket back to them and said that I could only accept their food if they would let me work for it. I cleaned the Red Cross offices every Saturday afternoon from July 1956 to January 1957. I was grateful yet ashamed for having to take their help.

I also started to teach ballroom dancing on Saturday nights at the Officer's Club. The money from giving dance lessons improved our financial situation. Dancing was in my blood I was good at it and my experience from competitive dancing in Germany provided me with an advantage. Ballroom dancing allowed me to transform myself into a free-moving body flowing with the rhythm of the music. It also allowed me to escape from the reality of my painful marriage. It was as if weights were lifted from my shoulders when I danced. There were no worries, no concerns, nothing else on my mind except letting the music move through my body and have it express its form.

Even though my marriage did not have the passionate and romantic beginning that I imagined other married couples enjoyed, my wife and I managed our first months of marriage without too much tension. I had become friends with Lieutenant Larry Beede, one of the pilot trainees in my squadron. Larry and his wife Beth invited us on many occasions to their apartment for Saturday night dinners and table games. Unfortunately, our home was a very small trailer and not adequate for entertaining. Having a social life, however, was extremely beneficial for my wife and me. It gave me an introduction to marriage among young educated adults. Larry and Beth were college educated, creative, and intellectually well-rounded. Both of them studied at The School of the American Art Institute in Chicago. Besides being husband and wife, they were each other's best friend. Seeing Larry and Beth being affectionate with each other, working together in the kitchen, and doing silk-designs and printing together gave me a whole new understanding of a relationship between a man and a woman. They were open and honest, and shared their feelings of joy and pain. It was so different from anything I knew. I realized they had a marriage, a partnership, and a deep friendship between them.

With Larry and Beth as role models, I found it very easy to develop feelings of love and affection for my wife. I was convinced we could have a life with warmth and genuineness. I envisioned myself being a husband like Larry, transforming myself into an educated, loving, equality-oriented, creative, and passionate man. My wife was carrying the seed of our family and I was convinced we could create such a family. I remember the many long hours of conversation we had with Larry and Beth; talking about their educational experiences, their feelings for each other, and the things they enjoyed. They were both artists, romantics, and fun-loving people. I learned there was more to a relationship than making money. There was the sharing of feelings and struggles, fun things to do together, and in my case, there was always the love of dancing to share.

On January 11, 1957, our son Robert Walter Kroner was born. The birth went well and mother and baby were healthy. When Robert's mother returned from the hospital, my commanding officer gave me a work schedule that allowed me to take care of them both. Four weeks after Robert was born, I was given orders to transfer to Misawa Air Force Base in Japan. Enlisted men could not take their families to Japan at that time because of the tense situation in Korea. Suddenly, we had to face a new set of problems. My wife did not want to stay in Enid where she didn't know anyone.

I had saved enough money by then so that Robert and his mother could fly to Germany to live with my parents. My plan was that after my tour of duty was over in Japan, I would re-enlist in the Air Force with the condition that I be stationed in Germany. The plans were finalized between everyone involved, and February 17, 1957 was set as my departure date for Japan. As soon as my wife received her passport she was to take the money from our bank account and buy airline tickets to Germany. I took my remaining vacation time and returned to Texas to spend the last four weeks with my small family. We decided to visit Robert's great-grandmother to show him off.

We drove our 1949 Chevrolet Convertible and on the way we picked up two young men who were hitchhiking. As I was traveling about eighty miles per hour, a woman drove her car out of a corn field and sped across the road directly in front of us. There was no intersection anywhere in sight. I swerved to avoid a collision, but it was too late and the impact pushed the woman's car into the adjacent corn field. One of the hitchhikers was in the front passenger seat, the other directly behind him. My wife was in the seat behind me and Robert was in a bassinet between the two rear passengers. Upon impact the front passenger was thrown out of the car, as was the hitchhiker in the back. Robert was thrown against the rear door that somehow had closed after the passenger was thrown out. Other than a few scratches, he had no apparent injuries. The car, however, was a total wreck. I was grateful that I had learned defensive driving while still in Germany. I believe it saved our lives.

Before I left for Japan, we replaced our car with a brand new Dodge, which I paid for in cash. My wife was to sell it when she was ready to buy the tickets for Germany. For some reason, I do not have any memory of my departure or my travel from Texas to Oakland, California, or from there to Japan. My wife and I were preoccupied with settling the insurance matters from the car accident and making arrangements for storing our personal things. I remember endless discussions about her going to Germany and reassuring her that my family would make her feel welcome. I cannot recall a romantic last dinner, if there was one. I don't remember a long walk in the Brazos River Park, something we often did. We stayed with my in-laws and that is all I remember about my last days before going to Japan. I normally have a memory like an elephant, and this blank period in my memory has always disturbed me.

I ended up at Clark Air Force Base, in Oakland, waiting for transport to Japan. The waiting was endless and to forestall the boredom I learned how to play blackjack. Unfortunately, I didn't learn very well and I lost most of my money, arriving in Japan with very little cash. On the long flight to Japan we stopped at Wake Island before continuing on to our final destination.

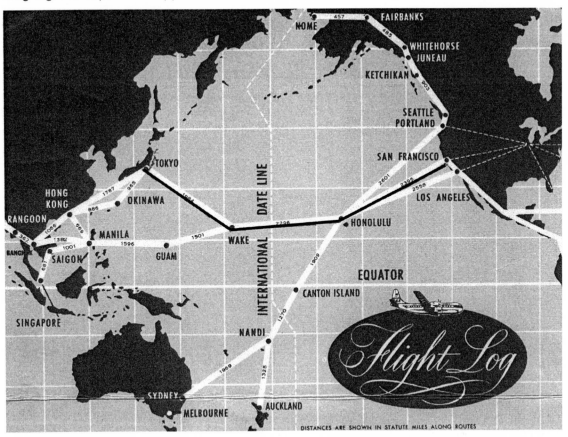

DISTANCES ARE SHOWN IN STATUTE MILES ALONG ROUTES

Cigarettes were given away free by the USO and I started to smoke. It calmed my nerves and eased the worrying about my family.

By the first of March 1957, I was at Misawa Air Base, Japan, where I worked as an administrative clerk with the 39th Air Division. I was surprised when there wasn't a single letter or postcard from my wife waiting for me. I wrote home at least twice a week and told my wife how much her letters would mean to me. I was going crazy, but calling home from Japan was not possible, at least not for me. At the end of April I received my first letter from her. She had found an apartment and had moved our furnishings. She kept our car, and Robert and she were getting medical care at the air force base. She said that she was getting her regular monthly dependent checks from the Air Force and everything was okay. The news about Robert was that everything was fine. I wished there had been pictures. She told me the trip to Germany was off because she was not comfortable with going to a strange country, staying with a strange family, and not knowing the German language. There was no explanation why she hadn't written earlier. It was a report, not a love letter. I could understand her feelings about Germany and realized I should have given the idea more thought. I was finally able to answer my parents question, "Where are they?" After they had waited almost four months for my wife and child, I had to tell them they weren't coming.

Work at the office of the 39th Air Division was very interesting, but somewhat confusing because of the difference between Air Force regulations regarding filing correspondence and the system the office was using to track correspondence. When I first arrived, Major Baker had a terrible time obtaining copies of messages, letters, and even confidential correspondence from the chief clerk. Since I was supposed to take over the chief clerk's position, I set out designing a tracer system for filing and keeping track of all correspondence for Major Baker's office operation. When I thought I had it designed for all possible eventualities, I presented it to Major Baker. He liked it and ordered it instituted immediately.

With the exception of the technical instructor in basic training, I had not encountered prejudice or discrimination against me as a foreigner or former Hitler Youth member. During my time with General Dean I felt that he was genuinely interested in Germany, the Hitler Youth, and I knew he found General Rommel fascinating. However, I learned something interesting in Japan. Two officers in my squadron had encountered young boys from the Hitler Youth during WWII. Both of the officers were shot down over Germany. They had been briefed about the German military, the SS, and the Hitler Youth. I remember that both of them agreed

Airman 1st Class Walter Kroner, 1957.

they were most afraid of the Hitler Youth - even more than the SS - because of their fanaticism about wanting to be heroes. I understood why they felt that way and I was glad their capture had occurred without bloodshed. I would have understood if these men showed animosity toward me; but they didn't.

My personal life was hell. In the year that I was stationed in Japan, my wife only wrote to me three times. I wrote to her mother and the bad news in my mother-in-law's letters made my life a nightmare. Her mother reported that sometimes my wife would leave Robert with her and she wouldn't return for days, or sometimes weeks. When she came back she removed Robert from my in-law's home without a thank you. I went to the base chaplain and inquired whether there was anything he could do because I was seriously concerned about the well-being of my son. The chaplain wrote to my wife, but he did not get a response. I tried the Red Cross on our base and asked if they could make inquiries with the Red Cross in Texas. They reported that they had found Robert abandoned with a babysitter, in deplorable conditions, and they had taken Robert to my mother-in-law. This pattern repeated itself several times. The Red Cross reported that each time my wife would reappear, take Robert from her mother, and then disappear again. The Red Cross was powerless. The Air Force chaplain in Japan was absolutely useless. I gave him the address of my pastor back home, but he never communicated with him. I gave the chaplain the address of a Red Cross worker in Texas, but he never communicated with them either.

I finally contacted my pastor myself and sought his help. I hoped that he could investigate Robert's conditions, perhaps talk with my wife, and just help me in any way he could. At first, he couldn't locate my wife as she rarely was at her apartment. The same observation was made by the Red Cross. I asked my pastor to write a letter explaining the situation at home to my commander so I could get an emergency leave to resolve my family problems. At one point I went to my commander directly to ask for an emergency leave to take care of my son. I explained the situation to him and showed him all of the correspondence. This triggered a few phone calls to confirm things with the chaplain and the Red Cross. I was doing everything that I had been taught to do in a family emergency. After he completed the phone calls and while I was standing in front of the commander's desk, I could feel myself becoming nervous, angry, tense, and tight as a bowstring. I will never forget the next moment. The captain leaned back in his chair, lit a cigar, and said, "Kroner. Face it. You're married to a fucking whore and ...."

Without wanting to hear the rest of what he had to say I flew over his desk, grabbed his neck with both hands, knocking him and his chair backwards onto the floor. I could feel my shoes knocking things off his desk as I landed on top of him with both of my hands on his throat. Suddenly I froze. He was still in his chair and we both were glaring at each other. I pulled my hands from his neck and raised them up as if I were a captured soldier. I stood up, straddling him, and then slowly stepping backwards. I came to attention, "Sorry Sir," I saluted and left the office. I went straight to the barracks to wait for the military police to come and arrest me.

"Fear will kill you." I realized that I had just ruined my life, for at least several years, and would probably get a dishonorable discharge. By lunch time, the military police had not shown up, so I went to the office where I worked to see my supervising officer, Major Baker. I shared with him the entire sequence of events in every detail; from not getting any mail, to hearing about the danger my son was in, to the erratic behavior of my wife, to my wife being called a whore, ending with my attack on the captain.

"YOU DID WHAT?" screamed the Major as he jumped out of his chair and closed the door to his office. "I lost my temper sir when he called my wife a "fucking whore." I only knocked him over in his chair, with my hands on his neck. I didn't hurt him, I just embarrassed him." "You attacked him Kroner! Did the captain call the military police?" "I don't know," I said.

The major picked up the phone and called the military police to inquire whether they received a report from my captain. There was no report as of noon. The major then called the captain and I listened to his portion of the conversation. The major said, "I understand Airman Kroner came to your office asking for help related to his family. Is that correct?" ---- "Did you call his wife a fucking whore?" ---- "Yes, I understand all of that. I asked you if you called his wife a fucking whore?"

There was a very long pause, and while I could hear the captain's voice, I could not make out what he was saying. The major asked, "Are you going to file charges against Airman Kroner?" There was a seemingly never ending pause. "Do you have a problem giving Airman Kroner a three-day pass?" the major asked. Another long pause.

The major hung up the phone and turned to me, "Kroner, I want you to go to your squadron's office and pick up a three-day pass. The Captain will leave it with the clerk." "Thank you sir." I continued, "Is there a possibility of getting an emergency leave for one or two weeks so I can go home and at least take care of my son?" "I don't know Kroner. Right now all I can tell you is to get away from the base, stay away from the bars, and don't get drunk. I suggest you go to the shore." He was a man of few words, somewhat like Vater.

The shore was only three miles away from the Air Base. I took the three-day pass and went into Misawa to sell my watch and a ring at the pawn shop. I took what cash I had hidden in my room and packed my bag to leave the base. Instead of the shore, I went to Aomori by train where some friends and I had been before. I made a decision on the train, amidst chickens in cages and people cooking things in the train car. I sat across the aisle from a goat tied to a rope, held by a Japanese passenger. Since Aomori had a harbor for ocean-going vessels, I decided to see if I could work my way to the States on a ship across the Pacific. I fully intended to go AWOL. I was going home to take care of Robert no matter what the consequences. I had tried all of the avenues open to me with zero results.

As I approached what I assumed was the Harbormaster's shed, two military and one Japanese policeman came up behind me wanting to know what I was doing. After I tried to talk my way out of the situation, they took my identification, three-day pass, put me in a jeep, and took me to their station nearby. I was placed in a cage while one of the MP's made a phone call. He came back and asked me questions a few times, including the names of my squadron commander and the officer I worked for. It was beginning to get dark when the MP took me from the cage into his office. "Major Baker wants to speak with you," he said and he handed me the phone.

"Kroner, I am going to ask you a few questions and I want you to tell me the truth. If you so much as attempt to lie to me, I'll hang up the phone and let the military police handle this. Is that understood?" he asked. "Yes Sir," I replied. Essentially, he wanted to know what I was doing in Aomori and whether or not I was trying to go on a ship to go stateside. I told him that I was and I felt not only sorry for trying, I felt stupid. He explained to me that there were no ships going from Aomori to the States.

"Kroner, I am trying to help you. I know you are upset and feel trapped like a caged animal, but for me to help you I need your help." He wanted to know if he could arrange for the MP's to find me a place to stay for two nights, and whether I would come back to the base by Sunday. I assured him that I would follow his command. I was to show up for work Monday morning and we would talk some more. He told me that the only reason he was doing this for me was that he didn't want to lose me. "You are the best clerk that ever worked for me." I thanked him and apologized for all the trouble I was causing. His final question was, "Kroner, can I trust you that you will not pull another stupid move?"

I assured him that I would no longer be a burden to him. The MP's took me to an inn that was really nice. For two days, I enjoyed a beautiful yet simple room, sleeping on a simple woven tatami with a few blankets and pillows, surrounded by moveable shoji screens that opened to a beautiful Japanese garden. The innkeeper provided tea and some type of bread and I had my own reading material. In the evening, a young lady dressed in a kimono removed the lid from the floor and prepared a fire in a pit. When the flames had died down she placed a perforated cover over the opening and I could feel the warmth of the coals. The landscape around the room was an art form with sculptured sand surfaces, rock gardens, small bushes, and a pond containing huge goldfish. I thought I had gone to heaven compared to the hell I had been in for the last six months. I had reached the end of my rope and it was clear to me that I could not manage my affairs alone. I was once again grateful that there were people who, for reasons I couldn't explain, were willing to do things for me that were out of the ordinary, especially when they had no obligation to do what they did. I was not in control of myself. I was taking without thinking, and it was the "giving" of my immediate officers that saved me. Mama-san, the inn hostess, came to fold back the blankets and she asked me if I wanted a "geisha." I smiled and said in Japanese, "No thank you."

I reported to my workstation at the office earlier than normal that Monday. Major Baker was already there and he told me he was calling a meeting of everyone involved with my situation to see what could be done on my behalf. I knew he did not have to do that. I knew that technically it was my squadron commander's responsibility, and I was lucky that Major Baker had taken an interest in me. I trusted him. He assured me that he would stay with the situation, to keep my nose perfectly clean.

I spent many hours in the Airman's Club listening to the music and working with the USO hostess on various programs. It took my mind off my problems. A group of airmen and I acted as hosts for a Christmas party given to the children in a Japanese orphanage. At the end of December 1957, I received a letter from my pastor, which was certified by a Notary Public. The letter stated that my wife had been arrested on charges of prostitution, drug possession, passing bad checks, abandonment of our child, and that Robert had been placed in the custody of my mother-in-law. My wife was legally prevented from taking our child away from her mother. I took the letter to Major Baker, and after he read it two or three times he said, "Kroner. I'll get you home."

The Japanese secretaries in our office knew about my family situation. They knew about my two-in-the-morning attempts to call stateside to reach my mother-in-law. One of them felt sorry for me and introduced me to another Japanese woman who worked on the Air Force Base. Another married airman from my squadron and I went to dinner with these two women. It must have been the most boring time they had ever spent with two men. We talked about our families, my son, our wives, home, and so and on. There was nothing in any way, shape or form sexual about the relationship, but I have to admit that my female companion was one of the most gracious, gentle, and understanding people I have ever met. My airman friend and I had dinner with them at least four or five times. It helped make the pain go away.

In January of 1958, eight months before my normal discharge date from the Air Force, I was given an honorable discharge under hardship conditions. Before I actually got my official discharge papers and discharge money, I went to the base bank to arrange for money to be wired from my stateside bank account to the base bank. I had no idea how long it would be before I would receive my discharge money. A message from my bank in Texas arrived that indicated all of the money had been withdrawn by my wife. When I left for Japan, in 1957, we had six-thousand dollars in our account (enough to buy three new cars), money that my wife really didn't need since she had her regular monthly income from her dependent check. I took the cheapest way back to Texas from Oakland using my discharge money. The train ride took about two days and while the scenery was certainly beautiful I could not enjoy it. The uncertainty that awaited me was all-consuming, and I had trouble thinking about anything else. The train fare may have been cheap, but the boredom cost me plenty in terms of eating and drinking during the two-day trip. I should have flown to Dallas.

I had informed my mother-in-law that I was on my way back and told her when I expected to arrive in Dallas. As I was about to step off the train I found myself looking straight at my wife, who was all smiles. There was no apologetic look, no externally observable posture of sorrow; just a happy face as if nothing unusual had happened. I didn't know what to do, so I just said hello, leaving the hugs and kisses for another time. From the Dallas train station we took the Greyhound bus south to Waco. On the bus ride, I didn't want to talk. The topics, the questions, and the issues were too personal to take place in a public conveyance. She wanted to caress, kiss, and play as if nothing had happened in the past year. I told her several times, "When we are in a position to talk I want to hear nothing but the truth, no lies, no playing games. I am prepared to hear it all, no matter how bad." She promised she would tell me everything.

I assured her that my imagination had run wild trying to analyze how bad things had gotten. I told here there was nothing she could tell me that would surprise me, or embarrass me, and that she needed to tell me everything. I mentioned to her that I couldn't get any money from our bank for the trip, and I wanted to know where the money went. That was when she told me we didn't have any money. I asked her how she obtained money for the bus to Dallas. She said that she had gone into a bar and "earned" twenty-five dollars for the trip. It was then I realized I was not prepared for that kind of honesty, for that directness, and for that shame. Thank God the bus stopped at Hillsboro; I needed to get some fresh air.

When the bus parked to let off passengers and take on new ones, I was surprised to see my father-in-law walking alongside the bus looking through the bus windows. It turned out he was looking for me. When he saw his step-daughter sitting next to me he turned as red as a Coca Cola sign and stormed onto the bus. He told us he would drive us himself. On the way he told me that the Health Department was looking for my wife because she might have a venereal disease. He wanted to make sure that we didn't have sex before she went to the Health Department.

Our first stop, however, was at the courthouse where my wife had to make an appearance. Robert, in my mother-in-law's arms, was waiting for us and at least outwardly he looked like a healthy boy. He reached his arms towards me so I could hold him. As I held him, I wished I could tell him how much I wanted to be with him and that I was sorry he had suffered. He was only one year old. As I turned so Robert faced his mother, his smile disappeared. As she held out her hands to take Robert from me, he screamed and cried, his body trembled, his feet kicked, and his arms were uncontrollable. I had never witnessed a child react in fear of his mother. He screamed as if he was in severe pain, and I had to walk away from everyone and calm him down by talking with him and bouncing him in my arms. I tried the most soothing voice I could create and held his cheeks close to mine. I felt like screaming at my wife, "What in God's name have you done to him?"

My mother-in-law made arrangements for a furnished apartment by paying the deposit and the first month's rent. She said she hoped we could pay the following months' rent ourselves. She gave me the key to the above-the-garage apartment and promised to bring Robert to us when we had settled our affairs at the courthouse and at the Health Department.

At the Health Department, my wife was tested for a venereal disease and received treatment. The doctor explained that she was accused of giving the disease to a man with whom she had a sexual relationship. The doctor insisted that I receive the same shots as a precaution. I told him I had no intention of having sex with her. The doctor said, "As a precaution I must insist that you take the shots."

I struggled with the doctor's recommendation as a matter of principal. I was not going to sleep with her and, therefore, I didn't need the shots. It was almost a matter of proving my capacity to resist my wife's sexuality. I would have been ashamed and devastated if I had been accused of the same thing, but it didn't seem to bother her at all. I could feel the stress building in my gut and I could feel anger forming inside of me. I felt ashamed, embarrassed, and demeaned to be in such a situation. The doctor, very patient and understanding, finally convinced me to take the shot as a safety precaution.

When we arrived at the apartment, I discovered that our 1957 Dodge, all of our furnishings, including our hi-fi set, and the dancing school music equipment had been turned into cash in order to pay for my wife's drug habit and lifestyle. She said that some of the money was taken by her pimp. She had even converted my clothing into cash. I only had the civilian clothing I had brought with me from Japan. The final blow was when I found out we had more than six-thousand dollars in debts, and neither of us was gainfully employed.

This short, yet painful part of my life happened because my wife was too young, too immature, and as ill-prepared for marriage as I was to immigrate. She got in with the wrong crowd and into drugs. She didn't have a very good role model in her mother, and I should have skipped the wedding as Bernhard suggested. I looked at my wife, the mother of my child, speaking of working for a pimp as an accomplishment. What had I done? What can I do? Where do I go from here?

I had to find a solution, I had to think of Robert, and I had to think of tomorrow. No one on my father's or mother's side of the family had ever been divorced. Divorce was considered a shameful event. I knew nothing about failed marriages except the disaster that I lived through. I just could not walk out on her and end the marriage. I felt I had to try to save it, if for no other reason but Robert.

The first step for me was to find a job. I had to support my family, pay off the large debt, and buy some clothing for myself. I found a job with the Dictaphone Corporation as a service technician working out of the Waco branch office. It was not very long before I experienced the full force of prejudice and discrimination. My boss, the sales manager for Dictaphone in Waco, had no difficulty with using the "N" word in referring to black people. What hurt was that he made it clear to me that foreigners were no different. When I told him that I was a foreigner, he dismissed it by saying: "Yeah, but you are a U.S. citizen." It hurt to be treated as if I was something less than human. My sympathies for Jews, Gypsies, and non-Aryans who had suffered in WWII increased even more.

Then one of our Dictaphone customers asked my boss to send an "American" to service his machine. I had maintained the Dictaphones at the Dr. Pepper offices before, and my German-accented English must have bothered the manager there. There wasn't anyone else my boss could send on the service call since I was the only serviceman in the office, so I was told to go. The Dr. Pepper office still had the old wax cylinder recorders and transcribers. I guessed they were too cheap, or frugal, to buy the highly improved belt-type electronic Dictaphone equipment. The secretary pointed out the machine that needed to be repaired and by the time the manager stormed into his office I already had the machine disassembled. "What in the hell are you doing here?" he yelled. "I am repairing your machine, sir." "I hate you goddamn Germans and…" he pulled up his trousers exposing an artificial leg "…this is why. Get out," he screamed.

I put my tools back into my tool box, put on my jacket, and said, "If you lost your leg in the war, I am sorry. And even though I could be angry at you, I am not. Why should I be angry? Because some American GI's in a jeep ran my grandfather off the road, causing his subsequent death. That was after the war. Do I blame you? No. Do I blame America? No. If I did, I wouldn't have come to America." I paused. He didn't say anything so I continued. "You sir are lucky that you were born in the United States. I am an American by choice."

As I walked out of the door, I sensed a pattern in my life. I walked out of Premco Manufacturing in Chicago, leaving my boss hanging with a disassembled machine. Now I had left a client with a disassembled wax-cylinder voice recording machine. I hated discrimination and the labeling of people. I saw what happened in Germany when no one spoke up against the hatred and discrimination. I went back to my office and reported the incident to my boss. I added, "He hates Germans as much as you do." With that I went home, since it was near the end of the day. The next day the big boss from Dallas, the Technical Manager, came to fix the Dr. Pepper machine. Afterwards, he, the Branch sales manager, and I had a long talk. I was treated much better from then on. A few days later the Dr. Pepper manager delivered a case of soda to the Dictaphone office with a card addressed to me, apologizing for his behavior. Evidently all was not lost in his case.

My wife and I went to a marriage counselor each week for several months. In one of the individual sessions, the counselor asked me, "How is it that after all your wife did, you still want to stay married to her?" "I have to try for Robert's sake," I said. Eventually, I realized that in order to forgive all that had happened I would have to forget all that had taken place, and I knew I could never forget what she had done to Robert.

The real surprise, however, occured when I filed for divorce. I asked for full custody of Robert. My attorney told me not to get my hopes up because no man in Texas had ever received sole custody of his child. He explained that it was common practice for the mother to get full custody. My wife did not contest the issue and in the divorce settlement it was stated that I had sole custody of Robert. I did not want any form of child support and I wanted sole responsibility for him. After the newness of the divorce had worn off, I realized that she never did want our child. I was responsible for all of the debts she had run up, but at least I was free to once again start again; free to float on the river of life.

Two of my friends were a young German couple, Helga and Walter Seeger. Helga's parents, the Thomases, offered me and Robert room and board. Robert and I had a room large enough for both of us. Frau Thomas cooked for us and she took care of Robert during the day when I was at work. It was a perfect arrangement because I didn't have to move Robert back and forth from our home to a babysitter. In the beginning, it was very hard because Robert was traumatized when he was left alone with a woman. Before my divorce, I had spoken with one of the neighbors where my wife had lived, and they told me they had witnessed her physically abusing him. I also spoke with the Red Cross workers who had found Robert abandoned numerous times, and they told me about the unbelievable conditions from which they had rescued him. When I presented Robert's history to therapists, doctors, and family counselors, they all commented that Robert appeared to be emotionally and physically abused. The abuse was inflicted not only by his mother, it turned out, but also by her friends and pimp.

While I was in Japan, Robert's mother had total freedom, plenty of money, new furniture, and a new car that allowed her to have a good time. The only responsibility she had was for our son, and she abandoned him. Before my marriage, I too had plenty of freedom, my own place, and a car, and my only responsibility was to the military. I had, however, an excellent upbringing and role models in my parents, relatives, and friends. What we both lacked was a way to tell the difference between people with positive potential and people with too many liabilities. Neither of us ever thought or talked about consequences. We never asked the question, "what if?" We both were blinded by the fun and games of life and the pleasure of the moment without a thought of tomorrow. In my relationship with her, I had focused on the sex, never considering

172

any other human qualities except being honest - which she was not. I had made a big mistake. I began to fully realize the importance of having family and friends who could give me guidance, or at the very least answer the questions that swirled in my brain.

Some good things came from those three years of hell. I learned what was important to me in a relationship. Being honorable, kind, honest, and open mattered immensely. Education and having a love for learning also mattered. Economic stability and security were paramount. Finally, the love of family and family history should never be compromised.

I still had concerns. My feelings toward and about women remained unchanged; I continued to admire the gender differences. It was my views on sex and intimacy that I began to question. I began to wonder if I placed too much importance on the quality of a sexual relationship to the point where it blinded me from seeing other qualities or noticing potential problems. I didn't know what to do with that concern and I didn't know where to turn for counseling and advice. I had to put that kind of question aside for a while, however, until I could be financially secure.

Starting Over

A new phase of my life began. The river of my life was free once again to move me towards my future. The falls, chasms, barriers, and dams that controlled the free flow of my river were in the past. My present included the challenge of balancing single parenthood with my job as a Dictaphone service technician. I had a service territory of nine-hundred square miles, which required a great deal of traveling. I also needed to increase my monthly income to pay the outstanding debts from my failed marriage. I began by offering ballroom dancing lessons at the local YWCA, and private lessons in people's homes. The Thomases were a very understanding couple and made it possible for me to be away at the dance studio at least three evenings during the week. Fridays and weekends were reserved for Robert and me. Frau Thomas was a wonderful, loving surrogate grandmother, capable of giving love and discipline to Robert, but he remained fearful of strangers, particularly women. Sitting in church, it was only natural for others, particularly women, to reach out to Robert or offer to hold him. His screams invariably stopped that from happening.

Towards the end of 1958, Frau Thomas' health prevented her from giving as much energy as Robert and I required, and they suggested that I find another place to live. I was convinced that a similar arrangement was critical for Robert's sake. I had met a young lady, Donna, in the medical record section of the local hospital when I was servicing their Dictaphone equipment. She suggested that I might want to join her church, which I did. Donna and I went steady and when it became known that I needed to find a new place for Robert and me, one of the members of the congregation offered us room and board. This arrangement lasted as long as my friendship with Donna continued. Once it became obvious that Donna and I were not going to be married, I was asked to find a new place once again. In the summer of 1959, a young couple from my dancing class contacted one of their relatives on my behalf. This elderly couple gave us room and board and indicated that they would be glad to babysit evenings if I wanted to take night classes at the University. This arrangement turned out to be perfect.

As a veteran, I qualified for the GI bill, which included getting tuition support. In the summer of 1959, I started my university education by taking summer evening classes at Baylor University in Waco. Initial courses included Physics, American History, and English. Baylor offered a series of tests to help students select appropriate majors. What surprised me was that both engineering physics and theater arts were fields for which I seemed to be well suited. In the beginning, it didn't matter because there were so many things I had to study based on graduation requirements. It had been over fifteen years since I first became interested in a university education. Until 1959 that goal had been unreachable because of my parents, the War, and life's twists and turns. I interacted with Baylor University students at church and I began to see what a life filled with knowledge and critical views might be like. I could sense that a university would be a place where my questions and curiosity would not be tabled, pushed aside, or remain unanswered. I had no understanding of the American educational system; terms like classes and sections, curriculums, papers, labs, and finals, just to mention a few, were very strange and unfamiliar to me. I decided that since I had come this far, I could go further.

The dance studio became an economic success, at least economically, and I felt privileged that I could teach some highly respected community leaders through my private classes. As a Dictaphone service technician, I had the opportunity to meet doctors, dentists, psychologists, and their staff. This exposure in itself was educational and I had the sense that some of them took an interest in me and my progress at Baylor. There was one woman, Miss Rose, who was in charge of all the legal staff in a large attorney's office. She was a beautiful, statuesque, classy looking lady with gray hair. She was well educated and reminded me of Frau Unkauf. Miss Rose took a genuine and caring interest in my work, my education, and Robert. We developed a strong friendship that time never erased.

In January of 1959, I received a call from Mr. Morris Maupin who was working on his doctoral thesis in the Baylor University Drama Department. He asked me if I was interested in doing the choreography for a musical he was creating as part of his dissertation. The musical would be performed at the Waco Civic Theater in the summer of 1959. He also told me that most of the dances would be to the music of West Side Story. I agreed to be the choreographer, not because I had ever choreographed anything, but simply because I believed I could do it. I didn't tell Morris that I had no experience in choreography, especially since he told me that he had heard a lot of good things about my dancing school and had actually watched me teaching some classes. If he saw a connection between my ability to teach ballroom dancing and modern jazz, I wasn't going to argue.

I had not been to New York City to see West Side Story. However, I immediately bought several LP records of West Side Story, and based on the lyrics and music I started to choreograph. Try-outs for dancers took place at the Waco Civic Theater, and that is when I recognized a young woman whom I had seen at a church youth group gathering. She had studied modern dance and certainly had the abilities I was looking for in a dancer. I remembered her and her two sisters because some of my friends had tried to arrange for me to date one of them. From those discussions, I knew that she was the daughter of a highly respected family in Waco. I declined the matchmaking attempt because I felt inadequate to socialize with upper society in Waco. Mutter's words, "Remember where you belong," were etched in my mind.

These insecure feelings went away when I was in the position of a choreographer and she was one of the dancers. I thought I could get acquainted with her by suggesting Sunday afternoon rehearsals with picnics afterwards at the community swimming pool. She volunteered to organize these Sunday afternoon social events and that is how we started to converse. I made attempts to get a date, but was given repeated excuses I soon found out she was dating a young airman from her church group.

There were six performances of "Party Tonight," staged by Morris Maupin and choreographed by 'Wally' Kroner. Judging by the press articles, it was a huge success. I was finally successful after more than ten attempts to get the young dancer to say yes to a dinner date. After that we began to date regularly. She was a Baylor student, and during that summer she studied at the College of William and Mary in Williamsburg, Virginia. I wrote to her every day, sought her advice on what color to paint my Volkswagen Karmann Ghia, and shared my feelings with her. I knew her father because I serviced the Dictaphone at his office. I didn't meet her mother until the day mother and daughter returned from summer school.

I had fallen in love with her and every waking hour I was consumed with our relationship. She was unlike any other young woman that I had known or dated. She was quiet and reflective, curious but not very revealing. We agreed on the value of family, honesty, and being self-sufficient. Periodically she and Robert would meet me after class, and that is when I discovered a new aspect of male-female relationships. As I talked with other students and made plans to study with them for tests she bombarded me with questions. It took me a little while to understand that her questioning were not related to my studyies. I had to develop a better understanding about jealousy. Thereafter she made sure that all my classmates knew, particularly the females, that I had been married and that Robert was my son.

Each day after her last class at Baylor, she picked up Robert from my landlady and took him to her house. We would meet there, eat supper at times, and spend the evening together. This ritual continued throughout the fall semester. Robert and I were welcomed by her family with open arms. Sundays we joined them at church, after which her parents invited everyone for lunch. Robert and I would spend the afternoons at the pool with her, or on walks through the park. Sometimes Robert and I would walk to the Brazos River nearby and I would admire the Roebling's smaller-scale prototype of New York's Brooklyn Bridge that spanned the muddy waters.

My new found love and I had become very serious. I was convinced that this relationship was a good one and the best thing that could happen to Robert and me. I became aware that one of the serious concerns her family had about me was that I had been a member of the Hitler Youth. The main issue was how her uncle would feel if she married a German. Her uncle fought against Germany in WWII. In the end, her uncle was okay with her bringing me into the family.

In April of 1960, I proposed to her with a diamond engagement ring. My parents sent us matching gold wedding bands. German tradition is that during the engagement period the bands are worn on the left hand ring finger, and after marriage on the right hand ring finger. The rings were made from the gold of a pocket watch that was the only surviving item from a relative who perished in a Berlin bombing raid. The rings were sized for us and inscribed inside with our initials and the engagement year.

My fiancée never wore her ring, either as an engagement or as a wedding ring. For me, the rings were symbolic of a relationship without an end, and it hurt me that she wouldn't wear hers. As everyone was planning for the wedding it appeared to me that the wedding celebration was for the benefit of her family and relatives, not for her and me. There never was a question of my taste for floral arrangements, rehearsal dinners, or any other planning decisions. I was told that I needed to buy a gift for the best man, and educated about the other responsibilities of the groom. At no time was I asked about sending wedding invitations to my parents, my siblings, or anyone else on my side of the family. Similarly, my parents never inquired about their part in the wedding, nor did they discuss coming to the wedding. I realized much later that my parents were very disappointed that they weren't invited.

The only concession to my feelings was that my German friends Walter and Helga Seeger and Mrs. Thomas were invited. Walter was my best man and Helga helped out by serving refreshments during the reception. When Helga suggested that Mrs. Thomas be considered my surrogate mother in terms of seating arrangements in the church, my fiancée's family was so opposed to the idea that it almost ruined the wedding. I also was told by my future wife that her very best friend, who she wanted as her maid of honor, was not allowed to attend our wedding by her parents because I was a German. I felt badly for her, but chose to ignore their ignorance and hatred.

The Destruction of Memories

We were married on August 28, 1960. I was in awe of my wife. I loved her and I was quite frankly captivated by her and her family. Never in a million years had I imagined that I would marry someone from what I considered the upper class; someone who was studying in college and whose family was wealthy. Similarly, I would have never believed that someone with her family's background would allow their daughter to marry a Dictaphone repairman with a child from a previous marriage. She was exactly the opposite of me. She was quiet and when she spoke it was usually briefly and at a low volume. I, on the other hand, was a high-energy go-getter with the tendency to passionately state my feelings and opinions; loudly I might add. I was in love, grateful, and thankful for my blessings.

After watching me work in the garage refinishing furniture for the family, my mother-in-law told my wife, "You'll never go hungry with him." That was true. Just like Vater, I would never put my family at risk. In the old fashioned way, I had asked her father for the hand of his daughter in marriage. After telling me that he saw that I loved his daughter, he asked me how I planned to support her. I made it clear that I had quite a way to go before I could provide for her with the lifestyle to which she was accustomed. But I promised him that I would try very hard to always provide for her, keep her happy, and support her.

Our wedding was a beautifully staged event in which I performed in my prescribed role according to the wedding script. My act was genuine in that out of respect and love, I did what I was told to do. With the exception of the best man, all of the other males in the wedding party were young men from my wife's church youth group. I must admit that I was oblivious to all of these details at the time because for me there was something much more important than the drama of the wedding itself. At the time I didn't even wonder why my parents and members of my family in Germany had not been invited. I appreciated the splendor and beauty of the wedding, but I was focusing on getting and keeping this marriage on a loving and giving path, so as not to experience a repeat of my first marriage.

Before the wedding, I received postcards from my fiance's sister who was studying at the University of Colorado. The cards highlighted the beauty of the Rocky Mountains. Before I knew it, we were talking about starting our marriage in Colorado. Little did I know that my sister-in-law had sent me the postcards at the request of my wife who wanted to get me interested in the idea of living in Colorado. She wanted to get out of Texas and to be near her sister. She would never come out directly and suggest the idea, but wanted it to be my idea.

I arranged to be transferred to the Dictaphone Corporation in Denver, Colorado. We lived in a duplex in Aurora, Colorado near the Denver Airport. She worked as a Varytypist and I continued working as a Dictaphone service representative while taking night classes at the University of Colorado Extension Center in Denver.

I had to select my major in order to plan my curriculum at the University of Colorado. My passion for acting, music, and the arts continued, as did my concerns that these endeavors would make it difficult to be a responsible and supportive husband and father. On a Sunday afternoon walk through downtown Denver, my wife asked me if I ever had considered architecture as a career. The first time I thought about that particular idea was when I watched our neighbor's son, an architect, work across the street from where I grew up in Neu-Ulm. I thought about her question and my own interests. The profession of architecture integrates the arts, science, and engineering. I enjoyed the arts and the sciences, but I considered engineering painful because of mathematics. We stopped at the Denver Public Library to do research on the field. The more I thought about her question the more I became convinced that architecture was the path to my future.

The books that captured my attention most were those by and about Frank Lloyd Wright. I learned it would take ten to eleven years to become an architect. I would have to go to undergraduate school for five years, then spend one year in graduate school, three years doing an internship, and then prepare for and pass the nine national licensing examinations. I would then be legally entitled to practice architecture. The most exciting discovery for me was that within the architectural profession there were many career options even if one never practiced in an architectural firm. An architectural education allowed one to do research, teach, do planning, architectural photography, or become an historian. I liked the idea of options and I felt comfortable with the thought of having multiple career options.

My wife and I discussed this decision in detail since it impacted her life and all our plans for the future. Despite the fact that I was studying with the support of the GI Bill, and periodic help from her parents, we both had to work for a while before I could attend the university on a full-time basis. Paying our debts, creating savings, taking care of Robert, and acquiring household furnishings were just some of the pressing needs.

A friend of ours, a structural engineer, suggested that if I was planning to become an architect I should work as an architectural draftsman instead of repairing Dictaphones. I took his advice and practiced drafting and drawing. By the end of 1961, I literally faked my way into an architectural draftsman position at the Plant Engineering Department of Stanley Aviation in Aurora, Colorado. When the personnel department called me and offered me the job they also told me the salary. I was scared. I don't remember the hourly rate, but it was more than I had ever been paid. I called my engineering friend and told him that I didn't think I could live up to their expectations. He kept reassuring me that I could learn and work at the same time. With much hesitation and fear, I took the offer and studied drafting texts, techniques, methods, and the differences between architectural, structural, and mechanical drafting. There were many times when my lies and deceptions were almost exposed, but somehow I persevered and discovered I was a fast learner.

One incident remains with me to this day as a reminder that I should admit something I don't know instead of pretending. During my job interview, my future boss asked me if I knew anything about surveying. I told him that I worked weekends with a friend of mine who was a civil engineer with the Texas Highway Department. I had such a friend, but the rest was a pure lie. I was on the draftsman job for about six months when my boss asked me to pick up a transit and go to the recreation building site to lay out the sewage disposal piping. There would be three laborers there to help me. When I went to check out the transit, the guy at the checkout asked me if I wanted a "rod." I didn't know what a rod was but I said, "Of course." He then asked, "Do you need a chain too?" Acting like I knew what I was doing I said, "Can't work without it." I put the rod, which is an elevation measuring stick, and the chain, which measures length, at my desk and hid myself in the men's room with the transit. I had never seen one, much less touched one. While sitting in the toilet stall I studied it closely. After maybe a half-hour I figured out that I had to mount it on the tripod, level it, and by rotating the telescope I would be able to read the scales on the rod.

When I finally arrived at the construction site the three laborers were very impatient with me because they had been waiting for me for more than an hour. I tried to take my time setting up the equipment because I didn't want to look like I didn't know what I was doing. When I finally had the tripod secured and the transit positioned, I decided I was in the wrong place and moved the entire setup. Pandemonium broke out as one of the more knowledgeable laborer said, "What in the hell are you doing that for?"

I knew I had made a big mistake. I learned later that the position of the transit didn't matter as long as I could have a clear view towards the rod's position. I had to come up with a fast excuse before I made a complete idiot out of myself.

"I would be looking directly into the sun from where I had my transit set up," was the best excuse I could think of. For some reason, they bought the excuse and I saved myself a big embarrassment. Before I left Stanley Aviation I was promoted to assistant plant engineer. I also received compliments for my work from Mr. Robert Stanley, the owner of the company and a former test pilot who rarely complimented his employees. Once again I survived on my conviction, "Courage can carry me beyond my capacities."

While in Denver we worked with an attorney to make arrangements for Robert to be legally adopted by my second wife. To do this we had to locate and seek my first wife's consent. I knew where my former wife lived, but my new bride made me swear not to divulge that information to the lawyer. I assumed she didn't want the possibility of having to deal with Robert's mother at any time. For the first time in our relationship, I was asked to deceive and lie beyond my comfort level. I would be lying to the court and to this day I feel guilt and remorse for letting myself be talked into this act of deception. It is difficult to describe how much I wanted to please my wife, how much I wanted to give to her what she desired in the way she desired it, and to demonstrate my love and devotion to her. My wife legally adopted Robert in 1961.

Soon after the adoption became final, I made a most disturbing discovery. I was browsing through my photo albums and discovered many missing pictures; memories of my past and my teenage friends. The photo albums covered my life from birth through 1961. The pictures of my favorite cousin Elfriede were gone. All of the images of my former girl friends in Germany were gone. Pictures with my friends in the Alps, and, to my great horror, all of the pictures from my first wife were removed. Even though I didn't value the pictures of my first wife, I wanted to keep them so someday Robert could at least have an image of his biological mother. I valued my history and my memories, good or bad, for they were the stepping stones of my life.

I told my wife that I had discovered that my pictures were missing. "You don't need them anymore," she said. I asked her what she did with them, and she told me that she had burned them. I felt sick. Part of my life had been destroyed. I was angry, but I believed I had to swallow my pain and find a way to forget the event in order keep my marriage healthy. I saw my role at that time as the breadwinner, the center mast of the family, the one responsible for every member in the family. Just as my father had been the ruler of the roost, at least to the outside world, I saw my role similarly. At the same time I had to admit that my mother was the ruler of the house when it came to family affairs and the children. I discovered that this attitude, belief, and mantra did not play well with my wife or her family.

I was constantly aware that feelings, either positive or negative, were not something my wife felt comfortable with. There was no passionate kissing, I was never embraced by her, and our intimacy felt like she was doing me a favor. I decided to not make an issue of the situation because of my previous experiences with women. In fact, I was in deep denial about my unfulfilled need for tenderness and love.

My wife became pregnant in 1962. For me the pregnancy was an unforgettable experience. There were times when I had no idea what was going on and had to depend on the local doctor to make a house visit to take care of my wife. Technology was not yet advanced to where one could find out the gender of the fetus, but to me it didn't matter as long as the baby was healthy, and had two legs and two arms. I spent nearly every morning rubbing my wife's back as she leaned over the toilet to throw up. It was painful to watch her suffering from morning sickness and I was frustrated that I couldn't change anything or make it go away. On the other hand, I thought the body of an expectant mother was just about the most beautiful sight imaginable.

We decided that we wanted her father to be present at the birth. I admired and respected her father and I trusted him with the life of my child. My wife's mother drove her car to Denver to take her daughter back to Texas late in the pregnancy. The birth went smoothly. I received a phone call on September 22, 1962, from my mother-in-law telling me that my daughter Michelle Reneé was born at 11:15 that morning. Mother and daughter were doing well and her grandfather was in attendance. My second child had dark hair and a big dimple in her cheek. I don't remember her weight, height, or length. It didn't matter. She was all in one piece, had the requisite parts, and a healthy voice; I knew then she was a Kroner. Whatever else was going on in my life and in my marriage, Reneé was a dream come true. I couldn't arrive in Texas soon enough to see this precious gift of life. A daughter conceived in and through love. I had watched and felt Reneé before she was born as she kicked the book that rested on her mother's belly.

I raced from Denver to Waco to see my Reneé. I arrived after having been awake for twenty-three hours. Reneé was in one of the small bedrooms in the back of the family home with her mom. A little bundle with cheeks that belonged on a Hummel figurine raised her arm and with fingers formed in a fist, punched the air. I fell in love with her that instant and for the rest of my life she will be Daddy's little girl.

In the year of Reneé's birth, with the help of a GI mortgage loan, we bought a home at 620 South 40th, Boulder, Colorado. I enrolled as a full-time student in the School of Architecture at the University of Colorado at Boulder in January 1963. My wife commuted to Denver for

work. We found a wonderful, loving, and deeply committed Nana for Reneé and Robert. Mrs. Warren had grown children of her own and was a widow living alone in Boulder. Reneé and Robert took to her like bees to honey. They loved each other and gave both of us peace of mind about the care of our children. Reneé embraced Nana as her surrogate grandmother.

Mutter and Marianne came for an extended visit in January 1963 to help with Reneé and to meet my wife for the first time. I had not seen Mutter and Marianne in the nine years since I had left Germany. Mutter had a visitor's visa, which meant she was planning to stay with us for six months. Marianne planned to work in Chicago for one year. Soon after they arrived, my mother-in-law came for a short visit. After the initial nicities there was an air of cautiousness, hesitation, and confusion. A series of events created a cloud that hung over the entire family. Some of the tension was in part caused by language difficulties. My wife did not speak German and Mutter did not speak English. Marianne and I were the only ones who could speak both languages. Besides the language problem there were personality and cultural clashes. My wife was a quiet, reserved, and shy woman, while Marianne was an energetic, loud, smart, and boisterous woman who had an opinion and answer for everything. Mutter had a strong sense of proper etiquette, specific opinions about raising children, and she believed in a clear delineation between the role of a husband and a wife. The three Kroners in this drama were by nature talkers who could out-talk and out-shout almost anyone. I was caught in the center of this milieu because of my relationship as son, brother, husband, and father.

The day Mutter and Marianne arrived, my wife learned about a common custom in Germany when family arrive for an extended stay. They brought with them facecloths and towels for their bathing needs. My wife took this act as an insult and instead of saying anything directly to Mutter or Marianne, she called me into our bedroom to express her anger and disappointment. She gave me specific instructions on how to tell Mutter and Marianne that they had insulted her. I tried to explain the custom to her and told her to just forget the incident, but she would have none of it and insisted on the confrontation.

When my wife came home from work during their visit, she immediately retreated to our bedroom and pretty much remained there for most of the evening, giving the explanation that she was tired and did not feel well. Often I was summoned to our bedroom and given orders or instructions about what to say or do. Mutter wanted to help with cooking, something my wife discouraged because she did not want to eat German food. Washing dishes, ironing, and doing the laundry were acceptable activities for Mutter. The evening meal was usually prepared by Mrs. Warren according to my wife's instructions.

During the short visit by my mother-in-law, the tension increased. Mutter began to suggest to me that the behavior of my wife was discourteous and improper, and, as "the man in the family," I should point this out to my wife. Mutter said my wife was wearing the pants in the family, and I was not standing up for my mother. I loved Mutter, despite our disagreements, and disrespectfulness was not something I would ever have considered. But my wife insisted that I explain to Mutter that I was her husband first and Mutter's son second. It all seemed childish, immature, and insensitive. I was trapped between my love for my wife and my respect and love for Mutter, as well as my admiration for my sister.

The morning my mother-in-law departed to return to Texas she cried, something I had never seen her do in the four years that I had known her. I sensed that something was terribly wrong. I assumed it was a mother feeling sorry for her daughter having to put up with my family. There was no love between Mutter and my wife and there was no friendship between my wife and Marianne. After three weeks of arguments, verbal fights, and disagreements about practically everything, the visit ended abruptly. Mutter returned to Germany six weeks before she had planned, and Marianne left for Chicago at the beginning of March. My wife got the last word by writing a letter to Mutter, that I had to translate and mail to Germany. Her letter made the argument that she was in the right and that they intruded beyond acceptable levels. It was now obvious to me why no one from my family, except me, had been invited to our wedding. The rejection of Mutter and Marianne during their visit suggested to me that perhaps I was acceptable as husband for their daughter, but my family was definitely a problem.

We had barely recovered from the disaster of my family's visit when new tensions and difficulties emerged in our daily life. When Robert started elementary school, the school psychologist expressed concerns about his behavior. He was a hyperactive child, inquisitive, and prone to getting into trouble. My wife and I started family therapy with Robert in an attempt to understand and cope with his outbursts and our own tensions. We started our life together with a child from a previous marriage; we both worked; and my nights and weekends were taken up with studying. We didn't have time to work on our interpersonal issues. Family conflicts began to take their toll on our marriage.

The Beginning of the End

In the fall semester of 1963 at the University of Colorado, the top two students from each year's class were selected for a special research/design project directed by Buckminster Fuller, the world famous architect, engineer, and author. It was through this project that I met Buckminster Fuller as well as world-renowned futurist Dr. John McHale and his wife Magda. Being exposed to them was an eye opener for me. There was much more to architecture than designing buildings or cities. There were responsibilities architects had towards "spaceship earth." Through architecture, human beings could create a sustainable future.

While I worked extremely hard in my studies, I had lots of fun, particularly in the design studios. I explored communications and speech-making, history, and photography through my free electives. In the summer of 1964, based on my performance in the architectural curriculum, I was offered a rare opportunity. I was invited to take a special summer design studio and if I received a grade of "A" in that studio I would skip third year design and move on to the fourth year design studio. Given the course work that I already had completed, it meant I could finish a five year curriculum in three years and a half. Other students had been offered this opportunity before me, but only three had ever achieved the goal. My professor in that special semester was Professor G.K. Vetter, one of my favorite faculty at Colorado. In the fall of 1965, I was again selected to work on a second Buckminster Fuller project. The design results went to the World Exposition at the International Union of Architects Conference in Paris, France. Our work was a prototype of a global video interactive display panel system about global resources. It was during this special project experience with Fuller that I decided I wanted to do graduate studies in architecture for an advanced degree. This would give me the option of teaching and doing research at the university level.

The second Buckminster Fuller project involved data that explained an underlying reason why the United States entered into the Vietnam War. It wasn't all about democracy, freedom, or fighting communism. By plotting factual data about resource location, the concentration of steel production, and the ownership of critical resources on a global scale, we discovered that Vietnam had the greatest deposits of manganese, a critical material for high-strength steel production. Several U.S. corporations had located themselves in Vietnam to mine this precious resource. When our interests abroad were threatened, we started to send military advisors to Vietnam. The rest is history.

My graduation with a Bachelor of Architecture Degree with honors from the University of Colorado took place in May 1966. To share in the joy of having reached another one of my goals, Vater came to join us for the graduation ceremonies. He also came to meet my wife and his grandchildren for the first time. Vater was a diamond in the rough. He spoke his mind and had a strong self-esteem. We went on a two-week vacation together, traveling and camping on our way to Texas to visit my in-laws. After Vater's visit, it became clear to me that the culture and family that I came from, the values that were ingrained in me, and my cultural roots were tolerated at best by my wife and her parents. Most frustrating was the fact that none of my in-laws would talk with me about this reservation they held towards my immediate family.

When Vater was living with us during his vacation in Boulder, he browsed through my library and discovered the photo album in which I kept my immigration mementos. On page one of the album I had written the following words, "Amerika das Land der Liberty in dem ich mein Glück und meine Zukunft suche." (America, the land of liberty in which I am seeking my fortune and future.) He pasted a note at the bottom of that same page that I discovered long after he returned to Germany. He had written, "Und gefunden habe, 10 Juni 1966; Dein Vater." (And you found it, June 10, 1966; your Father.)

This note was written by the man who also tried to break from the trend of his family and get a university education, only to have the opportunity denied. This man, who also let his river flow, saw his son finally achieve his dream. When I saw his note, I felt assured that Vater knew why I left Germany. He knew that what I was searching for could not be found in Germany at the time of my emigration. He knew it was not a rejection of my history or family. I felt at peace. During the graduation ceremony in the football stadium it was announced that Hans Kroner was the person in the stadium who had traveled the farthest to see his son graduate.

In July of the same year, we moved to Troy, New York where I had applied for graduate studies at Rensselaer Polytechnic Institute (now called Rensselaer). In addition to my course work, I participated in research projects managed by the Center for Architectural Research, under the direction of Alan Greene and later, David S. Haviland.

After extensive therapy, Robert's doctor and psychologists recommended to the Troy school system that Robert be placed in a special class because he was diagnosed with an attention deficit disorder. The Troy school district refused and placed him into a regular class.

I achieved my final education-related goal by obtaining a Masters in Architecture Degree with Honors from Rensselaer in May of 1967. Completing my internship requirements for the practice of architecture was my next hurdle. We moved the entire family to Arlington, Massachusetts where I accepted a position with a firm called Geometrics which partnered frequently with Buckminster Fuller. Geometrics was located in Cambridge. Before I left Rensselaer, Ray Caravaty, one of my professors, suggested that if I ever left Geometrics, I should give Rensselaer a chance to get me back. I told him I would. There was one other person at Rensselaer of significance to me personally and professionally; David Haviland, a fellow graduate student at Rensselaer. I remember observing David. I realized right away that this was a fellow to watch

R. Buckminster Fuller on the left, with Walter.

and learn from. He wasn't outwardly as vivacious, passionate, or theatrical as I was, but he had admirable characteristics, intellect, was insightful, and had fascinating points of view.

In June 1967, we rented a single-family residence on Washington Street, in Arlington, Massachusetts. As we drove out of Troy my wife said, "Troy is one place we won't even drive through on our way to someplace else." I knew she hated Troy, a city that was struggling economically. Her disappointment, however, was mostly because the Troy school system had ignored Robert's psychological condition.

It was in Boston, Massachusetts at the Boston Architectural Center (BAC) that I discovered my ability to teach and to inspire students while at the BAC's evening program where I taught design studio. My views on architecture and its future were of interest not just to my students

186

but to my teaching colleagues. Slowly my plan for the future began to form. However, it was important to me to be licensed to practice architecture. I needed a future with options. I could complete my internship, sit for the National Council for Architectural Registration Board (NCARB) examinations to obtain my license to practice, and either work in an architectural firm, open my own firm, teach at a university, or find a job in an architectural or building research organization. Having options increased my independence and prevented me from becoming enslaved to a position, firm, or economic condition.

The BAC promoted me to head critic in the senior graduate department in January 1968. On May 21 of that year, our third child Kevin Tracy Kroner was born at Melrose Hospital, Melrose, Massachusetts. At the time, my wife and I agreed that she would not bear any more children. If we found we wanted a larger family someday, we would adopt them. My wife wanted to raise Kevin without a nanny, so we decided she would stay home full-time and raise our children.

Sometime during the spring of 1969, David Haviland invited me to come to Rensselaer. It was great to catch up with him and he told me he was considering accepting the position of Director for the Center for Architectural Research at Rensselaer. He went on to explain that his acceptance of the position depended on who he could get to work with him. David offered me a position as Research Associate in the Center. I indicated that I also had an interest in teaching and inquired whether that would be possible. He assured me that he could work something out. I had sufficient practical experience by then to sit for the licensing examination, which meant I could accept the position as Research Associate. I had also decided that traditional practice was not my cup of tea. Geometrics did fascinating projects, as well as mundane ones. I was working on robot floor polishers, large-scale wide-angle lenses, airplane hangars for future SSTs, and interactive computer game rooms with video projection screens, a technology that was emerging but not yet available. Much of it was fascinating, like when we were asked to use the video projection technology to design a Peace Game Room as a counterpoint to a War Games Room.

But there were also projects that were taken on by the office just to pay the bills. I decided I wanted to have a small practice that could expand and contract as projects I liked came along. The projects I was interested in were those that most architects would decline because of budgetary constraints or because they were difficult projects and had no precedents. Nevertheless, my main endeavor would be research and teaching at the Institute.

Once again, the family moved. It had been difficult to convince my wife to move back to Troy where our experiences with the school system were less than positive. We did not want Reneé and Kevin to have to deal with Troy's system. My wife made me promise that if we moved back so I could work at Rensselaer, I would consider adopting a fourth child in a few years. I promised to consider it.

We found a beautiful place in a quiet neighborhood. It had a large lawn, a forest in the back, and wonderful neighbors. It was difficult at first to make ends meet because we had chosen a house that was much more than we could afford, but I worked very hard. Unfortunately, this meant spending many long hours away from my family.

On August 21, 1971, our family of five returned to the place of my birth. I had been in America for seventeen years. It was wonderful that our children were old enough to enjoy the trip and remember the occasion. My parents hosted a welcome home party that was attended by all of my relatives. On August 28, during our visit to Germany, my wife and I celebrated our eleventh wedding anniversary. We took a trip through Switzerland, Lichtenstein, and visited the Mountain Club's lodge in

Visit to Germany in 1971.

Gunzesried where I had spent a great deal of my youth. It was during this wedding anniversary trip that my wife told me she had never wanted to marry me. I asked her why she did. For some reason I was not surprised by her answer, "You were my way out of my parent's house and out of Texas."

The visit did not erase the pain from previous interactions between my family and my wife. She found me tolerable, but not the rest of my family. I still loved her and I was bound and determined to be the kind of man that she could love. I tried to change every time she made me aware of a "blemish" on my character.

I passed the architectural licensing examination in 1971 and officially and legally became an architect. I remember that moment not just because I reached the milestone, but because it was the only time I can recall that my wife had ever thrown her arms around me and kissed me. Normally, I initiated all physical contact.

Another event that took place in 1971 was my promotion to Assistant Professor of Architecture. The only professional goals that remained for me personally were to achieve tenure and become a full professor. There was no doubt that Rensselaer was the place for me. Its technological and scientific orientation, its strength in architectural research and building science, and its top quality students presented exactly the type of challenge I was seeking. To be promoted to full professor with tenure. I had to present a strong case in research, teaching, and service. Personally, I wanted to add a forth component; a successful architectural practice. I wanted to prepare and present a strong and convincing case to my institute that I was worthy of tenure and full professorship.

I sought out potential clients and opened a private practice out of our home. I also did architectural consulting for the federal and state government, industry, and the Roman Catholic Diocese of Albany, New York. At times, I employed former students in my office to manage architectural design projects. My work included churches, residential designs, small medical clinics, and planning studies.

In July 1975, I was promoted to Associate Professor with tenure. This was not only a tremendous opportunity, it was an awesome responsibility. Tenured professors are the stewards of academia. I had studied how bogus academic institutions were created during the Nazi regime. I felt strongly that I would do my part to ensure it would not happen here. I took President Eisenhower's mid-1950's warning to heart when he talked about the risks of the military industrial complex.

I became Director of Rensselaer's Center for Architectural Research in 1977 and began to do research in building systems, resource conscious design (what is now called sustainable design), and intelligent architecture. These were my passions and thanks to my mentors Buckminster Fuller and John McHale, I was able to achieve international recognition for my work. I had achieved my intellectual goals, attained economic security, and was surrounded by a loving family. While all of these things were a blessing, I began to question my marriage and my inability to manage my feelings and emotions. Being involved in three professional enterprises took its toll on my personal life. I missed out on time with my children on doing things with them that they loved and enjoyed. And despite numerous counseling and therapy sessions with my wife, our marriage continued to deteriorate.

Ashamed, Alone, and Abandoned

On the recommendation of our family psychologist, Robert was placed in a foster home in 1973. He was arrested a year later for breaking and entering a home, and for the theft and destruction of private property. Robert avoided going to jail by promising to enlist in the Navy.

That summer Mutter and Vater came to visit my family and to make amends with my wife. One of my clients made their cabin in New Hampshire available to us. During long walks in the woods, Mutter and I finally found common ground and related to each other as loving and responsive human beings. We shared with each other marital experiences and the difference between disappointment and hopelessness. I told her that my marriage was not successful and that my wife had unequivocally stated that she never really wanted to marry me. For the first time in my life, I understood Mutter's feelings and expectations of a marriage and discovered that we had a lot in common in terms of our hopes for intimacy and our marriages. I learned that Vater never discovered that special form of giving. Prior to my second marriage I had discovered it, enjoyed it, and was convinced that my sexuality was another form of communicating my love. I never experienced that level of intimacy in my second marriage, and neither had my mother in hers.

My family and I returned to Germany in 1978 for my parent's golden wedding anniversary. When the visit ended and we were saying auf wiedersehen, my wife turned to me and said, "I think from now on you should visit your parents more often, but without me." I took that comment as a kind and understanding gesture since they were getting old and I wanted to see them more often. I didn't realize that there was another purpose embedded in the offer. When we returned home she asked for a separation agreement. I didn't want to think about a divorce. I was convinced our marriage could be saved if only both of us were willing to seek help through therapy and a willingness to change. A year later on June 7, 1979, my wife asked me for a divorce. A few weeks later, she suggested that she might reconsider. By my forty-fifth birthday she had reconsidered and agreed to go to therapy again. She stopped wearing the wedding ring I had given her and sometime later she took back her maiden name. We never discussed these changes but when I asked her about them I was told that I wouldn't understand. She also told me that she didn't think I was ready for the changes that were yet to come.

On November 14, 1979, I started therapy with Dr. Mike Roselle. My wife went with me to the early sessions, but Mike suggested that she continue with his wife, also a therapist. I continued with him for five years. It was through his group therapy sessions that I acquired the emotional and intellectual tools to cope with my marriage, Robert, my relationships with Reneé and Kevin, and my interactions with my students and colleagues.

During the course of my life I discovered behaviors I didn't know how to handle. I had difficulty with being given "the silent treatment." I was also in a quandary as to what to do with my desire to be intimate. I had no sooner discovered my sexuality and the happiness that was derived from it when, after my first marriage, I denied my feelings because I felt my priorities were wrong. With my second wife, I was made to feel bad just for wanting to make love to my wife. I felt ashamed, alone, and abandoned by the woman I loved deeply and completely. However, therapy sessions taught me that my expectations of intimacy were very normal. I'm not proud of it, but after months on end being left with my desires, when someone offered their hand I reached out and grabbed it. However, the unfaithfulness and guilt sent me into greater stress.

I also could not cope with uncontrolled spending. Living within one's means was a lesson I had learned as a child. Both my first and my second marriages were financial disasters and no matter how hard I worked or how much money I made, it never seemed to be enough.

My wife had never completed her college education and the fact that she was without a degree became an issue for her as she socialized with faculty and their wives at Rensselaer. To rectify this she obtained an associate's degree from a community college in 1977. In May 1979, she graduated with a B.S. Degree in Sociology and became a New York State parole officer. She was assigned to Sing Sing Prison in 1981. To take this assignment she had to live in Ossining and commute home on weekends. Both of us were concerned how this would impact Kevin who was still living at home.

We explained to Kevin that he and I would have to live alone together during the week while his mother lived and worked in Ossining. We expressed our concerns to him and inquired how he would feel about the arrangement. I'll never forget the response of my twelve year old son, "Of course I don't like the idea." And looking at his mother he said, "You are yourself first and you are my mother second. If you are not good to yourself you won't be able to be any good to me." He shocked both of us with his wisdom and insight.

I stopped having affairs, and I stopped having expectations and hopes for improvements in my marriage. I realized that bringing her coffee in bed in the morning, not making physical demands, sending her flowers at work, asking her to join me on professional trips to romantic places in France, Greece, and Canada all did nothing to improve our marriage. We had a weekend marriage and our time together was filled with doing laundry and grocery shopping.

My wife was still working as a parole officer at Sing Sing, and Kevin and I went to Ossining to help her move to another apartment. As the last item was moved into the bedroom, and while Kevin was setting up the TV in the living room, I asked her for a divorce. It was in March 1982, and as soon as I had made the request it occured to me that Kevin was still a dependent and could be used as a pawn in the game of divorce. My wife touched me and begged me to forgive her and to give her another chance to be a wife. I was shocked. She had never before placed herself in a pleading position. It took me a while to figure it out, but I finally realized that by living apart and supporting herself, she had weakened her case in a divorce settlement. However, I agreed to reconsider my request.

Reneé had started her university studies at Marymount College, majoring in fine arts. She went to Italy during her third year to study in Florence, Italy. We took her to the airport with all of the externalized reassurance of our love and wanting to appear as parents who had all the confidence in the world in their daughter. On the way home from the airport, I cried my heart out as I was overwhelmed with loneliness. My wife asked me why I was crying. I just shook my head because I couldn't explain my fears about the problems Reneé might have due to her youth and language barriers. I finally felt what I imagined my parents had felt when they said goodbye to me and when Vater was crying at the Munich Airport.

The Winter Solstice

In the summer of 1983, my research team at the Center for Architectural Research had completed the design and construction of a passive solar demonstration project. Rensselaer asked me to design a passive solar facility that would demonstrate what a private university could do for itself in relation to energy conservation and energy conscious design. It was indeed an honor to be responsible for the project because in the 150-year history of Rensselaer, I was the first member of the architecture faculty to be asked to design a building on the

The Rensselaer Visitor Center, 1983.

campus. The building, known as Rensselaer's Visitor Center, was dedicated that summer and was one of the first buildings to use intelligent technology to control and monitor a building's operation. Because the U.S. Department of Energy supported part of our effort, the Visitor Center received national and international attention.

One month later the phone rang in my office. Dr. Ursel Köstlin informed me that Vater had an aneurism. He was in the hospital in Memmingen, Germany, where Ursel was chief of Pediatrics. Ursel had remained a lifelong friend of the family. She explained that she did not give Vater much hope and that I should come home immediately. "I know he needs to see you. And Walter, you need to reach closure with him."

The next day, I was on my way to München on a Lufthansa plane. Once back on the ground, I raced on the Autobahn to Memmingen. I wanted to tell Vater how much I loved him, and how much he meant to me ever since I could remember. And, if I had the chance, I wanted him alone so I could ask him about the secrets he had been hiding from me and everyone else. When I entered the room Mutter, was sitting in a corner with a worried look, and Vater was in his hospital bed with a small smile on his face, tubes extending from his body. I leaned over and kissed him on the cheeks as he whispered to me, "Now that you have come I can die."

I leaned back and said out loud, "I did not come six thousand kilometers to watch you die; you are going to live. I still need you and your grandchildren need you. Stop talking nonsense." I knew no one else in my family would dare talk to Vater that way. I didn't know that Ursel was standing in the room until she spoke. "Herr Kroner! Are you going to listen to at least one member of your family?"

Mutter commented that he needed a bath and Ursel said she would get the nurse. I said, "Give me the basin, washcloth, soap and towels. I will do it." Ursel smiled and within minutes I had what I needed to give Vater his bath.

Dr. Ursel Köstlin, Vater and Anke at the hospital in Memmingen in 1984.

There was no resistance; there was no talk, just tenderness. For the first time in my life, I was able to nurture my father. For the first time, I could do something for him at the most personal level. I had him where I wanted him, in my hands while he had to lay still. This time he could not walk away to avoid tenderness, loving, and sensitive topics. I noticed that his toenails needed cutting, as did his fingernails. I took care of that and then I gave him a massage. This hunk of a man, strong as an ox, told me he was willing to give up. Why? There must be something else that was going on. I was not an experienced masseur like my Vater, but I tried and to my surprise he never corrected or directed my massaging. When he was lying on his side facing away from me I let the tears flow down my face. I wasn't thinking of him dying; I was feeling closer to him as never before. I was doing something that I had never dreamed of doing; I was touching my father tenderly and lovingly; just trying to make him feel more comfortable. There was such joy running through my veins that I had to keep myself from shaking. Here was a man who had never needed me, who hardly needed anybody else. This stubborn, independent soul, my father, was putty in my hands. I didn't want to spoil the moment with words, questions, or even a sound. I wanted to feel him, make him feel me, and hopefully make the whole thing a wonderful memory for both of us. I think my mother, sitting in the corner, knew what was happening at that moment. Her tears spoke very clearly as they ran down her cheeks and dripped onto her dress.

Vater had never hugged me but I knew he loved me. The only time I had hugged him was in 1966 when he came for my graduation in Colorado. He hardly ever praised me, giving me his excuse that he didn't want my head to swell or my ego to get too big. There never was a congratulatory handshake for anything, just a touch on my shoulder and a smile that glittered because of his gold fillings. I knew that I was his pride and his joy. I knew I always had that bond with him, yet it never depended on things, words, or deeds, just a loving energy that flowed between us, and we both knew it. Finally Mutter spoke. She told me she never knew I was capable of such tenderness.

Ursel had arranged for a room in the hospital for Mutter and me so we could be nearby. The next morning Ursel asked to speak with me in private. She had several concerns, the first of which was that since my parents had moved in with my sister, Vater was having some difficulty. My parents had their own apartment on the second floor of Marianne's home. However, Vater's difficulty was that he needed his garden and driving there had become a big problem. Vater denied the problem, but there were too many close calls that could have resulted in bad car accidents. Ursel told me that everyone, including herself, had tried to talk to him about this, but he refused to give up his car keys. I asked Ursel, "What can I do?"

"You are the only one that your father will listen to. You have to get him to give you his car keys because if he does get better, he will want to drive." "I'll do it," I told her. I used the opportunity to ask Ursel about some serious questions I wanted to ask Vater. I told her that for as long as I could remember,` he had ignored certain questions, deflected them, or simply refused to talk about them. I told Ursel that the issues had to do with who his grandfather was, with his Nazi activities, and whether or not he was a member of the SA. Ursel asked me to go outside with her. We sat in a little garden area on a bench. She said, "I know your Vater has these secrets, but to my knowledge he is determined to keep to himself." "Is it ok if I at least try to get some answers?" I asked.

"Walter, what I do know is that if you ask him now, he'll probably stress out and you could kill him," she said. "Why is my father so insistent on keeping these secrets?" I asked her. "I can only tell you it is because of shame," she replied. "Thank you Ursel, I am glad I asked," I told her.

I nursed Vater for about three days, and according to Ursel there was a surprising and unexpected improvement in his health. The day before I had to fly home I went to his hospital room and found him sitting in a chair. We were alone and exchanged questions related to his health. Without changing the rhythm or volume of our conversation I said, "Vater, I need your car keys. It is best all around if you stopped driving."

The look on his face started out as a sad expression. He turned and looked out of the window. When he looked back at me the sadness had disappeared and he said, "I will." I asked him where they were and he reached into his robe pocket and handed them to me. I took them, put them in my pocket, leaned over and held him close while I kissed his cheek and said, "Vielen Dank." I gave Ursel the keys and asked her to take care of them.

Later, as I said my goodbyes to my family, I told Mutter, Heinz, and Marianne that they shouldn't mention the subject of driving, car keys, or anything else related to the car to Vater. I explained to them that he would be in pain for a long time because of the loss of his freedom and his inability to go to his garden. He didn't need to be reminded of the loss.

I was absolutely convinced that not being able to go to his garden and do as he pleased was like the river disappearing into the earth for him. For Vater that was the beginning of dying, for he was in his element when he was in the river. I knew he needed to have his hands in the earth and he needed to feed his menagerie of animals in the garden. He could no longer bring flowers to the love of his life. The inability to assemble gifts of vegetables, berries, and fruit for his sisters and brothers-in-law reduced him to a taker instead of a giver. I had struggled with these issues before I asked him for the keys, and I was glad I had not had to discuss them with him. I was glad that I didn't have to say to him, "What will actually kill you the fastest is if you, who has saved lives all of your life, end up taking someone's life in an accident."

Vater lived for another year. He transferred the lease to his Garden to my brother Karlheinz who, to everyone's knowledge, had no love for nature, landscape, or animals. Vater passed away on December 23, 1984, in the home of his daughter Marianne and her husband Hannes Müller. I made it in time for the burial of his ashes. There in the cemetery of the village of Machtolsheim, in a quiet corner by a lilac tree, Vater had selected his gravesite. Once again he was in a place where I could go talk with him whenever I visited my family in Germany, and he could not weasel out of my inquisitive embrace.

My inheritance of his personal items included the contents of his desk, but not the desk itself. Vater had decided to give the desk to my brother's son Ralf. As I went through the desk there were many items that I remembered from my early childhood that triggered many pleasant memories. I also discovered a secret compartment. No one, not even my mother, knew of this secret space. In it were some photographs, papers, and a small hand gun. There were photographic negatives that, as near as I could tell, where photographs of men in SA uniforms. I told my siblings about the gun, and we agreed I should not try to take it to America. The other items I packed away quietly in my suitcase.

One of the items in the desk was an officially certified Familien Buch (Family Register) that documented family births, weddings, and deaths, and each was stamped by the local authorities. This document was the official register that had to be submitted to the Nazi regime to prove one's Aryan ancestry. Included in this information was data about my grandfather. However, the places where my great-grandfather was supposed to be documented had this notation,

"Keine Eintragung beim Standesamt über die Vaterschaft des Jakob Kroner." Translated it means, "There is no record in the official village registry office concerning the father of Jakob Kroner." The record continues and identifies Jakob Kroner's mother, my great-grandmother, as Walburga Kroner who was unmarried. Jakob Kroner was born on August 3, 1864, in Breitingen near Ulm. Walburga, his mother, was born in the same town on December 23, 1834, and was thirty years old when she gave birth to my grandfather.

It was at the time of Vater's funeral that the family attempted to uncover the secret of who our great-grandfather was. Mutter did not know the answer and only revealed that everyone on the Kroner side of the family had concluded that the reason Walburga never revealed the father's name was because she must have received hush money from the father. Given the small size of the village, and its location, there were only two possible male candidates who had enough money to pay and support Walburga and her child Jakob. One was a Jewish banker, and the other an Earl with large land holdings. Mutter made the comment that in her opinion she was convinced it was the Jewish banker, but acknowledged that she could never get her husband to agree with that theory.

Vater took the secret to his grave, just as his father did before him. I was skeptical of these theories because there was no reason in the mid-eighties to either deny his Jewish heritage, or protect the Earl's ancestors from embarrassment. Other theories had never been discussed, for instance that she might have been sexually assaulted.

On a return trip from Romania in September 1985, I saw Mutter, as it turned out, for the last time. Two days before she died, Mutter telephoned and said goodbye. She was calm, sure, and told me not to worry about her. On December 5, 1985, Mutter joined Vater, the man who worshiped the ground she walked on. I have no doubt, if there is a heaven other than on earth, they are enjoying it together. I also have no doubt that Mutter willed herself to die. She wanted to outlive her husband so no one else would have to take care of him. She was no longer needed and she, like her husband, died in here sleep in the circle of her daughter's family.

Robert, Reneé and Kevin at Walter's 50th birthday party.

My wife did not express any desire to be at Vater's or Mutter's funeral. I was not surprised, given the fact that past wounds had never healed. However, once again when I needed a hug, a hand to hold, and an ear to listen to me, I was alone. Instead I had to sit on the bench next to my parent's grave, shaded by a lilac bush and cry in solitude.

Karlheinz, Marianne, and I were given instructions, instead of a will, about what our parents wanted us to have. There was no difficulty and it was a tranquil moment as we each took our memorabilia and little personal treasures. There was no sealed envelope to be opened after death and there were no hidden papers. I decided that someday, however, I was going to try and solve the puzzle of my great-grandfather.

When I enjoy someone's friendship I have no difficulty expressing my feelings towards that person. I have always been this way. It is not uncommon for me to put my arms around a man's shoulder, hug him and, in the case of deep friendship and in the European fashion, kiss him on the cheek. With women I am equally expressive, and since I am comfortable with expressing my feelings, there is no doubt how much I enjoy the company of friends. Throughout my career, socializing with faculty and spouses - including going to the events at the Chapel and Cultural Center on the Rensselaer Campus - always created conflict, arguments, and huge bouts of jealousy on my wife's part. As a result, we only had three or four couples with whom we socialized, but very infrequently.

We traveled to Paris, France, in June 1989. We were joined by Kevin, who at the time was studying in Leeds, England. I sensed that the end of my marriage was approaching. Russ Leslie and his wife Jan joined us on the trip to Paris, in which we combined professional travel with a little vacation. The four of us were a study in contrasts. Our friends were like lovers touched by the spell of Paris. I was hoping that the magic ambiance would rekindle my relationship with my wife. It didn't.

In 1988, without telling me, my wife started private therapy with a new therapist. In the fall of 1989, she asked me to join her in therapy, which I did. We drove to therapy sessions every two weeks, driving in silence for one hour each way. I will never forget a statement she made in a therapy session on August 6, 1990, "For as long as I can remember, I have never been happy; not with my family and not with the family of this marriage or with Walter. This marriage is not at all what I had hoped and imagined and I am not happy with it at all. I am disillusioned with it." We repeated the ritual of silently making the two-hour round trip until the summer of 1991. I remember the last three therapy sessions as if they happened yesterday. The therapist asked me, "What would be the most important thing your wife could do to show you her affection." I responded by saying, "It would be nice if once in a while she would come to me and hug me." The therapist looked surprised and asked me if I could demonstrate how I wanted to be hugged. I put my arms fully around my wife, pressed my body fully against hers, and placed my chin in the curve of her neck. I squeezed firmly but gently. I freed her from my embrace and sat back in my chair. The therapist directed her next question to her, "Do you think you could do this just once in the next two weeks to Wally?" She didn't say yes, but nodded her head as if to say yes. Two weeks later we reported to the therapist that the therapeutic exercise never took place. She gave us two more weeks to try it; but I never got my hug.

In the third and final session my wife and I spoke two sentences that were identical. She told me, "What you see is what you get." I paused, making sure I heard her correctly. I responded, "Well, I have to say the same thing. What you see is what you get and I will never again attempt to change according to your demands."

What followed was a series of mediation sessions that turned into a total failure. I went to an attorney in March of 1992 to start the process for a divorce. My wife's attorney ended up filing first. I moved my personal belongings into a smaller bedroom upstairs in our home. After a while, I became fearful for my safety since my wife was allowed to carry a gun as a parole officer. Our therapist and my attorney advised me to move out of the house as quickly as possible. On July 6, 1993, two days after Independence Day, I left the home I had known for twenty-four years. With the help of friends I moved my personal belongings and some furniture that I had inherited from my parents to an apartment complex in Clifton Park, New York. I was served with divorce papers in September with her as plaintiff and myself as defendant.

Life turned ugly and it seemed that every time we came close to some form of agreement she would change her mind and we would have to start all over again trying to formulate some type of agreement. I finally realized that she was not interested in a settlement but rather in prolonging the settlement process until I ran out of money. In October, Kevin told me that his mother had called the police to arrest him because he was trying to remove his personal belongings from of his own bedroom in the house. Kevin told me, "Dad, I lost my mother and I wish I could have her back. The woman in our home is not the same woman that I remember as my mother."

The next time we were close to reaching a divorce agreement, she changed her mind again. Even her own lawyer refused to go on unless she signed the agreement. I was willing to sign an agreement that gave my wife everything including the house, the furniture, the household goods, all of our antiques, almost all of the antique Persian carpets we had collected, as well as the antique jewelry we owned. I agreed to pay the remainder of the debts the family had. My only condition was that there would be no alimony payments. In essence I gave up everything materially for my freedom.

The divorce was finally granted on the day of the Winter Solstice – December 21,1994. The symbolism of the sun rising and setting on its annual journey, sinking as low as it can in the noon sky represented my thirty-five years of marriage. Yet, the Winter Solstice is also the beginning of a cycle where the sun moves higher in the sky and gives our daily life a longer exposure to warmth and light as the calendar moves towards the 21st of June.

My only regret is that in my process of becoming free I had caused suffering and pain. In the wake of letting my river flow I had left turmoil, confusion, and pain. We as individuals seldom see the consequences of the wake we leave behind. My children need to know, however, that they were conceived in love, raised with compassion and hope, and given a strong sense of family. There is, however, a lesson to be learned from the success and failure of a thirty-five year marriage. Neither of us were very well prepared for a marriage that on the first day started with a child from a previous marriage. Neither of our parents had provided us with the full set of tools that we needed for navigating the torrents of marriage and life. The adjustments we had to make because of the cultural differences, the Vietnam War, women's liberation, open marriage, and similar social experiments added to the stress within our marriage. We were a very good team as long as we were committed to the same goal, which initially was my undergraduate and graduate education, then my professional licensing goals. While we were very busy attempting to reach our goals, we didn't pay attention to the key differences between our personal priorities. I was simply unable to cope with our differences and the ways these differences became manifest. I was a man very much in love trying to prove I could make a marriage last, but I realized too late that my hopes could be used by others to control me. The most positive aspect about those thirty-five years of my life was that my loving relationship and friendship with my children remained unbroken. I feel that I truly learned who my children were and tried to give them the same gift Vater gave to me; letting their rivers flow freely.

During my time at Rensselaer, Reneé and Kevin had the opportunity to be exposed to the world of higher education. They were surrounded by my graduate students and colleagues who at times would stay in our home or share a meal around the family table. Robert had no interest in going to a college. He instead joined the Navy. Reneé studied at Marymount College in Tarrytown, New York. For her graduate studies she went to the Rochester Institute of Technology where she received her Master Degree in Fiber Arts in 1986. Kevin did his undergraduate studies at Vanderbilt University; spending one year at Leeds University, with a study-abroad program. After graduating in 1990, he continued his studies at the College of William and Mary Law School where he graduated with a law degree. As a parent who came to America with an incomplete basic education, an electrician journeyman certification that had no value in America, three words of English, ten dollars, and the address of his sponsor, there is nothing but pride in my heart for all three of them.

I thought that intimacy was a key feature of a happy marriage. I had been married twice and at the age of sixty-one I had experienced only partial happiness. I did, however, learn that in my marriages I had ignored or forgotten what was really important to me personally. I was in denial about my own needs, priorities, and desires. The first marriage was the result of an accident. The second was over-burdened with too many individual agendas. I was extremely grateful that someone would consider marrying me when I had sole custody of a child from the previous marriage. However, my second marriage turned out to be the means to an end. In my case it was the means to find care for my son, security, happiness, family, and success. In my wife's case it was getting out of Texas, out from under the influence of her parents, and to becoming liberated. She and I created a happy family, relatively speaking, and built success and potential security; but we just grew apart.

Giving Forward

While my marriage was slowly falling apart I continued to move forward in my professional career. In the summer of 1985, I was selected to be a member of a joint U.S. - Romanian research exchange program by the National Science Foundation. For ten days, American scientists and researchers met with our counterparts in Bucharest, Romania to compare our work and develop future collaborative programs. The cities and the rural landscape we traveled looked abandoned, neglected, and dirty. We became even more appreciative of our academic freedom related to research under a democratic system when we compared our experience to that of our colleagues under the communist government of Romania. Our visit to Romania made us appreciate the freedom and liberty we have in the U.S. My first day in the International Hotel in Bucharest included a telephone call to my wife. Included in my conversation was the complaint that the hotel toilet paper was like sandpaper. When I returned to my room that evening after dinner I discovered soft, western-style toilet paper.

Each of the American visitors had their own translator who was specifically trained in the technical field related to our specialty. In my case it was the design and control of passive solar energy systems. However, there were other participants on the Romanian side who didn't have a particular scientific specialty. We discovered that they were security personnel who not only spied on us, but were responsible for keeping us under control. Once, after an all day bus tour to scientific laboratories and historic sites, we reached a restaurant at dusk. I needed some exercise so I decided to jog down the road for a bit. As I vanished into the darkness, I heard voices calling for me to stop, which of course I didn't. When the voices finally caught up with me they explained that I was not allowed to move freely about the country, and that they were responsible for me.

I decided to put this restriction to another test. On my last morning in Bucharest I decided to take pictures of historic buildings around the City Plaza near the hotel. I was supposed to meet my translator, but instead of waiting for her in the hotel I started to walk towards the plaza. I observed that not a single person was walking across the plaza; instead everyone was walking along the edges, near the buildings. I walked to the center and started taking photographs of the buildings. Suddenly, a shrill whistle sounded from the perimeter. Two policemen started to walk towards me and I walked slowly away. They started to run, and I continued to walk away, taking pictures as I went. I heard them approaching and I suddenly stopped, turned around and pointed my finger at them. In a loud voice I said, "I am an American so stay away." I turned back towards the edge of the plaza and kept walking, never looking back.

1985 U.S. and Romanian exchange visit, Bucharest.

When I shared the event with my translator, she explained that the plaza was off limits because the Romanian authorities knew foreigners had listening devices and high-resolution cameras that could spy on the government offices surrounding the plaza. In addition, she pointed out that I had aimed my camera at the offices of Nicolae Ceausescu, the communist leader of Romania. I apologized and asked whether my actions would get her in trouble. She answered, "Don't worry. We'll take care of it."

Elisabeta Victoria Asadurian, my Romanian translator, expressed an interest in immigrating to America. I told her if she could get herself out of Romania I would help and sponsor her. In 1988, she managed to escape from the communist regime and my wife and I sponsored her immigration to America. We helped her find a job at my Institute and a few years later she was able to bring her daughter and mother to live with her in Troy, New York. It was a wonderful feeling to give Elisabeta the same gift that I had been given thirty-four years earlier.

I chose to focus my career on the study of alternative futures in the context of architecture. My studies allowed me to forecast how architecture itself might change, provide the basis for new architectural theories, and identify the important role of science in architecture. My passion was to constantly keep watch on economic, scientific, and technological developments as they might relate to architecture, building, or ways of thinking about buildings. This passion was first stimulated in me by my mentors Buckminster Fuller and John and Magda McHale.

A colleague once asked me, "What are you most proud of?" I didn't like the question because it was like asking which of my children I liked the best. I think a more significant question related to one's work and accomplishment is, "Who are the people who made your success possible?"

When I joined Rensselaer there were many colleagues who supported my out-of-the-box thinking and theories, notably Professors Raymond Caravaty, George Droste, and David Haviland whose guidance all through my career was invaluable. I was indeed fortunate that during my tenure at Rensselaer I had the support of President George Low and Provost Professor Jim Meindl. And there are two graduate students without whom I could never have had the success in my own career; Russ Leslie, who is now Professor and Associate Director of Rensselaer's Lighting Research Center, and Jean Stark, my Research Associate.

My reason for mentioning these wonderful and supportive colleagues is because of their guts, courage, and the faith they had in me and my work. My research proposals were mostly on the edge of critical inquiry and rarely had external theoretical support. My work had a high potential for success or failure.

I also liked to use unconventional teaching methods. For example, several times I gave a studio exercise where students had to design, build and live in emergency shelters. The shelters had to accommodate one person comfortably and be built from recycled materials. Once constructed, students had to throw their shelters off the roof of Rensselaer's architecture building to simulate what would happen if they were thrown out of a helicopter to waiting disaster victims. Each student then picked up someone else's shelter and transported it to a designated "rescue site" where they had to live in the shelter for 24 hours. The shelters had to be lightweight so they could be carried to the site, and they had to be able to stand up to whatever weather the students might encounter. Each shelter was "tested" to see if it measured up to a set of very specific criteria. The shelters had to have the capacity to increase or decrease internal temperatures, and all instructions had to be pictorial. Not all of the shelters survived, nor did all of the hypothetical shelter occupants. We always had a fall-back facility where students could spend the night if their shelters failed. Students learned a lot about human physiology, comfort, and building science.

I was also a maverick when it came to the professional presentation of my work at national conferences. In 1976 I was invited to present a paper on energy conservation strategies titled, "Beyond Safe Energy Conservation Options," at a technology assessment conference held at Rensselaer. To help illustrate the point of my paper, I decided not to wear a traditional suit and tie. Instead, I walked into the conference hall in a Dashiki, an African robe-like garment worn by men. As I entered the lecture hall some of my colleagues from Rensselaer's School of Architecture started to disappear. The critic of my paper, seated at the stage, inquired of the audience whether such attire should be condoned. I was allowed to proceed and as part of my opening remarks I explained that the content of my paper would focus on non-traditional forms of saving energy. I told them that formal lecture presentation clothing weighs between six and seven pounds. "What I am wearing, this Dashiki, underwear, and sandals, weighs about two pounds, reducing the material required to clothe me comfortably by roughly two-thirds. Most important, however, is the idea that in this hot assembly hall I am a lot more comfortable than any gentleman in the audience, as our female colleagues can attest." The rest of the examples I presented illustrated other ways to step out of the conventional "thinking box" that often plagues so many of us.

In 1986, The Gottlieb Duttweiler Institute in Ruschlikon, Switzerland asked me to participate in an international symposium on Intelligent Buildings. A former graduate student had spoken about my work to one of the lead researchers at the Duttweiler Institute.   The researcher came to visit me at Rensselaer to learn about my work, and invited me to attend the symposium. It was at there that my work finally received recognition, particularly in the areas of advanced comfort systems in architecture, intelligent buildings, intelligent building envelope systems, and resource conscious design. Leading thinkers in architecture, sociology, technology, and psychology worked for three days to envision the future workplace. The discussions focused on how information technology, computers, the paperless office, and wireless communication might impact our definition of work and living. Two of the leading individuals at this conference were Francis Duffy from the U.K., and Nicholas Negroponte from MIT. My interactions with these two gentlemen and their enthusiastic support of my work on intelligent architecture and the intelligent workplace will always be deeply appreciated.

Perhaps the most significant accomplishment of my academic career was the establishment of Rensselaer's Lighting Research Center (LRC) in 1987. Rensselaer was given a Request for Proposal (RFP) by the New York State Energy Research and Development Agency. One of the major reasons the RFP reached my desk was that one of the agencies technical managers, Mr. Jim Barron, was familiar with the Center for Architectural Research's energy research accomplishments. Professor Russ Leslie, Professor David Haviland and I wrote the successful proposal to establish the LRC. We received multi-year funding to support the creation of laboratories and an administrative structure. The grant also supplied funding for research support, product testing equipment, a graduate education program, and collaboration with other advanced technology researchers. I became Interim Director of the LRC and Russell Leslie held the position of Associate Director. We knew from the beginning, however, that the LRC had to be under the direction of a scientist. With that in mind, Jim Barron and I took the lead and brought Professor Mark Rea to Rensselaer. Since then, Mark has led the LRC to international prominence, and Russ continues in the Associate Director position, maintaining the architectural connection to lighting research.

I received support from the United States National Science Foundation (NSF) in 1987 for an investigative research project designed to identify the latest technological developments and theories related to advanced comfort technology. Gifford Albright from the NSF provided significant support to help me with this project. My research over the last fifteen years had shown that phenomenal amounts of energy could be saved if thermal comfort was supplied directly to building occupants. The idea was extremely unconventional and very few architects, engineers, or scientists were willing to support the concept. My idea was to heat and cool buildings according to the requirements of building materials and to give people their own small heating and air-conditioning packages at their desks. Gifford Albright had the courage to provide an investigative travel grant that allowed me to visit cutting edge thinkers in the United States, Europe, the Mideast, and Japan. The emphasis was on developments that had not yet reached the market place. The purpose was to identify institutions and individuals whose research related to the development of advanced comfort technologies in the workplace. National productivity was a big issue for our government at that time and my research related to the potential for increasing human productivity. Following the completion of the investigative travel report, the NSF provided funding for an international symposium on Advanced Comfort Systems for the Work Environment to be held at Rensselaer in May 1988. What made the symposium effort successful was the help, encouragement, and assistance of internationally recognized thinkers, designers, and futurists such as Frances Duffy (U.K); Baruch Givoni (Israel); David Wyon (UK); Wolfgang Radtke (Germany); Helmut F.O. Müller (Germany); Fritz Gartner (Germany); and Kay Mori (Japan). My network of colleagues expanded and it was fun working with them and exploring the synergy of our ideas.

Following the Advanced Comfort System Symposium, Magda McHale encouraged me to present my ideas on the future of architecture at the Tenth World Conference of the World Futures Studies Federation (WFSF) in Beijing, China in September 1988. My paper was titled, "Do Developed Countries Have a Future?" I argued that the developed world should not be used as a modernization model by developing countries. New models for development had to be found for a sustainable world and a large part of my challenge was that new urban forms and architectural designs were needed. I did not know that this topic was of particular interest to China's First Secretary Deng Xiaoping. One of the lead organizers of the conference was a very close friend of John and Magda McHale, and he invited Magda to meet with some distinguished Chinese friends at a Beijing Guest House. Whether by arrangement or accident, I never found out, we met with Secretary Deng Xiaoping and were escorted to a private room. There were formal greetings and expressions of appreciation for what the WFSF was trying to do in relation to planning China's future. I remember silk carpets on the floor, and large and thickly-cushioned lounge chairs arranged in a circle for about ten people, including interpreters. The Chinese interpreter advised us when to sit and when to rise. We were told never to look down on the Secretary. Handshakes were not allowed and we were shown how to bow. In our short session, while drinking Chinese tea in a smoke-filled room, I learned that Deng was intensely opposed to China adopting the capitalistic system. He felt that China could not modernize under capitalism. While I didn't necessarily agree with all of his theories, it felt good that my paper had made an impression. Deng told us that he hoped our efforts would result in fresh ideas and opportunities for China.

In 1990, Russ Leslie and I traveled to Moscow, Russia for a conference related to utilizing energy efficient daylighting strategies in buildings. There wasn't much opportunity to visit the countryside and very little time to tour Moscow. Whatever free time I had was consumed trying to find my passport, airline tickets, and money that were contained in a travel bag that was stolen in the dining room of the hotel restaurant. Dealing with the Russian police, female detectives working for the hotel disguised as prostitutes, and the private hotel police was enough to discourage future travel to Russia. In 1990, it was a corrupt environment and not traveler friendly. However, the architecture of the Kremlin, Red Square, St. Basil's Cathedral, the Gum Department Store, and the Subway System were most impressive.

During the Advanced Comfort System Symposium in 1988, I met the Vice President of Research for the Johnson Controls Corporation. A year later the LRC supported a seed-research project to document the development of task-comfort systems (TCS); heating/cooling/lighting/and noise control systems that provide environmental comfort directly to individual office workstations. The research project was a state-of-the-art survey that created the foundation for a later research project, sponsored by Johnson Controls, that looked at the impact of TCSs on human productivity.

The West Bend Mutual Insurance Company was in the process of constructing a new office building in West Bend, Wisconsin. Johnson Controls had developed a TCS that they referred to as a Personal Environment Module (PEM). Johnson Controls wanted to know if the use of the PEMs would significantly impact the productivity of the office workers at West Bend Mutual Insurance Company. The insurance company's leaders were also very interested in the impact PEMs might have on their bottom line. The results of our work clearly demonstrated that TCSs could improve worker productivity by five to fifteen percent. Two of the key investigators who assisted me with this project were graduate student Jean Stark and Professor Thomas Willemain, who did all of the statistical analysis on the project. The study remains the most convincing argument for improving productivity through architecture. Jean's paper on the subject was accepted for presentation at an international conference in Finland, making her one of the first graduate students at Rensselaer to achieve such recognition. While PEMs have not yet become the norm, I believe that one day we will all have personal control of our micro-environments.

My parents departed too early to share in my professional accomplishments. I had become full professor a few days after I returned from Vater's funeral. My reason for seeking a professorship was not the title or the satisfaction of my ego. It was the freedom that it allowed me to pursue, profess, and do research without being manipulated by outside forces. It was the pursuit of intuition and knowledge, regardless of the risks or the findings. It was the search for answers and the testing of ideas that were made possible through academic freedom. No one could control what happened in my classroom, studio, or laboratory. As a child, I hoped for a place where I could ask freely, a place where people could answer without fear, and for access to knowledge that otherwise would have eluded me. Academia was the one place where the pursuit of knowledge seemed to be the centerpiece of existence. The academy was, and is, the single most important institution in any society because the quest for truth is celebrated there. When I was ten years old I did not understand what academe meant, but I had a sense that it was the place where I needed to be.

I could have stopped my academic pursuits when I was promoted to associate professor with tenure. But that wasn't enough for me. It is the full professors who are responsible for maintaining the principles and values of academe. Theoretically, it is they who make policy, administrative decisions, and protect academia in the context of society. It is they who establish and maintain the quality of research, education, and knowledge. Senior and full professors make decisions related to their younger colleagues and protect those that challenge the established paradigms.

Academia has not always been the incubator for the pursuit of knowledge. At times, academia lost its way in some countries and became the instrument of dictators and power brokers. I had decided that I would never go into politics or become a career officer in the military. Those endeavors required skills that I didn't have. They required acts that were not always noble, and sometimes they required foregoing one's own ideas and values in favor of someone else's power play, dogma, or belief. I remember a very influential Rensselaer alumnus who kept warning me that if I continued with my outspokenness, my exploratory methods of teaching, and my challenges to the establishment I would never get promoted. I proved him wrong. When tenure was my next step, and then full professorship, the same warning was repeated. I enjoyed proving him wrong, again.

I discovered that certain qualities and concepts resonated more harmoniously in my mind and heart than others. For example, I believe feelings are as significant as quantitative proofs to the development of ideas, designs, and science. In Einstein's words, "Imagination is more important than knowledge." Synergy is a reality even though it is not easily measured. And, just because you cannot see something or feel it, doesn't mean it doesn't exist. I prefer "both/and" thinking and detest "either/or" attitudes and mind-sets.

In time, my interests shifted towards visionary ideas and futuristic thinking. I reached several administrative leadership positions in academia and had to learn the art of compromise. I must add that these accomplishments could never have happened by my efforts alone. Throughout my academic career there were colleagues, administrators, and friends in the U.S. and abroad who made my successes possible. I will forever owe them a debt of gratitude. In addition, I have to acknowledge that the Rensselaer students in my classes and studios were, for me, a precious gift. They were intelligent, tough and demanding. They had high expectations, and as a result they made teaching fun and challenging. I am convinced they kept me young and intellectually alive.

Distinguished Professor Walter Kroner, 1988.

My greatest sense of accomplishment, over and above my successful research and design work, was when the senior faculty at Rensselaer bestowed upon me Rensselaer's Distinguished Faculty Award in 1988. To be judged worthy of this award by my academic colleagues told me that I had distinguished myself in teaching, research, and service to academe. I had reached a goal, the seed of which was planted by my teacher Fräulein Hermann forty-five years earlier.

Whether it was stubbornness, perseverance, or belief in myself, I had learned that if I really truly believed in something and if I really truly worked very hard at what I chose to do, I would succeed. I knew from the beginning that coming to America was the right choice, even though I had no facts to support my decision. I know foreigners who have returned to their homelands with horrible stories about America. For me, however, America always felt right. I knew it was a good place to be and the place where I could pursue my dreams.

America gave me the freedom to think, speak, write, and profess. I in turn have the responsibility to uphold and support its basic values. I am an American by choice. I have been educated by America in the context of critical thinking, and I am here at this very moment because of America's commitment to freedom.

New-Ulm on the Hudson

After my second divorce, I was a happy man professionally. I liked who I had become socially, and I was blessed with wonderful children and the precious gift of true friends who stood by me throughout my career and personal development. I prefer a small number of very dear friends who are there for each other regardless of what might happen. These friends sustained me through my most difficult times and struggles. After the divorce, I had my personal possessions and my friends. All of the other things that had been acquired over the course of my second marriage were no longer mine.

I hoped for happiness within the context of marriage, but that dream had eluded me thus far. I also hoped that someday I would have my own "Häusle" again. I had given up our home in the divorce, but the dream of my own place remained.

Bobbi and Tom Ryan, my very close friends, had a home on the Hudson River north of Corinth, New York. I was sitting in their garden looking out over the river in the summer of 1994 relaxing with one of Bobbi's famous gin and tonics. I was waiting for the final granting of my divorce and was once again thinking about my future. I realized that my next home would probably be my last since I had just reached the age of sixty. As I contemplated the meaning of "my last home," the question was where should such a home be? I had grown to love upstate New York. I enjoyed the nearness to New York City, Boston, Montreal and the Adirondack Mountains. As I contemplated this issue I was struck by a consistency that I had never before realized. Whether it was for a vacation, just getting away from the pressures of the day, solving difficult problems, or to become re-energized, I had always chosen to be near a body of water. It didn't matter whether it was the ocean, a river, a brook, a lake, or even a small pond in someone's garden; water refreshed my soul. With that realization, I turned to Tom and Bobbi and told them that if they ever heard of a place for sale along the river, I'd like to know about it.

Two years later, Tom called me and told me that a house across the river from them was for sale. By the summer of 1996 I had purchased a home in the village of Lake Luzerne, New York. I named it "New-Ulm on the Hudson."

The house, first constructed as a summer camp in 1976, went through several modifications, additions and what the former owners considered improvements. Before it could become my "häusle" it needed work, in fact lots of work. It is located on a dead-end street that runs parallel to the Hudson River The river is crystal clear in this area and about 400 feet wide. Rockwell

Falls is three miles to the north and two miles south is a hydroelectric plant dam. In short, no boat traffic comes up or down the river from any distance, and there is no industry on the Hudson north of Lake Luzerne. The property fronts on the river for about seventy-five feet, making it a perfect swimming pool.. When I bought the house it had a one car garage and the first floor included a kitchen, dining room, living room, and bathroom,

209

complete with laundry and pantry. Upstairs were three bedrooms and a bathroom in a space that had once been an attic. A fireplace and electric baseboard heating provide the source of thermal comfort. The house has its own well and septic system, something that appealed to my sense of being as independent as possible.

On the river side of the house is a large wooden deck and a soft grass carpet that stretches to the water. From the deck, one can watch beautiful sunsets with constantly changing colors and cloud formations that are reflected in the mirror-like waters of the river. In the fall the multi-colored sunsets compete with the colorful autumn trees for attention. It is a perfect setting for lovers and for enjoying good wine while Vivaldi's Four Seasons drifts from the outdoor speakers.

As a young man, I assumed that happiness would be the consequence of working hard, being noble, giving, and being a good person. I had very few happy moments in my youth or in my teens. I was the happiest when I finally sat on that SAS airplane and felt the plane lift off the runway. It was then that I really, truly, felt happy, riding on the wings of a metallic eagle. I had not yet had the experience of intimate human relationships so I was assuming that two people would somehow create, or find, these happy moments. I witnessed Mutter's happiness whenever Vater would do something that had love written all over it. I knew Mutter was happy when her brother Ernst, Elfriede's father, would come to visit. Mutter was happy when her daughter, who adored her, built her häusle big enough to accommodate her family with two children, as well as her parents in a second floor apartment.

If there was anything I had learned about human relationships, it was that honesty and trust were by far the most important building blocks of a happy relationship. I am reminded of an event that occurred in 1990 that, for me, exemplified the meaning of trust.

Jean Stark and her husband had spoken with Mr. Herbert Liebich about my passion for creating affordable housing. Mr. Liebich was a very wealthy man and he too had an interest in affordable housing. Mr. Liebich contacted me and we arranged to meet at my office at Rensselaer. A tall, well-dressed, elderly gentleman introduced himself and indicated that he would like to hear my ideas. However, he started by saying, "Let me briefly tell you something about me so you understand where I am coming from." He went on to explain that his father, a Methodist minister, had immigrated to Albany, New York with his wife and raised nine children. His parents never took any support from anyone and all nine children became millionaires. He went on to explain that America had been good to his parents and to him, and his own children didn't need his money. Therefore, he was giving his money to three good causes: (1) support for hard-working students who needed a scholarship to afford college; (2) medical research to help move innovative concepts from the research lab to the consumer; and (3) affordable housing. I will never forget his next remark, "What makes America great is the American family, and what strengthens the American family is home ownership. That is where I want my money to go."

I told him about my own background and said to him, "I too am a millionaire, but not by the money in my bank. My wealth is in the opportunities and experiences I was allowed to have since coming to America." We shook hands and agreed that I would prepare a proposal to design and develop an affordable and responsive community/housing system (ARCH). After two reviews of our proposal, Mr. Liebich stood up, shook my hand, and told me that I would have all the money I needed to do the proposed work. Within two days he had transferred enough money to Rensselaer in my name to do the proposed project. I was taken aback by the informality of it all and the fact that he trusted me with over one-quarter million dollars. For the occasion of Rensselaer's formal acceptance of his gift, I wrote the following poem:

The Gift of Trust

Life given
and shared with others,
in a place we call
our precious earth,
is the gift of nature.

Talent, knowledge and dreams
are the gifts within us
we pursue in our search
for the gift of living.

Wealth and creativity
shared with others
are gifts
creating energy
for the making of new dreams.

Yet, there is no greater gift
than a gift
given
when feelings are gentle,
the heart warm,
when a gift is given
based on trust alone.

Inspired by Mr. Herbert Liebich
Professor Walter Kroner, April 9, 1991

When I think of "trust", the poem says it all. Several members of the Rensselaer faculty, graduate students, and my friend Tom Ryan, a structural engineer, were involved with this project. One of the key research associates was Jean Stark.

Let's go back to the dream of a lover who I was hoping would someday share the deck at New-Ulm on the Hudson with me. At the age of sixty-three years, with the experience of two divorces behind me, I had learned a few things about myself in the context of relationships. There were values and priorities that I would refuse to modify, change, or otherwise compromise.

I call them my non-negotiable values; they are:

1. A relationship must be based on total and complete honesty and trust;
2. Always strive to maintain economic stability and security;
3. Be sexually compatible and passionate; and
4. Be respectful to others, specifically our families and their history.

These for me are the foundation upon which I was hoping to build my next relationship, if there was to be one.

A Waking Dream Come True

There were the typical dates arranged by friends and family. I joined an Internet match making group. Through my sister Marianne, I was introduced to a divorcee who lived with her two grown children in Munich. I didn't feel comfortable with any of these avenues as a way to discover a new partner. In fact, part of the problem with the dating game is that you're required to put your best foot forward, emphasizing the positive and concealing one's blemishes. I wanted a situation where I could be me, with the message being, "What you see and hear is what you get." I didn't want to conceal anything, but that is easier said than done.

I invited a colleague from Rensselaer to my place at Neu-Ulm on the Hudson for a weekend. Naomi and I discussed a recent advertisement I had placed in an academic match making club. After reading it, her observation was reassuring. She said, "I would respond to this advertisement." However, Naomi quickly qualified her remarks by telling me that for her, an age difference of twenty-three years was too difficult to even consider. That eliminated the possibility of her being interested in me.

In January 1998, I found out that Jean Stark had filed for divorce. Naomi and I suspected that their relationship was not on solid footing when her husband would not take time off from work to care for her after she had a hysterectomy. Jean's doctor directed that someone had to be with her for an entire week 24/7. Her husband lived and worked in Vermont at the time and only came home on weekends. Naomi and I compared our calendars and developed a plan so one of us would be at Jean's house to take care of her at all times. For a week Naomi and I rotated living at Jean's house to provide her around the clock care.

By then, I had known Jean for almost ten years, first as a graduate student, then as a research intern. After she graduated with her Master of Architecture Degree she became a research associate in the Center for Architectural Research until she moved to Maryland in 1993 to work on her internship and be near her husband who had moved for a new job. I had discovered her immense research/design talents, her superb intellect, and her propensity for hard work. She was an artist not only in the usual artistic sense of the visual and graphic arts, but in every aspect of living. She exhibited tremendous sensitivity towards very important clients, consultants, co-workers, and fellow students. She was above all honest, sincere, and hated game-players, as did I. We had spent considerable time together traveling professionally and I truly believe one can learn much about a person's character in the stress of traveling, particularly abroad. It was during these traveling days when Jean and I engaged in long and varied conversations ranging from politics, culture, academia, and our profession - architecture. We shared personal thoughts and feelings, convictions, beliefs, and values. It was through these conversations that I believe we learned more about each other than most people could possibly discover by dating. Jean has four brothers and through our many conversations I discovered that she, in the most genuine way possible, enjoyed the company of men. I saw this when she was with her brothers, male students, or male colleagues. I was convinced that the woman I was going to marry someday had to genuinely like the male gender. It was interesting that the women I most admired enjoyed being around men. For me that included Frau Unkauf, Dr. Köstlin, Marianne, Elfriede, and Magda McHale.

During the early 1990s, Jean, her husband, my wife and I socialized together at cultural functions and at Jean's home. I saw and enjoyed Jean's talents as a hostess, cook, and homemaker. After my divorce, I was invited to spend Thanksgiving with her with her family in Delaware.

When Jean's mother came to visit Glens Falls, her mother and I went kayaking on the Hudson. We enjoyed each other's company and became friends.

When I heard about Jean's divorce in 1998, I immediately called my sister Marianne who had met Jean and her husband on several occasions. I told Marianne that I had fallen in love with Jean, and if she would have me, I wanted to marry her. Marianne asked me if Jean knew of my feelings, to which I replied no. My sister encouraged me to share my feelings with Jean right away. I suggested that I should wait until the divorce was final. "Walter, you need to tell Jean your feelings right away and don't wait," instructed Marianne.

I knew in my heart Marianne was right, but I was unsure because of how others might see this intrusion during a time of pain and stress. I decided that no harm would be done and Jean already knew that I would be there for her as a friend while she is dealing with her divorce. I called her and made arrangements for us to have dinner at one of Saratoga Springs' nicer restaurants. I went to Dennis deJonghe Jewelers and bought her a small gold ring with a gem as a friendship gift. Jean is a stunning woman even when she wears blue jeans and has paint splattered on her face. That evening she looked absolutely gorgeous in a flowing silk dress. Her short hair and a beautiful necklace framed of her lovely face. During dinner I gave her the gift and a scroll with the following poem:

Dearest and Loveliest Jean Anne!
My Love is forever; this I feel deep within my heart.
My life wants to be devoted and true to you, always; this comes from deep within my soul.
We harmonize and make synergy, those who know us, will testify and so do I.
Walking with you into eternity is a longing deep within my heart; I feel it.
My respect and admiration for you is without condition and expectation; this I know.
Our Love is true and our destiny is to be together; I know this also.
My promise is to do all that is within my power to live a long time, so we may enjoy
what I know we can create together.
What I would like to know is: Will you marry me?

Asked from the bottom of my heart
Love, Wally

Before she answered, I assured her that the ring was not an engagement ring. I would understand if she said no and the ring would remain forever as a friendship ring. She had tears in her eyes and she was silent for a while. Then, as she stared at the ring, she commented on its beauty and that I shouldn't have bought such an expensive gift. When she did respond to the question I was not surprised. "Wally, I can't answer you right now. I really need time to think about this. I admit I have strong feelings for you and a lot of admiration, but I really need time." I felt that I had already overstepped my boundaries with my poem. I told her that I understood and that I was willing to wait no matter how long it took.

In the years that followed we vacationed in Germany where Jean met my family. We went to the Stark family's 50th 4th of July Reunion at Cable Lake in Michigan. That was when I discovered Jean has pyrotechnic abilities and likes to arrange and set off large fireworks. While in Michigan I went with Jean's mother and her children to church one Sunday. Jean's mother, who was also named Jean, introduced her children to the priest. When it came to me she said, "And this is my 'son' Wally." Everyone thought this slip of her tongue was funny, and from then on I referred to her as "mom." I learned that Jean Sr. had enjoyed dancing in the same Aragon Ballroom in Chicago where I used to take Doris. Perhaps we had even been there on the same night. She and I had fun dancing on the grass at Cable Lake.

Reflecting on our beginnings, it was most unusual and perhaps the secret of a good marriage. Instead of starting with the usual dating game we first became colleagues, moved on to deep friendship, and only then did romance enter our lives. My non-negotiable values were matched and for the first time in my life I felt totally comfortable that my vulnerabilities were safe with her. We discovered that we were soul mates. I had finally found true and complete happiness and once again, I learned that perseverance will lead to joy and the fulfillment of hopes.

I highly recommend that lovers who think they want to bond for life should travel in a foreign country where neither of them speaks the language. It is truly a test of compassion, understanding, communication, and trust.

Jean and Walter in Germany.

The Stark Family at Cable Lake.

Jean and I traveled to Costa Rica, Germany, and Switzerland, and it confirmed not only how wonderfully suited we were for each other, it revealed the respect and appreciation we have for each other, as well.

In the spring of 2000, Jean's mother spent part of her summer in Kankakee, Illinois with her oldest son David, his wife Rita, and their family. Jean and I had planned to visit her mother on June 9 to celebrate her mother's birthday. While we were there I planned to officially ask Jean's mother for the hand of her daughter.

Once again my Mutter's favorite saying came to mind, "Die Menschen machen Pläne aus, Gott Vater schaut zum Himmel raus und sagt wird nichts daraus." (People plan, God looks on from heaven and says nothing will become of it.) Jean's mother passed away suddenly on May 10, 2000 before I could ask for the hand of her daughter. I loved that woman, and her daughter is so much like her. Jean Sr. was an artist and one of her favorite mediums was watercolor. She had painted several sunsets and to this day, when the sky is full of color we say, "Mom is painting the sky again."

I worked with Dennis deJonghe, an artist and goldsmith, to design an engagement and wedding ring for Jean. The engagement ring has a Ceylon sapphire and seven small diamonds, and interlocks with the gold wedding band. On November 11, 2000, I made arrangements with a florist to place the engagement ring in the center of an orchid set within a bouquet of flowers. In my living room was a table with a bar concealed in its center. When the middle of the table top is pressed, the bar rises to reveal its contents. I removed the bottles and placed the bouquet in the center of the elevator bar. I made a fire in anticipation of Jean's arrival. After dinner we sat in front of the fireplace and I asked her to fix us an after dinner drink. As she pushed down on the table center, out came the surprise.

I asked Jean again, but more formally and in private, if she would marry me. It had been two years since I asked her the first time. Given our age difference of twenty-one years, I had wanted to make sure she had a lot of time to think about the question. She answered, "FÜR IMMER," which means forever in German. My only regret is that my parents never had the pleasure of meeting the daughter-in-law they had wished for me.

Walter and Jean on their wedding day, June 9, 2001.

On June 9, 2001, Pastor Joyce DeVelder of the Old Saratoga Reformed Church married us during a weekend gathering at Friends Lake Inn in Chestertown, New York. Our immediate families and friends celebrated with us. I felt especially honored that Marianne and Hannes, her husband, as well as their children came to celebrate our union with us. Robert was able to join us and Reneé came from Kannapolis, North Carolina for the occasion. Kevin joined the wedding and, together with a friend presented Jean and me with a musical performance of songs and guitar music. Naomi Miller was the matron-of-honor and Tom Ryan my best man. Jean was, and still is, a stunningly beautiful woman. Our union was filled with the loving and lasting spirit of our families and friends, which together created a most memorable three days, never to be forgotten.

Kevin, Jean, Walter, Reneé and Robert.

We spent part of our honeymoon on the Greek Island of Kassos in a villa of a dear friend, Spyros Loukos and his family. Spyros studied with me at Rensselaer and is a successful architect in Athens, Greece. We are life-long friends. Kassos is the best kept secret in Greece and usually only Greeks go there for vacation. Jean and I were greeted as old friends by the villagers because Spyros had informed restaurants, general stores, and taxi drivers that we were coming. If there is heaven on earth, it was in Kassos where Jean and I discovered beauty, silence, and clear starry skies. We were treated like a king and queen and we shall never be able to return this favor to Spyros and his family. Jean and I don't have a long list of dear friends, but we have a precious small group of friends that will forever remain close to our hearts, another treasured aspect of our shared values. On the return trip, we stopped in Germany for a wedding reception with my friends and family.

We combined our resources, went into debt, and since Jean is also a licensed architect, we designed a major renovation for our home "New-Ulm on the Hudson." There have been numerous additional exterior and interior projects, and several that are waiting to be realized. We created our place with our resources, our ideas, our hands and sweat, and with our love. I remember the villa in my hometown of Neu-Ulm where stairs lead out of the river and led to the mansion. New-Ulm on the Hudson has such stairs rising out of the river to our häusle.

Jean is the third generation of an immigrant family. Her mother's side comes from Poland and her father's side from Sweden. There is pride in all of the following generations and an appreciation for America and its open arms. I know Vater is smiling in heaven because I have found a wife that has his green thumb and talent. And I know Jean, if need be, could sustain us with vegetables, berries, and fruit. And I can imagine my mother smiling in heaven whenever Jean puts me in my proper place with love and affection.

Jean and I have three little ones running around the house. She brought two of them, eighteen-

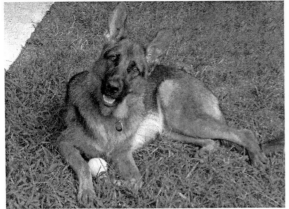

year old cats named Jessie and Freddie. Jean knew about my surrogate German Shepherd Arko whom I loved as a child in Neu-Ulm. She insisted it was time I had my own German Shepherd. We named her Anke.

Vater lived according to Goethe's concept that a human being must, "...be noble, giving, and good." All that Vater did in his lifetime is embodied in these words. My soul-mate Jean embodies these same qualities and I am constantly reminded of them by her love, giving, and treatment of people and animals. I am truly happy about whom I have become,

Anke, Walter's beloved German Shepherd

that Jean and I found each other, and that I have persevered with my hopes, dreams, and convictions. Life along the river is sweet indeed.

Secrets Revealed

The two questions that I had formulated as a child, but were never answered, now needed attention. The first question was whether or not the SA uniform in the armoire belonged to Vater and was he a member the SA? When I mentioned my curiosity about Vater and the SA to Marianne she vehemently denied such a possibility. My family knew, of course, that Vater was a Nazi because he had to join the NSDAP in order to hold the civil servant position as Schwimmeister. We also knew that the requirement to join was not made law until June of 1933.

I took the glass slides that had been concealed in Vater's desk and had them photographically reproduced. The images were improved with computer technology. The photos show seven men in Sturmabteilung (SA) uniforms, including Vater. Each man had a backpack, as if they were going on bivouac. Clearly, the uniforms were winter issue since they all wore overcoats and each of the men had an Edelweiss insignia on their circular cap. I know this insignia meant that this group of SA men belonged to a mountain division. The uniforms included the famous Long Knives of the SA, suspended from the belts with metallic buckles and an insignia I could not decipher. Each man wore the Nazi armband. This was proof that Vater did belong to the SA and that the uniform I had seen in the armoire was his.

Vater in the uniform of the SA.

Under the terms of the Treaty of Versailles signed in 1919, the German Army was limited to 100,000 men. Hitler's solution to that limit was to establish the "Protection and Sport Division," a paramilitary group, in 1921. This group was called Sturmabteilung (SA), and their primary function was to protect Hitler and to disrupt other political functions. By 1934 the SA had grown to a force of more than four million men. Hitler became fearful that the head of the SA, Ernst Röhm, had too much power and could potentially seize control. Historic documents show that Hitler masterminded the "Röhm Putsch," also known as the "Night of the Long Knives," on June 30, 1934. Four-hundred leaders of the SA where invited to an assembly hall under false pretenses and were murdered by the SS. Others, including some generals who disagreed with Hitler, were also murdered.

With Vater's active participation in numerous sports organizations, it is easy to imagine that he could have joined the SA in his early twenties. If I were to speculate, I would have to say that Vater was in the SA sometime after 1922 after reaching the age of twenty-one. This was the time when one week's wages was just enough money to buy one hard roll. By 1927, he was married and worked as a civil servant for the City of Ulm. Between 1930 and 1932, the SA was banned until Hitler became Reich Chancellor in 1933.

I believe Vater experienced a turning point between 1927 and 1934. First he married my mother, who had no use for politics or the military. He began to associate with a highly intelligent woman, Frau Emma Unkauf, who I am sure had a strong influence on his political orientation. Vater's first son, Karlheinz, was born in 1929 and I was born in 1934, two days before the Night of the Long Knives. By then Vater was a highly visible, well-known figure in the cities of Ulm and Neu-Ulm. I believe Vater realized that he had been too quick to embrace the promises of Hitler's politics and not critical enough to question his motives.

The second question I wanted answered was about my paternal great-grandfather. Was he really a Jewish banker or an Earl of the State of Württemberg? In my previous visits to Germany I had made several trips to Breitingen near Ulm, the birthplace of my paternal grandfather, where I searched for his birth records. I had the little red book, the official Family Register, in which the entry about my grandfather Jakob Kroner read as follows, "Keine Eintragung beim Standesamt über die Vaterschaft des Jakob Kroner." Translated this means, "There is no record in the official village registry office concerning the father of Jakob Kroner."

My inquiries during my visits produced no new information. I was reminded of an earlier story told to me by my favorite Aunt Marie Kroner, my Vater's sister-in-law. It was during the early thirties that Tante Marie discovered she and her husband could not have their own children. My Aunt and Uncle worked out an agreement with my parents that if my parent's second child was a boy, my parents would let Aunt Marie and Uncle Jakob adopt the child. That boy was none other than me. However, when the time came everyone found it impossible to complete the adoption. I had always felt a special bond between my Aunt Marie and Uncle Jakob. Perhaps that was the reason.

In January 2007, I had my Y-DNA analyzed by Family Tree DNA because I wanted to know whether the theory that I had a Jewish great-grandfather could be true. After all of the analysis results were returned from the lab, I received a document that stated the following:

"Your Y-DNA results determined that the origin for your direct paternal line (father's father'... father's line) is of Western European origin and not of Jewish origin. This Western European origin is found in males from Germany indicating that your direct paternal line is of German origin, rather than of German Jewish origin."

This eliminated the Jewish origin theory. I provided all of this information to my sister Marianne who not only was surprised about the SA membership, but that the Jewish theory suggestion had perhaps been a diversionary tactic.

As part of my research for this book, I shared some of my notes with Marianne, particularly the story of the spaziergang to Pfuhl when I was seven years old (cited earlier). I realized there must be a family secret involving the details of where grandfather came from and where he lived. We discussed this 1941 event and she decided she was going to initiate her own research. Marianne was able to reach the current Pastor, Dietrich Oehring, of the Evangelische Church for Holzkirch, Breitingen, and Neenstetten in Germany. The Church Registry is located in Neenstetten. Pastor Oehring provided Marianne with photographic copies from the church register along with explanations. The news was totally unexpected and disproved all previous theories about my great-grandfather. The registers are complete and detailed, including dates related to births, confirmations, marriages, and deaths.

The answer begins with the wedding of George Junginger and Walburga Kroner who were married on June 12, 1793, in Holzkirch. That marriage produced ten children. Four of their daughters never married. These four daughters were Anna, Angelika, Scholastika, and Magdalena. Angelika Junginger was born on December 10, 1795 and died on October 24, 1848. The records indicate that all four sisters were dirnen, which means prostitutes. The church register indicates that these four dirnen produced between them fourteen children out of wedlock. Angelika Kroner, one of the four prostitutes, had four of those children, one of whom was named Walburga Kroner, who was born on December 23, 1834 and died in 1913. Angelika's other three children were registered under different surnames. Walburga Kroner, also marked in the Register as a dirne, had four children out of wedlock, three of whom died within one year of their birth. The lone survivor's name was Jakob Kroner, born on 3 August 1864. It was Jakob who married my grandmother Anna Mayser on 11 November 1888.

The answer I was searching for was that my great-grandfather was a solicitor of a prostitute. He vanished after an interlude with Walburga, my paternal great-grandmother. It is no wonder that my grandfather was so adamant about not wanting to talk about his parents, where he grew up, or anything else about his youth.

Clearly it is a chronicle lined with shame and embarrassment. I was happy to be confronted with the truth rather than the fantasy theories we considered previously. After all the truth will set you free. Yes, I had imagined my great-grandmother Walburga as a strong, independent, liberated woman who would rather keep my great-grandfather's name a secret, perhaps out of love, as opposed to revealing it. It is clear why my grandfather disappeared from the record books in Breitingen and re-appeared in Neu-Ulm. He was, like my father, a proud man and determined to flow with the natural path of his own life and his own innate compass.

My feelings about my lineage have not changed. I am proud of my name, proud of what Vater accomplished over his lifetime. I understand now that he must have lived in fear that someone would discover he was the descendant of a line of prostitutes. During the Nazi regime prostitutes, Gypsies, Communists, and others were accused of "offending traditional morality." Sometimes they were sent to work camps and murdered, while others were treated medically, never to be heard from again. What no one knew was how the regime would deal with the children or grand-children of prostitutes. The Nazi's kept changing the rules of who was undesirable. In the context of a society that was possessed with the concept of pure Aryanism, Vater's life must have been a nightmare. This burden of fear and uncertainty was carried by him, his parents, and his siblings in silence. Vater was the only one of his siblings who had to provide proof to the Nazi regime that he was Aryan because he worked as a civil servant for the City of Ulm. I am convinced that he had found the same information that Pastor Oehring had given to my sister and that he needed to hide his lineage. Joining the SA and the NSDAP could also have been a strategy he devised so no one would question his ancestry.

I am convinced that this secret was discussed between Vater's siblings when Hitler came into power. When I re-examined the official document that Vater had to submit as part of his proof of purity, the comment that there was no record for Jakob's father was in his own handwriting, and that part of the chronicle had no official stamp. There must have been a pact between my grandfather and his children that the truth would never be revealed. The fear of being euthanized or sent to a concentration camp was very real for all of the Kroner family. At the very least, there would have been the risk that he would not be allowed to work for the City of Ulm, as Schwimmeister, or as part of the physical therapy profession.

I am proud of my family, for in the process of surviving they became even stronger and more determined. My Vater, who lived with fear, had many proud moments. The greatest of these occurred when he was awarded the German Service Cross, 2nd Class, the highest honor Germany could bestow upon a civilian. It was given to him to him for having rescued eighty-six people from drowning under extremely dangerous conditions over a twenty-five year period.

My desire to live my own life as free as a river and to follow my own innate compass certainly mirrors my father's and grandfather's history. I've lived through times of great uncertainty. Sometimes I feared my future could only be measured in hours, perhaps a week, at best a few months. It was difficult to dream, but it was essential that I kept hope alive. Keeping hope in front of you may sometimes lead to more misery, but keeping hope alive allowed me not only to survive, but to exceed my own expectations. Life, like a river, encounters many rocks along its path; some self-made, some natural, some intriguing, and some as dangerous as whirlpools. But when we trust ourselves and the river's natural path, we can float over the most turbulent waters.

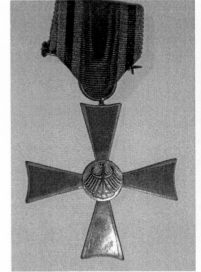

The German Service Cross 2nd Class, awarded to Vater in 1954.

I am reminded of a poem my father wrote to my mother during a time of great uncertainty:

> Let no one rob you of your courage.
> In misfortune be the strongest,
> mindful that the best of the grapes
> always are squeezed the longest.

Hans Kroner, 1926

I have been squeezed, at times longer than I care to remember. However, I have tasted that wine, properly aged, and I can attest to its savory qualities of love, beauty, peace, and tranquility.

References

Neubronner Eberhard. *Ulm in Trümmern*. Endras Verlag Pfaffenhofen (Germany), 1992.

Black, Jeremy, General Edito. *World History Atlas, Mapping the Human Journey*, Dorling Kindersley Book, New York, NY, 2005.

Heck, Alfons. *A Child of Hitler: Germany In The Days When God Wore A Swastika*. Renaissance House, Frederick, CO 80530, 1985.

Fulbrook Mary. *A Concise History of Germany*, 2nd Edition Cambridge University Press, UK, 1991.

German Bundestag Publications' Section Bonn. *Questions on German History – Ideas, forces, decisions from 1800 to the present*. Historical Exhibition in the Berlin Reichstag Catalogue, 4th Edition, 1992.

Höhn, Karl. *Ulmer Bilder-Chronik*, Band 5b, 1939-1945, Verlag Dr. Karl Höhn KG, Ulm/Donau (Germany), 1989.

Treu, Barbara. *Stadt Neu-Ulm 1869 – 1994*. Texte und Bilder zur Geschichte. Stadtarchiv Neu-Ulm 1994, Stadtische Sammlungen Neu-Ulm (Germany), 1994.